Globalization
and Multicultural
Societies

Globalization
and Multicultural
Societies

SOME VIEWS FROM EUROPE

| Marina Ricciardelli | Sabine Urban | Kostas Nanopoulos |

EDITORS

University of Notre Dame Press
Notre Dame, Indiana

Published in the United States of America

Library of Congress Cataloging-in-Publication Data
Mondialisation et sociétés multiculturelles. English
    Globalization and multicultural societies : some views from Europe /
edited by Marina Ricciardelli, Sabine Urban and Kostas Nanopoulos.
        p.   cm.
    ISBN 0-268-02952-0 (cloth : alk. paper)
    ISBN 0-268-02957-1 (pbk. : alk. paper)
    1. Globalization.   2. Multiculturalism—Europe.   I. Ricciardelli,
M. (Marina)   II. Urban, Sabine M.-L.   III. Nanopoulos, Kostas.
IV. Title.
JZ1318 .M6613   2002
303.48'2—dc21
                                                        2002155289

Contents

Foreword to the American Edition   ix
Sabine Urban and Marina Ricciardelli

Introduction   I
Sabine Urban

1   Is the Future a Given?   9
      Ilya Prigogine

PART I.   READING GLOBALIZATION

2   Economic Science and Real Economy   19
      Franco Modigliani

3   Globalization and Regional Responsibility: 33
      Challenges for Leaders
      Peter Eichhorn

4   Strategic Management and Change of Structurally   41
      Global Organizations: The Case of Development Banks
      Taïeb Hafsi

5   Global Investors and E-Networks: Winners and Losers in   59
      the New World Economy
      Ernst-Moritz Lipp

6   Managing the Multinational Enterprise in a World of   75
    Different Cultures: Some Fundamental Remarks on the
    Pluralism of Cultures and Its Managerial Consequences
    Horst Steinmann and Andreas Georg Scherer

7   Governance in a Border-Free World: Economy and Currency 102
    Dario Velo

8   The Ambiguities of Globalization   121
    Philippe de Woot

PART 2.   INSTITUTIONAL DESIGNS

9   Globalization and Cultural Diversity: The Contribution   137
    of European Institutions
    Romano Prodi

10 European Unification: A Response to the Challenges   147
    of Globalization
    Emilio Gabaglio

11 Europe in the Face of Globalization without a Political 156
    and/or Historical Program
    Mihail Papayannakis

12 Globalization and Environmental Protection   170
    Alexandre Kiss

13 Actors in a Globalized Society: "Médecins du Monde"   185
    Jacky Mamou

14 Globalization and Its Statistical Challenges   200
    Photis Nanopoulos

15 The Globalization of Justice   223
    Dinah Shelton

16 Globalization: A New Framework for Women's Rights   240
    Elisabeth G. Sledziewski

PART 3. VIEWS AND TESTIMONIES

17   The World of Music   251
Pierre Boulez

18   Theater and Creativity: "From the World of   267
Approximations to the Universe of Precision"
Sergio Escobar

19   Inventing the Future of Surgery   271
Jacques Marescaux

20   Food: Language, Thought, Ideology   287
Davide Paolini

21   Mayoral Voices   293

22   Considerations on Method and Events   312
Marina Ricciardelli

Foreword
to the American Edition

Globalization and Multicultural Societies: Some Views from Europe presents a series of essays written in 2000. It is being published in the United States a little later than either the original French edition, *Mondialisation et sociétés multiculturelles: L'incertain du futur* (Paris: Presses Universitaires de France, 2000), or the Italian translation, *Idee per un futuro già iniziato: 28 voci sulla globalizzazione* (Rome: Edizioni Lavoro, 2002). The interest displayed in this book encouraged us to publish it in English, the obvious first language of globalization.

The American edition diverges only slightly from the original. There are several reasons for this. Globalization is in fact a long-term, complex, and evolutionary phenomenon that, in diverse ways, has accompanied humankind for centuries. We continually need to pay it renewed attention, though we can only comprehend it by seeking to understand its roots in historical and cultural developments. The authors, all distinguished figures in their fields of science, art, or action, dedicated their reflections to fundamental problems of enduring importance. With their rich and rigorous vision, they help us to understand better the reality of globalization.

The editors are grateful to the University of Notre Dame Press for recognizing the importance of the project and for the great attention they have shown to this publication.

Marina Ricciardelli   Sabine Urban

Introduction

SABINE URBAN

The present book was conceived as an essay of sorts to be included in the lively debate that is now taking place throughout the world, particularly in Europe, concerning the globalization process, a major catalyst in the transformation of contemporary society. In this work there are varied, sometimes conflicting, observations, ideas, analyses, and accounts written by individuals from different fields of specialization. Yet the authors all share the role of thinkers or players who exert, or are likely to exert, an influence on the evolution of this unfolding society. The uncertainties of the future seem to be even greater as the reality we confront becomes more complex and the interdependence of diverse and multiple factors (cultural, technological, economic, political, etc.) increases. But, beyond an awareness of this, unexpected and unpredictable events occur that change the course of events and of our lives.

Before opening the debate and introducing those who are participating in it, it seems necessary to clarify some of the concepts that underlie this reflection and to present the general philosophy that has presided over the conception of this work.

First, one fact is firmly established: man is evolving in a world that is increasingly interconnected. This process of communication and integration has been translated into many languages using the term *globalization,* which is, no doubt, evocative of a planetary phenomenon, i.e., one that affects the entire globe. But this term is imprecise since it lends itself to

Sabine Urban is professor emeritus at the Université Robert Schuman in Strasbourg and until 2002 was director of the affiliated CESAG-IECS Research Center. She is a visiting professor at the University of Pavia, Italy. Her main research fields are international business and European economy.

multiple interpretations. In French, the semantic problem is perhaps more pronounced than in other languages because two words are used to indicate the process: "globalization" and "mondialisation."

The use of the words "mondialisation" and "globalization" is relatively recent, although they are both related to the phenomenon of *internationalization* which is itself quite old. The Holy Roman Empire encompassed several continents; in the Middle Ages trans-European networks of banks, merchants, and cultural exchange were created; Europe spread to the New World as early as 1492, then over the rest of the world, with its unique Judeo-Christian-Greco-Latin cultural texture and its civilization founded on humanism, rationalism, science, and liberty.[1]

"Mondialisation" refers rather to the notion of space; it is defined in Paul Robert's dictionary as the fact of becoming worldwide (relative to the entire Earth), of spreading over the entire world. But even in the nineteenth century, at the height of the "globalization" driven by the colonial powers, the phenomenon touched only a very small minority of the population of the world. And "globalization" remained superficial. Until the mid-twentieth century (marked by the two world wars), the notion of borders retained all its significance, with sovereign states, residing behind their frontiers, flaunting their power and their ambition for power. Companies then became essentially national. Multinational or transnational companies did not appear until the second half of the twentieth century; until that time, the majority of markets (labor markets, financial markets, public procurement, etc.) were national and were controlled by government agencies or national commissions. Social systems remained distinct, each characterized by a national identity: there was liberal Anglo-Saxon democracy, the German, Scandinavian, and Japanese models, French-style capitalism, the Chinese and Soviet planned systems, and so on. In every case, the national reference was present.

Following the fall of the Berlin Wall (1989), we have seen an explosive expansion of *"mondialisation globalisée."*[2] Due to its nature and its depth, "globalization" has proven to be more radical than "mondialisation" because it refers to all aspects of life and involves a large number of people throughout the world. Novel phenomena are disseminated through several factors. We should no doubt consider as most important the prodigious deployment of new information and communication technologies (NTIC), allowing for the interconnection of all world players, even those who are in space. The NTIC foster dynamic interrelationships: we now have a society made up of interdependent networks, via the movement of goods and services, the mobility of people and capital, and the transfer of images, sound, and knowledge.

Technology has facilitated exchange, all exchange, to such an extent that controlling the flow of money and financial information, polluting elements, contagious diseases, information, and so forth, has become impossible. Technology has enabled the *integration* across the world of all the functional processes which were becoming more and more fragmented—research and development, production and diffusion of tangible and intangible goods—as well as the *delocalization* of the creation of value, and it has changed the balance of revenue among nations.

Furthermore, technological progress has occurred at an extraordinary rate, so that its evolution has become uncontrollable, and does not provide the time or space needed to gain perspective on events. Time for reflection and rest has become a rare commodity; time to adapt is even shorter. Structures are breaking down and being rebuilt within a context of perpetual, rapid change. The speed of the evolution of technical and economic phenomena tends to surpass the ability to adapt in both civil society and the political arena. Moreover, this high-speed change creates disturbances, disruption, and tension. Risks of all kinds are exacerbated.

With globalization the *organizational architecture of the worldwide society* is redefined.[3] Globalization does not, however, mean that the individual parties are included in the whole. Interdependency creates complementarity and antagonism. Multiple realities, both organized and disorganized, coexist within an open space of possibilities. The whole is not homogenous, and individuals—still a little Promethean—tend to refuse uniformity.

Next, we should note that this book places particular emphasis on *Europe*. This choice was made for three primary reasons. The first is linked to history. Europe has been a constant major player in world history for almost three millennia. In the areas of knowledge and know-how, fundamental (universal) values, and art, Europe has shown exceptional creativity; Europe is a depository of our human heritage.

The second reason relates to the concept of Western culture; in this regard, Europe has not only created universal values (as incarnated in such heroes as Ulysses, Don Quixote, Faust, and Don Juan), but has also introduced a multitude of ideas that have fed controversy, opened dialogue, and indicated new avenues of thought. Europe has never converged toward uniformity but, on the contrary, has always fostered diversity. Europe has never ceased to be a "society of learning" (a *Lerngemeinschaft*, to borrow a term from Wolf Lepenies);[4] Europe is the embodiment of that culture of learning which is so highly regarded in the information society of today. With the growing interpenetration of world cultures, Europe is, in a way, overcome by the shock of pluralism (a "clash of civilizations," according to Samuel Huntington)[5] and hesitates between the paths of tradition and modernity.

The third reason is related to the present, to Europe's ambitions and to the external forces that Europe must confront, thereby exposing a real existential fragility. Curiously, Europe is poorly defined: it is not a clear geographical notion, but rather just a small part, with moving horizons, of the Asian continent ("un petit cap de l'Asie," as Paul Valéry called it); it is a historical notion with changing borders. "It is a notion with multiple faces that we cannot superimpose without creating a blur. It is a notion made up of transformations. . . ."[6] At the same time, Europe is a reflection of the dynamism of reality, that is, of a process which is perpetually destructive and constructive, and which is characterized by the diversity of the individual and the group. It is within this context that we are witnessing the creation of a new social architecture: a European Union, currently limited to fifteen members, who are sometimes unsure as to what action to take, but nonetheless a Union which is attractive to the countries that are excluded. The fate of Europe as a community is now being rethought and reorganized. There is limited space for maneuvering, bounded as Europe is on the one side by the concept of supranationalism and by shared responsibility, and on the other by subsidiarity, or grassroots movements—actions taken at a lower level by individuals concerned with their particularity. An interactive solidarity, new in its breadth and original in its process, is being created in Europe, not only by political institutions but by companies, unions, universities, cultural organizations, and associations of all kinds.

Europe has thus become a laboratory for social experimentation in a world of mutation, aspiring no doubt to a true "civilization-focused" policy that is not exclusively dominated by the "golden calf," the cult of money. Europe, then, is very much an open entity, open to the world, open to the future, open to dialogue, and is therefore an interesting model to clarify, one likely to become a force for ideas that apply elsewhere.

The discussion presented here is also *transdisciplinary*. Globalization has emphasized the relativity of territorial borders; disciplinary borders are reacting along the same lines, combining the general and the particular via new systems of communication. The sciences describe a fragmented universe, rich in qualitative diversity, in which multiple connections and similarities are being defined. Science and its techniques evolve without borders; ways of living and thinking are coming together. Paradoxically, while draconian demands for quality are reinforced in some cases, in others second-rate mediocrity is increasingly invading our world. These diverse aspects of global reality are not mutually exclusive; rather, they most often coexist. Globalization may have opened the door to the best and the worst. It has indeterminate consequences, which are being expressed in a setting of clearly defined strength and power, but which are nonetheless going in undefined directions. It is these ambiguities, realizations, and questions that are expressed by the authors in the chapters that follow. The future world is emerging out of events most often unforeseeable, out of sporadic scientific discoveries and technological innovations, and out of human involvement, the strengths and effects of which are difficult to assess.

This book is intended for people who are intellectually curious and who wish to better understand the evolution of the world (the global environment) in which they live, that is, the cultural spaces which are marked by their own local history, but which maintain relationships with a multitude of other such spaces, all quite varied in nature. Our intention is not to provide certainties or to present a study with exhaustive claims. Rather we aim simply to present reflections, concerns, and experiences that bring to light the thinking and action taking place within today's rapidly changing context, in which all players attempt to make their mark. The responses to the questions arising out of the globalization process are both convergent and frankly paradoxical, optimistic, or tinged with concern. The chapters that follow—all original essays—can be read separately and in any order because they address *different approaches to understanding,* different ways of life or ways of living together as world citizens. Nonetheless, the editors propose an order of presentation that has a certain logic, following one guiding principle.

The introductory essay, written by Ilya Prigogine, raises a fundamental question: Is the future a given? This question justifies the initiatives and ambitions of individuals as well as organizations. Events have shifted balances and led to bifurcations in the evolution of society. If "individual and corporate history escape from any sort of determinism," the "players," or the actors within an organization, are responsible for implementing change.

Following these introductory remarks by a scientist, epistemologist, and philosopher, the first part of this book, entitled "Reading Globalization," is devoted to the analysis of contemporary society's evolution toward globalization. Part 1 begins with the contribution of Franco Modigliani, who discusses the relationship between economic science and the management of real phenomena. The changing dynamic of reality is then illustrated from different angles—societal, monetary, financial, and managerial—by Peter Eichhorn, Taïeb Hafsi, Ernst-Moritz Lipp, Horst Steinmann and Andreas Scherer, Dario Velo, and Philippe de Woot.

The architectural recomposition of systems for the production and distribution of goods and services around the world—which continually creates new relationships between the players and brings about new paradigms—means that, beyond positive analysis, normative thinking is necessary. The second part of the book, entitled "Institutional Designs," begins with an essay by Romano Prodi, president of the European Commission, who discusses the role of European institutions with respect to cultural diversity. Europe is also at the center of the reflections of Emilio Gabaglio, secretary general of the European Trade Unions Confederation; he discusses the requirements of a European social model. Mihail Papayannakis, member of the European Parliament, expresses concern over Europe's historical and political design.

At a planetary level, the challenges facing institutions are even more significant; they touch on all vital aspects of *humanity;* environmental and biosphere protection, respect for human rights, the quality of social relations, the fight against disease, and so on. Nongovernmental organizations (NGOs) seek to replace or complement institutional action. Jacky Mamou, president of Médecins du Monde, discusses the philosophy and functioning of an NGO for humanitarian action. In technical domains such as statistical information, institutions are having difficulty facing new requirements for treating social problems amplified by globalization. Photis Nanopoulos, director of Eurostat, shows that statistical decryption of today's global socioeconomic complexity remains very partial and imperfect, in spite of developments of the new information and communication technologies. The current primacy of financial considerations is detrimental to the environment and to the quality of the biosphere. International environmental law is being established, but its very conception presents numerous problems, as Alexandre Kiss points out before discussing the rules for implementation. Respect for human rights and universal values is also addressed in a different light with the redefinition of state sovereignty and the appearance of more global governance. Will a new global juridical system be likely to respect fundamental human values? Dinah Shelton asks this question. Geographical interconnection and the free circulation of ideas leads Elisabeth Sledziewski to wonder in particular about the new universal framework as it relates to women's rights.

The third part of the book, entitled "Views and Testimonies," focuses first on culture, looking at how the globalization process is actually seen and lived in the world of art: by artists, designers, actors, admittedly, but also by specialists, experts with an able mastery of their craft, the art of doing. Five fields of artistic expression are represented here, each affected by new technologies that have deeply influenced forms of expression and the distribution of art in the larger sense of the word. First, Pierre Boulez, composer, conductor, and creator, leads the reader into the domain of contemporary music (a universal language?). Sergio Escobar, director of the Piccolo Teatro di Milano–Teatro d'Europa, brings us onto the stage and behind it, to a place where, certainly, individual and social—but also universal—questions are asked in a specific language (a barrier?). For Davide Paolini, gastronome and culinary expert, food is simultaneously "language, thought, ideology," and is therefore a factor for integration (global or local?). For Jacques Marescaux, surgeon and professor, the medical art (or science) is being revolutionized by its entrance into the information age, with worldwide networks of experts and technology sharing knowledge, with the development of virtual reality, and even with the worldwide exchange of surgical techniques thanks to telesurgery. The future is inventing itself rapidly, and nothing seems impossible.

Part 3 also offers discussions by the mayors of several European cities (cities selected for their historical interest but purposely not capital cities) on a wide range of the topics introduced in this volume. Several mayors insist on the importance of local and regional communities in the treatment of social problems exacerbated by globalization: unemployment, immigration, and public safety. Cities may appear to be new centers of hope and welfare for their citizens. The mayors also discuss their responsibilities relating both to supranationality and subsidiarity, and they strongly emphasize the essential role that culture should play in the future. In a global world, with a tendency toward uniformity, culture appears to be a means to attract people "locally," a source of inspiration and creativity, an antidote for monotony, and a factor for individual enrichment and social integration—in short, an essential element in a society.

In the concluding essay Marina Ricciardelli wonders about the complexity and the uncertainty of events, and about humankind's ability, will, and method for mastering these events in order to shape the future.

Finally, it has been very inspiring to realize that in spite of their different points of view, the authors in this work have all perceptively linked the new world of interactivity, of sharing, and of co-responsibility, to the idea of quality: quality to create or to preserve, quality of services or quality of relationships, quality of the future that needs to be invented. Along with a deep concern for quality, there are also frequent discussions of the necessary activation of an ethics of responsibility. Actors must commit themselves to the ongoing process of building a more humane world for which they share responsibility.

NOTES

1. E. Morin, *Penser l'Europe* (Paris: Gallimard, 1987), p. 72.

2. The expression comes from Jacques Robin, "De la gauche numérotée au projet d'écologie politique," *Transversales Science/Culture* no. 60 (Nov.–Dec. 1999): p. 6.

3. Cf. J. Habermas, *Die postnationale Konstellation: Politische Essays* (Frankfurt: Suhrkamp, 1998).

4. W. Lepenies, *Die Drei Kulturen: Soziologie zwischen Literatur und Wissenschaft* (Munich: Hanser, 1985); *Aufstieg und Fall der Intellektuellen in Europa* (Frankfurt: Campus, 1992); "Von der Belehrungskultur zur Lernkultur," in *Wozu deutsche auswärtige Kulturpolitik,* edited by H. Schmidt et al. (Stuttgart: Neske, 1996), pp. 33–54.

5. S. P. Huntington, *The Clash of Civilizations and the Remaking of World Order* (London: Touchstone, 1996).

6. Morin, *Penser l'Europe,* p. 27.

CHAPTER I

Is the Future a Given?

ILYA PRIGOGINE

Madame Sabine Urban asked me to write an introductory chapter for this book, and I write it in all modesty. I greatly admire the economists and sociologists who are facing problems of terrifying complexity. But, there is one topic that has always interested me. That is the relationship between culture and nature. According to the Judeo-Christian tradition, this is a duality. Culture dominates. It reflects man's privileged position. Nature, on the other hand, is an object, an object destined to be dominated. This duality is reflected in the duality of the language of the social sciences as compared with the language of physics. The social sciences include the unforeseeable, the qualitative, the possible, and the uncertain. On the other hand, the ideal of the physical sciences is certitude and temporal reversibility. The past and future play the same role. Nature is an automaton. Yet, in spite of this duality, economists and sociologists have always been attracted by the Newtonian vision. According to John Herman Randall Jr.:

> The two leading ideas of the eighteenth century, Nature and Reason . . . derived their meaning from the natural sciences and, carried over to

Ilya Prigogine is a Nobel laureate in chemistry. He has been the director of the International Solvay Institutes for Physics and Chemistry in Brussels since 1959 and the director of the Ilya Prigogine Center for Studies in Statistical Mechanics, Thermodynamics, and Complex Systems at the University of Texas, Austin, since 1967. He has received numerous awards and distinctions, including fifty-one honorary doctorates. Five institutions bear his name. He is the author of *The End of Uncertainty: Time's Flow and the Laws of Nature* (New York: The Free Press, 1997), which was originally published in French as *La fin des certitudes* (Paris: Odile Jacob, 1996).

man, led to the attempt to discover a social physics. . . . In all things the newly invented social sciences were assimilated to the physical sciences. . . . The rational order of the world, as expressed in the Newtonian system of nature, scientific method, and scientific ideals . . . [was applied] in the comprehensive science of human nature that embraced a rational science of the mind, of society, of business, of government, of ethics, and of international relations.[1]

And Immanuel Wallerstein adds that it is in this perspective that we lived for three centuries. The recent evolution of physics and mathematics, however, allows us to envision another perspective, one in which physics draws nearer to the image that we have created of human history. My work falls into this perspective.

Let us enumerate some of the characteristics of the description adopted by the social sciences. First of all, there are sciences that describe behavior at the level of populations and not at the individual level. Human history is not reducible to the individual. Even if we analyze the behavior of one particular person, we have to include an analysis of the milieus in which he has lived. By definition, in human history there is a breakdown of symmetry between past and future. On the other hand, in Newtonian physics, even if modified by quantum mechanics or relativity, there is reversibility, symmetry between past and future. Fernand Braudel speaks about the "long term" of the historical trend as well as chronicles of events. Both suppose a specific orientation of time. The importance of the event remains a controversial issue. Is it dust, as Fernand Braudel wrote long ago? Are there abrupt changes? Does history express itself through a mix of determinism interrupted by events? Events that correspond to the reorganization of society? I believe that the essence of an event is that it introduces a difference between what is predictable and what is not. The position of the moon a million years from now is not an event. It can be deduced today, and with great accuracy, according to Newton's laws. On the other hand, the fall of the Berlin Wall, just to mention one example, was an event. Very few people foresaw the possibility of its fall. The event is associated with the uncertain. The existence of events on the human scale shows that on this scale social structures escape from determinism. What is interesting is that the event is the result of numerous circumstances. A scientist would say that the event is preceded by "fluctuations." The Russian Revolution was an event, but it was made possible by a series of coincidences: the weakness of the czar, the general hatred for the empress, Kerinsky's weakness, the violence of Lenin and Trotsky. It was certain that the czarist regime had to fall, but the manner in which it fell corresponded to one of the possibilities. The event has a micro-structure. It is the event, in a certain sense, that makes it possible to distinguish the past from the future. We can "explain" the events of the past. We can almost consider them as the issue of a latent determinism. But we cannot predict the events of the future.

It is interesting to compare the idea of the event with the idea of bifurcation currently used in physical and mathematical sciences. The bifurcations are placed in the perspective of evolution described by nonlinear laws. In such systems we can describe an economic variable or any other variable by a trajectory, but this trajectory generally leads to singular points, the bifurcations, from which several branches emerge.

For a physicist, there is another condition to which we will return, that of being far from equilibrium. This word has a very simple meaning when applied to human society. It is the flow of energy that society uses in a given situation. This flow of energy has been growing during the course of history. The transition from the village to the state was an event that corresponded to a flow of energy that was reinforced by agriculture and metallurgy. Of course, history does not consist merely of economic evolutions. The number of variables to consider and their relations are problems for sociologists and economists, and I dare not venture into that realm.

In physics we speak of "self-organization." That is, for the same external conditions, there are several solutions of the system of nonlinear evolution, one of which will be achieved—the one that corresponds to the branch realized after a point of bifurcation. We could probably speak of self-organization on the scale of the millennia of ancient Egypt, not that there were not outside influences, but the evolution of Egypt up to the Roman era was essentially internal evolution. Self-organization is a concept that applies to different scales, even to the entire universe. What can direct the evolution that we observe in the universe if it is not the universe? Here we are touching on a difficult philosophical point. Anyway, the lack of equilibrium, the flow of energy, is at the base of evolutionary phenomena.

Probably the most important and most evident characteristic of life is concern about the future. We find this even among the single-cell organisms that must evaluate the nutritional value of the environment and change their environment when its nutritional value decreases. This concern for the future reaches its peak in humans. Evaluating the future plays an essential role in man's decisions. I have always admired Le Pichon's words:

> But man has the ability of projecting himself in time, and this ability is, without a doubt, the source of his existential anguish. It is this

ability to see himself and to project in time that, I believe, comprise man's true originality. It may be his only true originality.[2]

In the life of societies, memory of the past, anticipation of the future, and the present intermingle, like determinism and events of which the outcome is uncertain. It is curious that many economists look at the idea of a linear and determinist world, which is contrary to everything we observe. Society is necessarily nonlinear because everything I do influences what others do and vice versa. But creating nonlinear models is certainly much more difficult than creating models on the basis of linear extrapolation. The emergence of the nonlinear is particularly clear at times of crisis. The larger society is, the more the nonlinear effects are important, and the greater the number of points of bifurcation. From all this, we must conclude that the "determinist" laws are not sufficient when we want to scan the future. They must be replaced by laws that imply probabilities. They must be probabilities that include a clear dissymmetry between past and future and describe populations rather than individual behavior. In physics and chemistry we are able to formulate laws that satisfy these conditions. Perhaps they will be sources of inspiration for the social sciences. The mathematician would like to qualify these probabilities as irreductible in the sense that they cannot be reduced to a decomposition into individual behaviors because the interaction plays an essential role.

Now let us return to physics. For three centuries Newton's laws dominated physics. Since the beginning of the last century, radical transformations have appeared, quantum mechanics and relativity, but the aspects that are at issue here have not been modified. The central object of Newtonian physics was the trajectory of a point. In relativity it is a space-time line; in quantum mechanics, a wave function. In every case it is a deterministic description that is reversible in time. In modern physics, geometric aspects play a fundamental role, while in the social sciences it is the historical and narrative aspects that play the fundamental role. And it is toward the perspective of a narration that the work of our group in Brussels and Austin is oriented.

We must recall that since Gibbs, who worked at the beginning of the century, physicists have described nature in two ways. We will obviously simplify things a bit. There is the individual description—which I have just mentioned—and there is the description in terms of ensembles describing a population of points or wave functions. But these ensembles were only introduced to express our ignorance of the initial conditions, for example, in a thermodynamic system that comprises an immense number of particles.

Hence the often defended idea that everything we deduce from ensembles can also be deduced on the individual particle level, and that the reversible temporal description would continue to exist if we knew the initial conditions. It would be our approximations that determine the evolution of nature. In such a description there is no event. This is a concept that I have always found a bit naive. It seems absurd to imagine that we humans determine the arrow of time through our approximations. The arrow of time is not only a human phenomenon, it is found on all scales in nature. There are novelties in nature, just as there are novelties in all human history. It is an interesting psychological problem that this issue has never really attracted the attention of researchers. I would like to quote a passage from I. Stengers's *Les Cosmopolitiques*

> In this context, it would have been sufficient, and still is, to recall that the famous physical laws that affirm the equivalence between "before" and "after" were made possible—and we are not talking about human history or applied physics—solely by measurements and that the least sophisticated of the measuring instruments denies this equivalence.[3]

The task I have set myself is to contribute to reconciling the Newtonian world with human reality. The sociobiologist Edmund Wilson wrote in his recent book *Conscience:* "There is no problem more urgent than that of lessening the gap between scientific and humanistic culture." I hope that the twenty-first will be the century of this reconciliation.

As I have already mentioned, we usually concluded that studying ensembles was the equivalent of studying trajectories. But, as demonstrated by the thermodynamics of equilibrium, this is not true. Everyone has seen phase diagrams, representing pressure as a function of volume with its discontinuities corresponding to the passage of a gas to a liquid and then of a liquid to a solid. But these discontinuities exist only in the theory of ensembles and even then, in a theory of ensembles in which we have reached the limit of an infinite number of particles and an infinite volume while the relationship between the two, the concentration, remains finite. It is only when we reach the thermodynamic limit that we see the physical states of matter appear. It is not the theory of trajectories, but the theory of ensembles that may tell us whether a body is in a given physical state. This is the reason why we, in our studies, are seeking to extend this observation to the system of non-equilibrium and to formulate the laws of physics in terms of these irreducible probabilities that I mentioned before. Obviously, we realize that this is an ambitious project because we must formulate an extension of the fundamental laws—that is, the laws of Newton, Schrödinger, and Einstein—and formulate them in terms of irreducible probabilities that lead to a breaking of temporal symmetry. This project is not an issue of personal ambition; it is a necessity. I cannot conceive of any other means of reconciling physics with the observation of nature. We have recently demonstrated that it is possible to do this in a mathematically rigorous manner. Naturally, such a generalization is not always necessary. The problem of two bodies, the problem of a reversible pendulum, are governed by Newton's laws and there is nothing to change. But already the "chaos" corresponds to unstable systems that are "sensitive" to initial conditions. What is more, this is so in the thermodynamic systems, which are far from equilibrium. Here we can demonstrate that irreducible probabilities do exist, which allow us to generalize "fundamental" laws. By using ensembles we obtain a physics of "populations," a concept needed for every social or economic model. If there are irreducible probabilities, this notion is applied differently for prediction and for "retrovision." In effect, we show that the evolution of these probabilities breaks up temporal symmetry. Each new theory in physics requires appropriate mathematics. Here, the theory of operators and their representations is the necessary tool. Everyone has heard about fractals that represent generalized functions. These irreducible probabilities are fractal-type functions. Now we have a mathematics "of time." But I do not want to go into the details here, and I suggest that the reader consult the original publications.

Reality is much more complex than we could have imagined. Matter is quite different from single points that wander without cease. The nineteenth century left us a conflicting heritage: on the one hand, the statistical, reversible laws of dynamics, and on the other, the evolutive description of thermodynamics based on the growth of entropy. This is the second law of thermodynamics. That is, irreversible phenomena, with a broken temporal symmetry, produce entropy. We can recall Clausius's statement that "The evolution of the universe takes place with an increase of entropy." Entropy is the arrow of time. Alongside the reversible laws of dynamics there are laws of irreversible processes including the arrow of time. We find it everywhere, in heat flow, in "transport" phenomena, in chemistry, and in biology. In fact, Newton's reversible laws cover only a small fraction of the world we live in. Let us consider the planetary system. Newton's laws give us a good description of planetary movements. But what happens on the planets—the geology, the climate, and life—all this requires the introduction of laws that include irreversible phenomena. Even at the microscopic level, we are discovering irreversible phenomena everywhere. Just think of radioactivity, of unstable elementary particles. As I mentioned earlier, the dilemma facing physicists was the following: do the irreversible phenomena come from our approximation of the introduction of ensembles as a result of our ignorance, or must we revise the laws of dynamics? We have already seen that the thermodynamics of equilibrium requires the introduction of ensembles, hence of probabilistic concepts. This position, which requires an extension of dynamics, becomes even stronger as a result of the unexpected results of thermodynamics far from equilibrium. Let us summarize the description that thermodynamics gives of nature. Close to equilibrium, thermodynamics describes a stable world. If there are fluctuations the system responds by returning to its state of equilibrium characterized by the extremum (maximum or minimum) of entropy or of any other thermodynamic potential. But the new fact is that this situation changes radically when we place ourselves far from equilibrium. Fluctuations could, thus, give rise to new space-time structures. In order for this to happen the laws of evolution must be nonlinear. Thus we arrive at "dissipative structures" that correspond to these new "supramolecular" organizations.

In the laboratory we reproduce these structures easily. For example, there are oscillating chemical reactions in which millions of particles simultaneously change "color," or the famous Turing structures in which chemical compounds organize themselves in groups, or "chaotic" phenomena in which two nearby trajectories separate exponentially during the course of time. All these new structures develop at points of "bifurcation." It is there that the old structures become unstable and new structures arise. We must note that, thanks mainly to the flow of energy coming from the sun, we live in a world "far from equilibrium." We are surrounded by structures formed during the course of the history of Earth, be it in chemistry, geology, or biology. We must seek their origins in the subsequent bifurcations. As a matter of fact, we have seen that the bifurcations introduce an element of uncertainty. Once again, it is the "end of the certainty" and the appearance of a plurality of futures. Let us insist on the constructive role of irreversible phenomena. This gives us a quite different view of matter. I have often written that "Matter in equilibrium is blind; far from equilibrium it starts to see." We generally have sequences of bifurcations. This leads to a "historical" view of nature. The model of classical physics was a geometrical view of nature, the model of which Einstein's general relativity gives the supreme example. Now we can see that "narrative" historical elements appear even in the hard "sciences of nature."

This is only possible by introducing a probabilistic view. So we find again, far from equilibrium, characteristics that we enumerated for the social sciences: the arrow of time, points of bifurcation, and events. Thus we are witnessing a significant rapprochement of the two scientific cultures.

It is time to conclude. To me, the arrow of time seems to be the most "universal" property there is. We are all aging in the same direction, including the rocks and the stars. But the arrow of time does not correspond only to aging. There are also events and new situations that manifest nature's creativity. We are only at the beginning. We understand quite well the mechanism of events leading to new structures in physics and chemistry. We have acquired notions such as points of bifurcation and self-organization. These concepts can probably serve as a metaphor for the social sciences. In any case, it is a much more natural metaphor than that of Newton's world.

We are still far from an understanding of the fluctuations that have led to the transition from the pre-quantum void to the universe in which we live, or even the fluctuations of matter at the origin of life. In any case, we are starting to come closer to the reality that surrounds us. The history of life and of societies is not subject to any type of determinism. We are rediscovering the "time" that was the exclusive domain of the social sciences and that extends to the whole of science. This rediscovery of the arrow of time coincides with an awareness of the transition toward the information society. Are we not approaching a point of bifurcation involving fundamental aspects of our societies? We are "living uncertainty" in a particularly intense manner at the start of this new century. The uncertainty introduced by globalization is inevitable. But what we must not forget is that fluctuations will determine the branch on which this point of bifurcation will develop. It is a call to individual action which, today more than ever, is not necessarily condemned to insignificance.

NOTES

1. Quoted in I. Wallerstein, *Unthinking Social Science* (Oxford: Polity Press, 1991).

2. In "La quête des origines," *Le Nouvel Observateur*, Hors-Série, no. 31, pp. 68–89.

3. I. Stengers, *Cosmopolitiques*, vol. 1 (Paris: La Découverte, 1996), p. 107.

PART I

Reading Globalization

CHAPTER 2

Economic Science
and Real Economy

FRANCO MODIGLIANI

INTERVIEW CONDUCTED BY MARINA RICCIARDELLI

I. The Relationship between Scientific Analysis
and Management of Real Phenomena

The phenomenon of globalization that actually began twenty-five years ago seems to have been influenced primarily by economic processes (intensive reorganization of production systems, internationalization of the financial capital markets, computerization, etc.). There are therefore different types of issues that relate to this subject.

Marina Ricciardelli: Are the theoretical models of economic science suitable for analyzing the increasing complexity of this evolving context?
  Franco Modigliani: In principle, yes. Many economists have dedicated themselves to this type of problem both as a main theme and as a secondary issue with regard to other problems that concern us. On the whole, the answer we can give is affirmative. According to general opinion, we could say

Franco Modigliani is a Nobel laureate in economics, professor emeritus at the A. P. Sloan School of Management, Massachusetts Institute of Technology, and honorary president of the International Economic Association and of the Econometric Society.

19

that globalization is, aside from a few exceptions, a salutary trend or, in other words, a process that improves things. On the one hand, we consider it the herald of egalitarian trends, in the sense that it is pushing countries to raise their levels of wealth and prosperity. On the other hand, we recognize that it can sometimes act in the opposite direction, by producing unfavorable results within countries. It can cause a redistribution of income in favor of the rich, or rather in favor of those who are intellectually advantaged or who have enjoyed the benefits of higher education. Therefore, the results of this distribution can be unfavorable. Movements of capital, especially over the short term, can also lead to problems. But, and I repeat, globalization on the whole acts as a catalyst for the growth and specialization of a country.

M.R.: If you agree, we will stay on the subject of the ability and willingness of economic science to comprehend and solve the problems raised by this new context.

The process of globalization we are witnessing is inspired by free market rules that are considered the guarantors of the best allocation of resources to the extent that they are based on the interest of each economic actor. But the free market's definition of the theoretical models differs from the dynamics of reality. For example, we suppose that a system of free competition develops spontaneously when, in fact, it requires extremely rigorous controls.

In your opinion, can a "world liberalism" that considers the behavior and rationality of the business as the driving engine of the economy be the basis for an adequate macroeconomic approach?

F.M.: It can be the basis as long as we are ready to make numerous exceptions. Let me explain. The first answer is yes. But as soon as we reason in a less approximate manner, the statement takes on many nuances. In general, the effect of liberalism is to increase competition. But of course there are exceptions. The fact of opening the markets forces businesses to follow precise rules that reduce their freedom. In fact, in many countries the monopoly is an essential element for maintaining the separation of classes. It is sufficient to think of the banking system which, in poor countries, is the prerogative of only a few rich people. They own the banks and consequently can exploit the poor "devils" to an extent that is indecent. Introducing rules of competition in this type of regime and opening the country to foreign banks is therefore very important.

When I speak of the need to make exceptions I refer, for example, to the possibilities of subjecting the market system to the phenomenon of speculative bubbles. Their specificity is that of being consistent with macroscopically rational behavior and, at the same time, being carriers of macroscopic dysfunctions. In this regard, a good example is the behavior of the American stock market, which in my opinion is currently [June 1999] highly over-valued. But from the viewpoint of those who continue to invest, no price is too high as long as it goes even higher tomorrow. In other words, the expectation that tomorrow's price will be higher is sufficient. However, in order for this expectation to be met, the price must go up. And it must continue to do so. As long as it keeps on rising everything is fine. But as it gradually rises it becomes more and more absurd, farther and farther from the base value, a price that will be difficult to maintain over the long term. According to my analysis, the rational capitalized value of the American stock market is about twenty to twenty-five times the level of the expected gain. Currently, it is at thirty. This is not rational. It could only be so if the growth rate of returns were much higher than what it actually is. What happens with speculative bubbles is that people continue buying in the hope that others do the same and therefore keep the prices rising, but at the slightest doubt, things could change, the whole world will want to get out immediately, and the speculative bubble will burst. The fact that it bursts is typical. A gradual descent is practically inconceivable.

In my opinion, these speculative bubbles are at the base of the recent troubles in the East and in some East Asian countries. Starting with Thailand, the country in which there was a massive influx of capital mainly because it was believed that it would procure big returns. But the capital was poorly invested, for example in those huge skyscrapers that no one needed, and at a certain moment the doubt that it was a perverse mechanism insinuated itself and the people wanted to get out immediately. And once people want to withdraw it is no longer possible to manage the fast outflow of capital. That is practically impossible and consequently causes extreme reactions. The exchange rates must drop to such a level as to prompt people to say, "it is so low that it is better to wait." Enormous difficulties. All this must be avoided in the future. I have various recommendations and one of them is to avoid speculative bubbles. But it is obvious that such recommendations interfere with the free choice of private agents, and there are many who are opposed to them. I therefore disagree with the treasury ministers and their staffs who do not want to interfere with the market in any way.

M.R.: Questioning the ability of theoretical models to provide an appropriate interpretative framework underlines the transition from positive science to regulatory science. Today, are we able to detect a weak link in this chain? Don't the current great emphasis placed on the microeconomic

*models, the limited rationality of the "representative" players, and the deter-
minism in making forecasts seem more appropriate for defending certain
axioms presented as "truths" rather than for seeking a new architecture of
rules?*

F.M.: Regarding the theoretical model, the model of rational expectations, it is perfectly correct and elegant because, if we may say it this way, it
completes the rational behavioral model. Before it was introduced, we referred to a rational behavior for the given expectations whatever they were,
and no one bothered about whether or not they were "rational." The new
model establishes that even expectations must be rational and that rationality is well defined. As I explained in one of my fundamental works, the
future depends on today's expectations. The expectation of an event can be
considered rational when the following result coincides with the expectation. At this stage, the value of the model of rational expectations, as one of
my very intelligent colleagues (Benjamin Friedman) emphasized, is the fact
that this model is a viable shortcut to what economists call the long term.
What does this mean? It is a time period long enough for us to learn to understand the consequences of our actions. Therefore, the expectations progressively become more coincident with the facts. Fundamentally, however, I
must say that I reject this proposed model on the one hand as useful for
explaining short-term behavior and on the other as a policy guide. I reject
it for two distinct reasons. The first, because it assumes a capacity for rationality on the part of individuals, something in which I do not believe. I do
not believe that individuals taken singly are stupid, but they are certainly not
geniuses. Their intelligence is average and their behavior is generally reasonable. Having said this, understanding the idea that their future depends
on what they expect and for which there is a single expectation coinciding
with its realization is much more complicated. The fact is that the rational
expectation and the corresponding action depend on what one believes the
structure of the economy to be. Mr. Lucas and I will never agree because he
believes that prices are flexible, that they decrease when there is unemployment. I believe that Keynes was completely right and that prices are not
flexible. Thus we have different models, and consequently the rational forecasts cannot be the same. And so, since I believe that people can always err
in their expectations, I believe that policy can help them. When wages are rigid
and many jobs prove it, if monetary policy takes wage rigidity into account,
it is useful because it stabilizes prices. Therefore, I believe that one of the
roles of economic policy is to take expectations into account, be they what
they may—sometimes they may even be rational—and then try to do its best.

M.R.: The propensity for insisting on relations that link scientific research activities and management of real phenomena derives from the growing bond between the experts and their research institutions, on the one hand, and the categories of people and bodies interested in establishing a client relationship with them, on the other. On the scientific level this could imply that interests in the outcome of research often converge with underlying criteria of utility. Do you believe that the role of "researcher" can shift responsibility and attention away from theoretical thinking or, in other words, lead researchers away from researching and seeking certain goals and toward choosing the methods and modes for achieving goals that have been set previously? Could this diminish the social validity and the general importance of scientific thought?

F.M.: That is a very long question, with at least twenty different points. Let's try to reorganize it. I believe that researchers, who are serious, respected, and therefore listened to, are not the slaves of the clients. At least this situation is very clear in the United States: "If you want my personal advice you can have it, but please don't quote me. If you want me to do research, you must give me full freedom. I will not even let you see the results." In America this problem does not exist either for serious researchers or institutions that are recognized as such.

What I do see as a reason for concern, and it may be inevitable, is the fact of submitting to certain schools of thought, or yielding to certain ways of seeing things, and perhaps wanting to see them from a not entirely impartial point of view—even if what occurred is perfectly clear. For example, in the early 1970s a phase began and lasted for fifteen years with two oil crises. Inflation made its appearance. I insist on repeating that it is absolutely untrue that inflation is a tendency of our economic system, but it was a rather delicate situation. By trying to reach a low unemployment rate, the economy found itself at the mercy of inflation: an inflation that continued up through the 1990s. In my opinion, it all derived from oil, which was the initial cause that engendered a spiral that can only be controlled by a nonaccommodating monetary policy and that leads to unemployment *cum* inflation, the phenomenon defined as *stagflation*, which lasted for many years.

All this happens simply because there is a component of the cost of living that is totally exogenous and that drives the rest. It is a situation in which we define certain behavior patterns as irrational. We call them irrational solely because the people do not fully understand the economy, or because they do not realize that prices rise because a tax had been established and levied by the "sheiks" and we must pay it: we cannot escape from it by demanding a compensating rise in salaries; this type of rise only produces inflation and unemployment.

But I do not see anything concerning economic, industrial, or commercial interests that affect research in relation to the issues we have mentioned.

M.R.: The question does not arise solely for economic and private interests. It also arises for public institutions. For example, we could mention the studies on employment that the European institutions commissioned research centers to conduct according to a framework of hypotheses and strictly determined cause and effect relationships.

F.M.: Many people insist on saying that unemployment is, above all, the effect of wrong policies in which the elements of the labor market also come into play. But there are a very few of us who say that the basis of the problem is a lack of global demand. Few, not because they pay or do not pay us, but because we are convinced that we understand how the economy works. It is an understanding that differs from that of others. The problem is that we have different interpretations; there are not different motivations and commissions which could bind us. Hence the possibility during a congress, as I recall, the one in Frankfurt,[1] of dividing us into those who believe that the entire problem is a matter of the amount of money in circulation, reasoning on the M1 and M2 weighted average and the need to create targets; and those who had presented papers that emphasized the importance of other phenomena, with unemployment at the top of the list, and who proposed reflection and thought on the errors of economic policy.

2. The Lights and Shadows over the Economic and Monetary Union

In relationships among different geographic areas, globalization has introduced the concept of externality. All economic systems have a mutual impact on each other due to the multiplication of the communicating vessels and the interrelation of actions and reactions. This has progressively put both traditional macroeconomic analysis and the economic policy that derives from it, and that has accompanied the development of the industrialized countries since World War II, into a crisis mode. Recalling this phenomenon will allow us to focus our attention on the Economic and Monetary Union, which, due to the adopted procedures, has accelerated and accentuated certain characteristics of globalization in the member states by introducing increasingly marked forms of supranational power.

Eleven of the fifteen members of the European Community introduced the single currency on 1 January 1999. To participate in this phase they had to prove that they had met the institutional deadlines (abolition of customs barriers, etc.) and the nominal convergences set forth in the Maastricht Treaty.

M.R.: Our first question is about the physiognomy of the Economic Union. Do you think this project is more important and more valid than the European Community of 1958? If yes, why? Is the adoption of the euro a determining element or an essential variable of this new reality? Do you think that the introduction of the single currency on the European level is a valid choice? Do you believe that Europe is hoping to oppose the dominant role of the dollar?

F.M.: I do not believe that the role of the euro is to oppose the American currency. I do not agree. Its goals are quite different.

I have always supported the movement for the European Union, which, I am convinced, will culminate in a single nation: in other words, a country in which the existing states will disappear to make room for the territories that comprise a true reality. We must remember that the differences among the European countries are becoming hazy.

Compared with the differences between northern and southern Italy, the differences among the European countries are blurring. In European countries the unemployment rate ranges from 4–5 percent to 25 percent, in Italy it ranges from 4 percent to 50 percent. The difference between Lombardy and Calabria is enormous. In my opinion Europe's future rests on its ability to free itself from constraints and to turn toward a concept of territorial areas with much more autonomous regions. In this context the single currency is inevitable.

Questions arise at this point: What are the dangers in this process? And, if the road is strewn with snares and pitfalls and hence costs, is it worth embarking on it? Consequently, is it better to acknowledge or to deny dangers? There is no doubt, I believe, that danger does exist: in essence it is the rigidity of the relative prices that derives from the absence of flexible exchange rates, a rigidity that was unknown up to now. On the other hand, it is clear that exchange rate flexibility has its own negative aspects. When the exchange rate in Italy was more favorable, in 1993, unemployment was as high as it is now. Because fluctuations do not, unfortunately, make it possible to compensate for all problems. For example, fluctuations create an exchange risk on the financial and currency markets and therefore a rise in interest rates, which, in Italy for example, did not decrease significantly until the euro was introduced. Thus, there are disadvantages in all this. I think that the problem of rigidity can be largely eliminated if the workers and unions accept flexibility on the labor market to replace exchange rate flexibility. Instead of devaluing, they should accept a limit on wage increases that amounts to a smaller increase than in other countries. And in some cases it should be the opposite: growth rather than over-valuation. Wage flexibility instead of exchange rate flexibility would be the best. Obviously we must see how we can organize and effectively control this.

Currently, the central bank is raising a particular problem. What we believe to be an intelligent and lucid central bank is in fact blind, narrow-minded, and has no intention of doing anything about what it should be concerned with, namely, employment. Instead of thinking about inflation that does not exist (price control is already run by the unions), it would be sufficient for the central bank to avoid engaging in erroneous policies such as, for instance, printing money without reason, because that would cause inflation. However, during periods of unemployment it should avoid concentrating on something that does not matter while ignoring what does. This depends partly on the EMU Treaty that only gives the European Central Bank responsibilities regarding inflation. Oskar Lafontaine and Dominique Strauss-Kahn had started a dialogue on these topics. I regard the fact that we lost both as a serious setback for the cause of high employment.

M.R.: Please allow me to complete the question you are answering. Do you think that nominal convergences and their fixed relative values are the inevitable criteria for the credible introduction of the euro on the financial markets?

F.M.: It is true that fixed exchange rates were needed to arrive at the euro, and it is also true that fixed rates mean a single monetary policy, and that does not necessarily mean an incorrect policy, but that is what happened. The Bundesbank became the de facto central bank and applied an incorrect monetary and fiscal policy. On the budgetary level two aspects have to be considered: for the deficit we must first of all distinguish between current and capital accounts, something that the Maastricht Treaty does not take into consideration. The three percent rate for the budget deficit on GDP is completely arbitrary, under the pretext that it may, perhaps, correspond to investments. And that, instead of establishing that current accounts must be balanced and that real investments must be handled according to the criteria of social efficiency. To apply this rule, the authors of the "Manifesto,"[2] who include me, recommended the creation of a higher authority to verify the legitimacy of investments. Furthermore, since the deficits in the past had been very high, the people fighting the current deficit refuse to understand that a large portion of the past one was false. We must also distinguish between nominal and real revenue. We must say that a significant part of the deficit was nominal and not real. I said this several times. And the answer I get is that if I said this to the parliaments, they—the parliaments—would have immediately approved new expenditures. As an economist I must state things the way they are, and then let the politicians assume their responsibilities.

I repeat that the convergence of exchange rates, inflation, and interest was absolutely necessary. But the convergence of very short-term budgetary policy is hazardous, and even more so when we impose a highly restrictive fiscal policy in the face of high underemployment in terms of job shortages and unexploited production capacity. The Germans and their arch-conservative disciples have never understood the concept of built-in flexibility, not even in the Stability Pact. This does not mean fixing the balance, the expenditures or the income, but rather establishing the parameters that determine expenditures and income in such a way that the current expenditure accounts are balanced when we are close to full employment, in deficit during the low cycle, and in surplus during the high cycle. In addition, as we have already said, we must distinguish between current expenditures and capital expenditures. Therefore, the creation of the euro was much more painful than it should have been.

M.R.: The Stability Pact, which redefined the macroeconomic framework of the EMU in a restrictive manner for the coming years, tightens the discipline of each national budget as regards the rules established by nominal convergences. Each country must solve its economic problems that derive from asymmetrical shocks without burdening the partners or without counting on federal fiscalism of the European budget. The supranational control calls for recourse to sanctions and penalties against the "defaulting" states. Do you believe that these strong constraints that accentuate the deflationist model that had been followed throughout the 1990s are necessary?

F.M.: In accordance with the reasons I gave earlier, the Stability Pact has aggravated the errors of Maastricht. Imposing a common limit to deficits is generally a mistake since the countries cannot turn to their central banks for financing, but must finance themselves on the market—proof of this is the American experience where the federal government does not impose any budgetary restrictions on the states.

M.R.: The EMU has adopted the competition model to achieve the single market and to define relationships among the member states. It has been said that "healthy" competition between the national institutions decreases their "monopoly" vis-à-vis citizens and businesses, and makes them more efficient with regard to unproductive public expenditures and taxation. This model was the determining element in the rejection of harmonization (or at least coordination) of the different national structures of direct taxation, for instance as regards the taxable base which is characterized by high transnational mobility. But tax evasion and fraud have increased, and respect for nominal convergences has taken, and will continue to take, a difficult, obstacle-filled path.

To counter the economic problems, the European states are stuck between the challenge of competition and multilateral/supranational monitoring with powers of sanction. Economic science, on the other hand, theorizes the development of cooperation among the states in the sense of a course toward more efficiency and economic use of resources. What do you believe could be the best approach?

F.M.: The idea that competition among the regulatory bodies could be useful for limiting the tendency to overregulate does carry a certain weight, and has even been applied in a beneficial manner in some cases in the United States. But, in a regime of totally free circulation, it is ridiculous to want to apply it to the taxation of capital gains and revenues. This concept is not applied in the United States, where the taxation of a large part of this income is regulated by federal laws that are identical for all citizens.

As to cooperative policies, we have, for a long time and specifically in the "Manifesto," expressed the conviction that the states must cooperate and undertake joint actions to increase demand and employment. We do not at all share the idea that unemployment is a strictly domestic phenomenon. Our opinion has produced some effects, to the extent that at recent meetings of the European chiefs of state, a principle was confirmed: the states must take joint measures and respond as to their implementation.

M.R.: The complexity of the EMU model is apparent in the frequently conflicting relationships among the various institutional levels and in particular among the new supranational and traditional national powers. If we look at more recent periods, the objections and polemics seem to touch the technical/bureaucratic bodies, on the one hand, and the legitimately elected bodies, on the other (the European Central Bank and economic ministers, the European Parliament and Commission, etc.). What is in question here is whether or not to defend a conceptual framework that opposes the "neutral" laws of the economy, which are considered priorities and free of dangerous "ideologized" values, thereby sacrificing the need for mediating the multiple interests of a pluralistic society. Do you believe that such conflicts are normal within a dynamic process that is modifying the traditional institutional systems? Or do you believe that we must face the more important issues regarding the evolution of democratic participation in the management of phenomena that so closely touch the fundamental aspects of society?

F.M.: That is a complex question and you cannot answer it with a simple yes or no. In essence, I think it always desirable that the Community impose rules of higher behavior for everyone: for example, that public tenders be open to all enterprises in the Community even if that goes against the custom of giving the markets to the local "mafias." But I also think that we must strengthen the more democratic institutions, such as the European Parliament, and that the Central Bank, which is currently totally independent of the democratically elected governments, be reformed and held liable.

M.R.: Does the creation of the European region as a single market accentuate the segmentation of the world into rich and poor zones, and within the context of competition among the large geographic areas does it augment the economic power of the former to the detriment of the latter?

F.M.: There is no reason to think that the single market or the euro will cause any further deterioration in the third world. On the contrary, what is generally good for one area is good for the rest. For example, the demand for the other's products increases. What could happen in relative terms is difficult to foresee and depends in part on the policies of aid for development implemented by the more industrialized countries.

3. The Problems of the Labor Market and the Multidisciplinary Aspect of Reality

In the EMU the criterion of supranational monitoring has been extended from nominal convergences to real economic convergences. The Treaty of Amsterdam complemented the Maastricht Treaty by institutionalizing the commitment of the states to define long-term programs aimed at fighting the problem of unemployment and by submitting this commitment to multilateral monitoring, that is, to the supranational European level to which they must answer.

M.R.: In order to adapt to globalization, European industry is engaged in a great movement to bring together businesses in many and different forms: cooperation contracts, groups of common economic interest, transnational investments, mergers, acquisitions, etc. Gradually, as competition increases, the number of competitors will decrease. Organizations are developing and are also exercising their power outside the market. Must we suppose that this process is as inexorable as it is positive, or, on the contrary, can we deduce that economies of scale and the effects of synergisms can rapidly be transformed into diseconomies of scale and dysfunctions (because of different administrative procedures, opposing entrepreneurial cultures, etc.)?

F.M.: This is a matter with which I am not that familiar, and specific knowledge is needed in this area. The experts I know are divided: some of them think that there are real economic advantages and others doubt that there is any clear advantage at all. I think that it is still too early to make a general judgment, but it is interesting to note that the slogan "small is beautiful" is no longer very fashionable.

M.R.: In a complex and chaotic context, the speed of change makes forecasts increasingly uncertain. The speed of adaptation to change fits poorly with burdensome organizational procedures; instead, it demands much creative imagination and flexibility. In relation to the United States or Asia and in the case of recomposition of economic players in networks, will Europe reap any particular advantages (such as the Italian industrial tradition) or specific disadvantages (multiple languages, different industrial regulations and accounting systems, etc.)?

F.M.: Currently, American industry is proving that it has a greater ability to adapt than Europe, but that does not mean it will continue to in the future.

M.R.: We have already stressed the problem of employment in the EMU. Please let me go back to it. The interpretive model at the base of European policies against unemployment stresses the structural components of this serious phenomenon. It proposes corrections that affect the profitability of the job offer (in terms of professional skills and qualifications, etc.), the institutions that govern industrial relations (flexible contract rules, etc.), and the development of the efficiency of the general system (endogenous theory of growth). We hear talk about the "insider" and "outsider" conflict. In the redistribution phase we affirm that the wage partner must give up parts of productivity to encourage investments and increase profitability. We absolutely do not take discretionary action against cyclical unemployment into consideration.

It is a mosaic of choices and actions that will bear fruits over the long and the medium term. Do you believe that flexibilizing the labor market at a GDP growth rate much lower than the potential GDP could increase rather than decrease the unemployment rates? If opening the economies reinforces the trade-off between jobs and productivity over the short term, how can we render the time required for adjustment socially acceptable?

F.M.: On more than one occasion, and specifically in the "Manifesto," I stated that in order to bring unemployment down to physiological levels we must implement simultaneous measures aiming, on the one hand, at increasing overall demand and, on the other, decreasing the numerous rigidities of the labor market. The global demand must be encouraged above all by relaunching investments that are languishing in Europe and flourishing in the United States. To do this we must first implement a more expansive monetary policy, encourage the formation of new businesses in disadvantaged areas, and relaunch public investments, which means modifying the Stability Pact. Flexibility means flexible working hours, including part-time, the possibility of reducing work forces when they are excessive (decreasing the protection for the insiders), and adjusting salaries and wages according to productivity. Some things have been done recently for flexibility but too little has been done for demand, and, as the "Manifesto" states, flexibility alone cannot go very far without an increase in the overall demand (and vice versa).

M.R.: With the aim of competing with the American model, we emphasize that the job offer in Europe must adapt its behavior to the creation of an optimal monetary area and therefore must deal with the mobility of other productive factors (financial capital, in the first place) or compensate for its poor mobility by greater flexibility in the salary systems. Could refusing these types of change mean defining unemployment as a voluntary phenomenon and separating it further from the macroeconomic issues and policies, which is the exact opposite of what is happening in the United States?

F.M.: My last answer already included something to this regard. The reluctance of the southern Italian workers to accept vacant jobs in the north could be defined as voluntary only if we qualify it as a consequence of an insufficient overall demand. Experience teaches us that in the past these people worked, and they would still be working if there were jobs of the type that would exist in the case of a higher demand.

M.R.: The problems of the labor market do not solely concern the economic system. They establish important bonds with social problems, with the criteria for cooperation, solidarity, democratic evolution, etc. Are we certain that ignoring these issues means marginalizing situations that have nothing to do with the creation of efficient systems? Or that in this way we "irrationally" squander resources, to use economic language, and consequently develop new and more severe imbalances?

F.M.: The measures that we consider necessary for a return to full employment do not demand that we sacrifice essential values. The "overprotection" of insiders is a problem that becomes inflamed when there are no jobs. It is a vicious circle in which job security (protection from layoffs and firings) decreases mobility and jobs. This reduces the flux of hiring, therefore making it even more difficult for outsiders, particularly young outsiders, to find jobs, and this in turn leads to exacerbated protection. When there are job openings, job security is not that important or harmful because mobility is obtained thanks to voluntary resignations. One classic example is Austria, where salary protection is quite strong but there is little unemployment and a highly mobile labor force. The "Manifesto" suggests that measures for decreasing protection should only be implemented after having reduced unemployment through measures for encouraging the overall demand. An enlightened demand and labor market policy could reconcile full employment while protecting human and democratic values.

NOTES

1. F. Modigliani, "The Shameful Rate of Unemployment in the EMS: Causes and Cures," draft document, International Conference on Future European Monetary Policy; Association for the Monetary Union of Europe, 30 November–1 December, Kronberg, Germany.

2. F. Modigliani, J. Fitoussi, B. Moro, D. Snower, R. Solow, A. Steinherr, and P. Sylos Labini, "An Economist's Manifesto on Unemployment in the European Union," *BNL Quarterly Review* no. 206 (September 1998).

CHAPTER 3

Globalization and Regional Responsibility: Challenges for Leaders

PETER EICHHORN

I. Introduction

This essay investigates the effects of globalization at the local level, its impact on people's work and private lives, and the action which can be undertaken by opinion leaders and company managers in order to avoid negative developments. The intention here is not to discuss general societal aspects, in the sense of the growing together of a global community of peoples with the goals of justice, freedom, and peace, but rather to address the problems for local populations and consumers arising from companies' globalization strategies.

Growth is a general organizational objective because it promises improved achievement of goals, be these formal or substantive goals. Apart from *endogenous factors* which are manifest in people's actions—or more precisely, in such characteristics as the striving for material wealth and

Peter Eichhorn is a professor in the Department of Public Management at the University of Mannheim, a former researcher at Nuffield College, University of Oxford, and visiting professor at Bocconi University (Milan), Nippon University (Tokyo), and the Université Robert Schuman (Strasbourg). He is also a consultant for nonprofit organizations.

possessions, the desire to make a useful contribution to society, the need for recognition, the exercise of power, the role model function—*exogenous factors* increasingly influence globalization. Technological advancement enables the worldwide exchange of information, capital, services, goods, and people. It is via these processes, very often conducted in English, that economies open up and grow together. Tighter national procurement and sales markets force organizations to pursue international strategies. Numerous countries formerly belonging to the category of newly industrializing countries are now involved as modern economies in international competition. To this trend must be added those of deregulation and liberalization in world trade (through the World Trade Organization [WTO], the Organization for Economic Cooperation and Development [OECD], and the abolition of trade barriers in developing countries) and in the European Union, which further lead to expanded trading opportunities for companies. Exports and imports are on the increase, as is the interconnectedness between national economies and geographical areas of economic cooperation. The radical political change in former socialist countries has exposed these to the market economy and has led to a spread of capitalism.

However, what is good for a global organization, its shareholders, employees, and the government in its role as tax collector is not necessarily positive for third parties. What exactly are the consequences of such a global process?

2. The Consequences of Globalization

The opportunities created by expanded markets are also accompanied by threats. The markets for labor, capital, goods, and services in distant countries are literally unknown territory and are often subject to different rules. On the one hand, increasing global competition between commercial organizations mobilizes initiatives for improved initial and further training, spurs ideas for research and technical development, and forces ossified bureaucracies in business and administration to change, as well as protectionist measures to be dismantled. On the other hand, those locations and regions with declining sectors or natural disadvantages may be the victims of this development. Local authority enterprises in the areas of electricity, gas, district heating and water supply, sewage treatment and waste disposal, local public transport, and banking and housing management, and even nonprofit enterprises such as retirement homes, homes for the handicapped, nursing services, rescue services, and hospitals are finding themselves continuously confronted by capital-rich, globally operating "buyers" eager to take them over. The logical result is that external factors exert an increasingly determining influence on local authorities and their activities.

Expanded business opportunities lead to the emergence of ever larger enterprises (multinational groups), which organize themselves as networks and establish strategic alliances with suppliers. The cooperating organizations can serve to unite this community of nationalities. International opportunities are opened for young people (e.g., jobs with global players and international work experience). On the other hand, however, because of this interconnectedness in sales, production, and finance, medium-sized organizations risk having their scope curtailed. Powerful large organizations, in particular those requiring standard, system-based components, place suppliers in a difficult position. Unless mass production can be combined with customized production, large batch sizes lead to conformity. The customer experiences this in the form of high prices for products or services tailored to his individual requirements and the general reduction in differentiated product/services offers.

Global organizations obtain their resources from the four corners of the globe, wherever these are offered at the best terms. Raw materials, capital, and labor are sourced and employed worldwide depending on where the particular factor happens to be the cheapest at the particular time. Countries that appear attractive to organizations are prioritized as locations for activities (bridgeheads), for example, those with low taxation and social insurance contribution regimes, low levels of environmental regulation and taxes, and generally fewer rules, regulations, and bureaucracy as well as less codetermination. Put bluntly, this rule of the market in the area of factor procurement and service provision goes hand in hand with a demise of the state. The community becomes sucked into the whirlpool of commercial interests. The business environmental conditions and the exercise of influence are solely dictated by market requirements in order to ensure that market forces alone determine supply and demand. As a result, it is extremely difficult to guarantee the basic provision of reasonably priced, high-quality, safe, accessible, continuous, reliable, and environmentally and consumer-friendly infrastructural services in the areas of energy, water, transport, banking, and housing. The principle of the welfare state with its social assistance measures, equalization of burdens, social insurance, free schooling, and support of further education, as well as the principle of codetermination by employees in matters of labor law and organizational decision making, down to free collective bargaining by employers and employees, disrupts the all-powerful law of *competition*.

Large companies with worldwide contacts and organizational functions, and with their plants scattered throughout the globe, dominate both prosperous and economically stagnant areas through their operations. In both cases, the reaction on the part of local authorities is passive rather than active. The more the economy of a community is based on one activity, the more influence the organization will have on local authority decision and policy making. The result can be that the power of the city or even the state is minimized. Small and medium-sized local communities or, more precisely, the bodies representing and administering these communities, as well as public representatives, often lack access to the people with decision-making power, since the top management of global public companies usually resides elsewhere. In the course of organizational mergers and acquisitions, group headquarters are relocated without due consideration being given to historic tradition, as witnessed, for example, in the merger of the Frankfurt-based Hoechst AG with the French company Rhône Poulenc. The new company, Aventis SA, established its headquarters practically within Strasbourg's "green field."

Although the top management, subsidiary management, and plant and works managers of subsidiaries and second-tier subsidiaries or other local operations of a given company may be familiar with local matters, strategic decisions regarding jobs, employment, diversification, investments, mergers and joint ventures, and to a certain extent even the payment of taxes are made by the management of the remote holding company, which has no proximity to or identification with the specific location. These management boards are in the position to place the community and its region under pressure by either actual or threatened measures that destroy basic material resources, in particular the income of the workers and local authorities. The sale of local organizations to international holding companies can lead in the medium term to the closure of developed business locations. Examples are the sale of the Speyer Siemens operation to the American investment company Tyco, and the takeover of Standard Elektrik Lorenz (SEL) by the French group Alcatel and its repercussions for the Mannheim plant. Such closures may be partly due to a lack of competitiveness by local production plants, but it is also possible that they are the result of questionable strategies, such as the elimination of undesirable competition between internal groups within the company. Regions which are particularly affected are those that are either unprepared to adapt to or incapable of meeting the needs of companies.

The more the power balance between commonweal and organizational interests shifts in favor of organizations, the more serious the whole question of the *legitimation of the power holders* becomes. The impact of market logic, the specific interest of large organizations, and the power of associations and organized interest groups may lead to a decline in the significance of democratically legitimized decisions and institutions. The self-propelling dynamic of economic processes has the potential to destabilize society and state.

Without a doubt, markets make a visible efficient contribution to the balance between supply and demand, and globalization does this on a worldwide scale. Consequently, new opportunities especially for developing countries are opened up, as long as these countries gain free access to the markets of industrialized nations from which they have been hitherto cut off. The same is true for the former Eastern bloc countries, although examples of societal dislocation associated with sudden exposure to the market mechanism are in evidence here.

People are communicating on a global level, distances are shrinking, and time differences are no longer a hindrance. Flows of information, capital, goods, and people take place on a continuous basis. The introduction of the profit motive into all areas of life is changing the way in which individuals live. The markets demand from them not only know-how but also flexibility and mobility. People´s thoughts and actions are driven solely by principles of material quid pro quo. Materialism increasingly puts its stamp on moral behavior. The "survival of the fittest" becomes the tenet of society. In the fight for survival brought about and intensified by global competition, there are both winners and losers—and these categories are determined by the presence and absence of purchasing power.

3. Ways out of the Globalization Trap

For globalization to benefit everyone, it is necessary on the one hand to face up to this development, and on the other hand to refuse to allow it to become the decisive factor. *Identity must be preserved* within the context of global conditions. Identity, understood as an attribute of a person consisting of an ongoing sense of belonging to a specific cultural area, manifests itself in different ways depending on the person's origin, race, language, home country, background, upbringing, and worldview. For many people identity is localized to their home town and to the space they occupy in daily life, but it also includes larger areas such as the region and nation. In the past, this sense of belonging did not extend beyond these borders, on the other side of which people spoke differently and looked different; their customs, education, and legal systems were foreign; in short, people lived differently. In the present day, geographical areas essential to personal identity have been extended beyond the borders of the state to include larger geographical areas (e.g., the European Union). This is already so today and will continue to be so in the future: identities will no longer end at borders. For example, to the identity of being a European will be added that of being a citizen of the world or a cosmopolitan. What is essential in this process is that the *primary* (local, regional) and the *secondary* (national, supranational) identities will remain, in spite of the added *tertiary* (global) identity.

The basic regulatory and economic environment must therefore be structured to take these specific identities into account. Globalization will make positive headway if it does not have conformity as its aim but rather pays due attention to and utilizes cultural differentiation. The epigram for castle and garden layout, "ars vincit naturam" (art conquers nature), should be adapted for globalization as follows: "cultura dominat oeconomiam" (culture dominates business interest). Specific duties must therefore be conferred on global organizations to ensure that they integrate themselves with relevant local, regional, national, and supranational business activities and adapt to the cultural specificities of the countries in question.

Some large organizations have already adopted these goals and have developed on their own initiative a set of governing principles for their group structure and the behavior of their employees. Such organizational concepts could be described as "coordinated self-regulating networks of decentralized organizations." This means that global organizations are connected financially (via capital participation) and in terms of personnel (via supervisory boards and appointments), determine business locations, and provide the strategy for production, product range, or areas of activity; but control over resources including recruitment, financing, delivery contracts, production conditions, and sales management is wholly delegated to the units on the ground (subsidiaries and second-tier subsidiaries, plants, and profit centers). With respect to employee management, the following are important: tolerance (in particular toward those of different beliefs and minority groups), prohibition of discrimination (especially discrimination on the grounds of race, religion, age, and gender), furthering of intercultural relations, fair competition, prohibition of private gain, prohibition of the use of the company plant, facilities, and information for business purposes other than those exclusively related to its activities (e.g., no exploitation of insider knowledge, and preservation of data protection regulations), and in general, outlawing activities running counter to the business interests of the organization.

Organizations that are involved in procurement, production, and sales on a global level and have chosen their business locations for reasons that include plentiful supplies of raw materials and other intermediary inputs, skilled workers, favorable natural and political conditions, sales markets, and relatively few restrictive regulations concerning codetermination, taxation, and environmental protection, have taken onboard the idea that local culture is more or less yielding to economic constraints. But a cultural clash emerges, sometimes stirred up by religious or neoliberal fundamentalists, both of whom desire to dictate their own "rules of play." The careful harmonization of cultural values and organizational goals would appear to provide a more promising solution, and one that the majority favor. This is the main task for statesmen, church leaders, heads of industries, opinion leaders, and other prominent figures. The preservation of identity and responsible assimilation are the keys to escaping the pitfalls of globalization.

The means for achieving this is *education* or, more precisely, the education of young people. The study of world languages, history, politics, business, and religions should form a more important part of the educational curriculum. The sciences, with their universal frame of reference, could serve as a model here. Openness to the wide world must be accompanied by urbanization aimed at people's local environment. More than ever, the ambivalence between local origins and globalization should be taken into consideration and openly recognized. *Globalization should be balanced by regionalization,* and that means the fostering of local self-help groups, local supply alternatives, medium-sized businesses, and local self-administration, with its own planning, financial, personnel, organizational, and legislative independence. It is precisely this self-organization of local community affairs that is the counterpart to globalization and yet is increasingly put under pressure.

The law of competition does not even call a halt when it comes to local nonprofit services, primarily in the areas of health care and social welfare, which enjoy special tax privileges. These services are viewed as distorting competition. The centralization of legislative and administrative enforcement powers and "top down" financial balance systems are further proof of the erosion of regional responsibility.

One can no longer talk about regional reinforcement of local businesses in Germany by means of local authority enterprises and business promotion measures, because local enterprises are treated in exactly the same way as private organizations from the point of view of the law of competition—that is, no consideration is given to their social function. From the point of view of budgetary and local authority law, however, local authority enterprises are subject to numerous restrictions. Thus, the question of allowing the local authority to participate in business activity depends upon the nature of the public task, the "purchasing power of the community and the predicted need," subsidiarity clauses, and municipal borders. With regard to the choice of the legal form that this undertaking should have and the appropriate regulations in the memorandum and articles of association, various matters must be taken into consideration: whether and to what extent the sponsoring agency should have powers of influence, how it should fulfill its democratic legitimation responsibility, and how it can limit its liability. Public companies question the justification of these restrictions, which contradict the fact that when it comes to competition, the public companies receive the same treatment as private competitors. A crucial explanation here is the necessity not only of the diversification of public enterprises into new operational areas, but also of their expansion beyond the confines of the local boundaries of the sponsoring agency in order to guarantee improvement and sustainability of their core tasks.

In conclusion, it should be stressed that both the actors of globalization and those affected at the local level should not behave as if they were diametrically opposed to each other. Globalization and regionalization should be organized in a compatible fashion. Global networks with decentralized power and responsibility on the one hand, and local services committed to the local commonweal and its general economic interests on the other, should stand side by side. In the case of the former, it is necessary that operational managers are competent and responsible for the "res publica," in addition to possessing specialized knowledge and social competence. Local, nonprofit service providers must fulfill their briefs in such a way that global competitors are unable to provide better alternatives. In the area of banking, regionally organized savings banks could defy the large international banks by positioning themselves as specialists for business setups with targeted support for SMEs. Similarly, in the deregulated electricity market, local providers such as the Großkraftwerk Mannheim must defend their market position by sharpening their abilities on the environmental front—a strategy that can succeed only if consumers become aware of their responsibility for the environment and base their purchasing decisions on factors other than price.

CHAPTER 4

Strategic Management and Change of Structurally Global Organizations: The Case of Development Banks

TAÏEB HAFSI

The globalization of markets and industries has revealed the difficulty of managing geographically scattered organizations with multiple activities (Doz 1986; Bartlett & Ghoshal 1989). The diversity of both their activities and the places where these activities are carried out increases the importance of relations between nations and stimulates competition between them (Porter 1990; Doz & Prahalad 1991). Companies are being forced to reconcile the demands of competition in an industry that is globalizing with the sociopolitical demands of the societies in which they are active (Hafsi & Toulouse 1996).

Taïeb Hafsi is the Walter J. Somers Professor of Strategic International Management at the Ecole des Hautes Etudes Commerciales de Montréal. He is especially involved in the following fields of research: strategy of complex organizations, management of change, and public and nonprofit organizations management. He is a consultant for governmental organizations in Canada and the United States and for EU-LDCs (Least Developed Countries) in Africa and Asia. He is a former professor at McGill University (Montreal) and ESSEC (Paris), and researcher at the Harvard Business School.

The globalization of markets and industries creates organizations that are more global. Internally, such organizations must also reconcile the interpersonal dynamics of employees who have different cultures, histories, traditions, and practices (Doz 1986). These organizations face a complexity with multiple determinants: the multiplicity of activities, places where the activities occur, local cultures, structures, and competing dynamics. These determinants inevitably result in a multiplicity of strategic perspectives and management styles at all levels. For the organizations' leaders, the relations between cause and effect are nonlinear and often have consequences that are obscure. In the best of cases, this requires careful, "mediated," and very specific management, which is sometimes called meta-management (Bower 1970; Hafsi 1985).

Nevertheless, the evolution toward global organizations has benefited from long experience in international management (Vernon & Wells 1976) and from the development of knowledge about management in complex situations (Hafsi & Toulouse 1996). Setting up global management in companies like Ford or IBM has been progressive, through a natural extension of related practices (Doz 1986). A simple, local organization does not become a complex, global organization in a day (Chandler 1962). Along the way, experimentation and progressive learning play an important role (see the spectacular example of Corning Glass Works, ICCH 1987).

However, some organizations are naturally global. It is part of their makeup. This is the case for all organizations created to manage global concerns, such as the World Trade Organization or the European Commission or, from a different era, the branches of the United Nations or the World Bank. In these organizations, as in global enterprises, the complexity is in the richness of the environment with which they must come to terms and the great diversity in the employee populations that make up this environment. Because globalization is, in short, decreed, the managers have no other choice but to live, without previous preparation, with the diversity and multiplicity of the organization's activities and characteristics. In this essay, I would like to examine how this happens.

Development banks are an interesting example of naturally global organizations. The mission of these banks is to finance projects that have a real potential to boost the economy in a number of chosen countries. The projects are financed under conditions that either resemble market conditions or are very advantageous for the borrowers, called beneficiaries. The shareholders and clients of these banks are the same sovereign countries. Thus, the Caribbean Development Bank has twenty-six shareholder countries that in some cases are also its business targets. Likewise, the African Development Bank has fifty-three shareholder countries that are sometimes clients. The World Bank counts nearly all the countries on the planet as shareholders, and its clients are those countries whose gross national product is below a certain level. The managers and employees generally also come from the shareholder and client countries. What complicates the operation of these organizations even more is that the country is the client only in appearance; the real client is often a private or state company or a public institution in charge of specific operations. This results in dynamics wherein the countries' personalities, cultures, and histories intervene decisively in the strategic management of the organization.

Using cases of change in the African Development Bank (AfDB) and the Caribbean Development Bank (CDB), I will describe particular characteristics of the strategic management of these institutions and will draw lessons from them for the strategic management of organizations with global dynamics. The first section is devoted to describing the dynamics of the operations of development banks, focusing particularly on AfDB and CDB. The second section describes a crisis at CDB in order to reveal the problems particular to the strategic management of these institutions. The third tackles the difficulties related to change at AfDB and highlights how natural globalization affects an organization's management. The fourth section brings out patterns that may be of interest for strategic management and change in all organizations facing globalization. Finally, in the concluding section I offer some implications for research and practice.

I. Development Banks: Dynamics and Operations

When the West Indies Federation was dissolved at the beginning of the 1960s, it was soon apparent that the small Caribbean countries, members of the Commonwealth and recently independent, would not be able to survive without some mechanisms for economic regrouping.[1] In 1967, a study by the UNDP,[2] under the leadership of Canada, the United Kingdom, and the United Nations, suggested the creation of a development bank. On October 18, 1969, an agreement between sixteen Caribbean countries, Canada, and the United Kingdom was signed in Kingston, Jamaica, and the Caribbean Development Bank was inaugurated on January 26, 1970. Sir Arthur Lewis, a leading economist (later a recipient of the Nobel Prize in economics), was named president.

At the beginning of 1963, many African countries had just become politically independent. A new generation of leaders was taking control of the continent. These leaders were most often nationalists who had taken part in the struggle against colonial powers. Ahmed Ben Bella (Algeria), Gamal Abdel Nasser (Egypt), Kwame Nkrumah (Ghana), Ahmed Sékou Touré (Guinea), Félix Houphouët-Boigny (Côte d'Ivoire), Jomo Kenyatta (Kenya), Mohammed V (Morocco), Habib Bourguiba (Tunisia), Modibo Keita (Mali), Léopold Sédar Senghor (Senegal), Gaafar Muhammad al-Nimeiry (Sudan), and Julius Nyerere (Tanzania) would soon become familiar names and would carry the hopes of an optimistic, enthusiastic continent. The dominant feeling in Africa, generally shared worldwide, was that Africans had all the means necessary to mark history and become a respectable force.

In August 1963, in Khartoum, the capital of Sudan, these leaders decided to begin building the institutions that would help unite a continent fragmented by its colonial past. This was the birth of the African Development Bank. One year later, twenty countries had contributed 65 percent of the bank's U.S. $250 million in capital stock. Mamoun Beheiry, a Sudanese, was elected president. Operations began in Abidjan, Côte d'Ivoire, with a staff of ten.

Since then, AfDB has become one of the most important financial and development institutions in Africa and the world. In 1997, its personnel numbered 1,055, including 600 highly qualified professionals. It had U.S. $22 billion in capital and had made over U.S. $33 billion in loans. Its net income was about U.S. $140 million.

The members admitted were countries in the region and traditional donors. In order to carry out their activities, CDB and AfDB used two main types of funds: concessionary funds, provided at very favorable conditions (nearly donations) by rich countries and reserved for the most needy; and ordinary funds, provided at close to market rates. The activities of a development bank generally revolve around the acquisition of funds (from donors or traditional financial markets), and the utilization of those funds in projects with a good potential for development.

Most of the employees are citizens of member countries, according to an implicit "quota" agreed upon by the bank's board of directors. The clients are public or private institutions located in the member countries. An effort is also made to balance the loans among the members. The loans at concessionary conditions are reserved exclusively for the poorest countries, with, again, an effort to distribute the loans and assistance equitably.

The loans are made to carry out projects which are generally conceived or promoted, as well as evaluated, by the bank's professionals. Each project becomes the object of a detailed study, followed by a recommendation which, after approval by the bank's top management, is presented for approval to the board of directors. The board of directors watches over both the balanced use of available funds and the quality of the management. Each board member is supposed to watch over the integrity of the bank as a whole and also watch that benefits are fairly shared among the countries. However, board members are often representatives of their countries, and tensions inevitably crop up between them and the bank managers.

The bank's employees are representative of the mosaic of member countries' cultures and traditions. The employees expect the institution to welcome, or at least be highly tolerant of, their different cultural values and practices. At the same time, the bank is a commercial institution whose practices, including human resource management, must be largely standardized if it is to succeed. The top managers do not want to have to use different management styles for each of the numerous nationalities represented. On the contrary, they often believe that, in the name of fairness, individual differences should be left at the doorstep of the institution and uniform rules should apply to all. This results in a certain tension. Sometimes top managers who are strong draw on local cultures and become cultural and political leaders in the eyes of the professionals. The top managers are often torn between the formality of written rules and the informality of traditional relationships. For example, in Africa, tradition favors collective, almost tribal, behavior, with interpersonal relationships and friendships that are warm and intense, while the dominant models in management favor neutrality, the coldness of logical reasoning, and the importance of rules.

Because of their affective proximity to the countries concerned, their sensitivity, and their knowledge of the problems of underdevelopment, the professionals and the employees of the bank in general are very emotionally involved in their work. Most consider their work a commitment to development or against poverty. They have strong opinions and do not hesitate to share them regarding the bank's strategy and operations, and to criticize when something seems to go against their values. If this criticism is not institutionalized, it can fill the hallways and poison the bank's working climate.

The top managers themselves are in a special situation. The bank's board of governors, where each country is represented by a minister, usually elects the bank's president. Although the president proposes his or her vice-presidents, the board of governors or, in certain cases, the board of directors must also approve them. Because of this, the president is both politician and administrator. He or she needs both political and managerial approval to succeed. The professionals often consider the president simply as the first among peers: in a prestigious position, yes, but a peer just the same. At the same time, the president is often an important model for the professionals.

The institution is a glass house, with no room for secretive practices. The professionals are naturally in contact with representatives from their countries and quickly inform them if internal practices seem questionable or inappropriate. Nonetheless, they are attached to the institution and will not hesitate to protect it from outside attacks.

The professionals in development institutions share a strong passion for improving the lot of the populations they serve. Basically, they consider themselves rather like militants fighting for a cause. They expect to be consulted often and generally believe that they have a better understanding of the realities of the countries being served than top management does. They resist all management that is autocratic, except in times of crisis. For them, the best management is, of necessity, decentralized and democratic. They fear politicization, but the fear of autocratic domination by one or another of the groups can lead them to encourage it. In general, they expect their leader to listen, have good judgment, and be able to take all points of view into consideration. For them, the best leader is wise, sensitive, and caring, like the prophets.

Institutions on the Edge of Chaos

Development banks should be considered as complex adaptive systems.[3] Living systems are the typical example of complex adaptive systems. Organizations become complex adaptive systems in trying to make a large number of people cooperate (Barnard 1938). Theories of complexity (Waldrop 1992; Morin 1994) suggest that the main characteristics of complex adaptive systems allow them to respond to their environment by being creative and taking initiatives based on very small clues. To stay alive, they must keep in constant motion. Equilibrium is the forerunner of death. In dealing with the environment and its complexity, the system tends to generate novel motifs whose variety eventually creates something that is qualitatively superior. Faced with difficult tasks, the complex system evolves right up to the edge of chaos, without, however, falling in.[4] Thus it avoids both a stable equilibrium and an explosive instability. Finally, the relations between cause and effect are extremely tenuous, making centralized management of complex systems nearly impossible, and perhaps a source of destruction.

Our observations of development banks, in particular CDB and AfDB, suggest that their operations are not really adaptive. They are often on the edge of chaos, but as we will later see, in trying to avoid chaos, they tend instead to tumble right in. Our observations reveal a tendency to swing between two extremes of destructive behavior. The first is characterized by the desire for structural order, imposing management that is professional, neutral, bureaucratic, and centralized. In the second, the actors no longer believe in the structural order and impose political order, with relationships being politicized and informal management dominating. Like a mobile, this kind of organization swings back and forth without really adapting to what is happening in its environment, and it ends up losing its pertinence and disappearing. Before developing this swing theory, we will present and discuss some events that are typical of the history of CDB and AfDB.

2. CDB and Government Crises in the 1980s: From Bureaucratization to Politicization

The second oil crisis and pressures from the United States caused the first major, modern-day crisis in the independent Caribbean countries. The countries in that corner of the world suddenly found themselves responsible for, but unable to completely honor, debts and payments for the acquisition of energy.

The CDB managers and professionals first tried to respond to the needs of the poorest countries and those newly affected by the situation by increasing support and development loans. This led instead to an increase in payment defaults that put the bank itself in a critical position. Because the bank obtained its resources in part from the financial markets, it found itself with revenues that cast doubt on its viability as a financial institution. This in turn forced it to put considerable pressure on the region's governments to respect their commitments.

Some of the larger countries, such as Guyana and Jamaica, were in difficulty, which meant CDB had to be more careful so as to decrease its exposure to payment defaults. Other countries, such as the Bahamas, Trinidad and Tobago, and Barbados, were themselves careful and concerned about controlling their debt. The poorest countries had the biggest fiscal problems and therefore the fewest opportunities for projects.

As regards the donors, a desire to manage aid more closely led the United States to focus on bilateral aid, to the detriment of the multilateral aid that usually went through CDB, although going through CDB was often more cost-effective. For example, USAID no longer channeled its interventions through CDB because it did not perceive CDB as being sufficiently private-sector-oriented. Many other countries and institutions followed the U.S. example. The accent on bilateral aid also contributed to drawing away clients, who saw an easier way to obtain resources without the constraints imposed by CDB. Finally, competition between traditional banks also became more active, especially toward the private sector.

However, in 1984, CDB was still recognized as the most well-informed group in regard to the region's situation and the group best able to understand the needs and come up with the most appropriate projects for development. Its professionals, essentially from the region's elite, made up the most important "think tank" in and for the region. The bank's employees made up one big family. The president was a sort of father, and all relationships, even tense ones, were similar to those in a large family. When pressure from the environment became stronger and it was necessary to adapt, in particular to reduce costs, a major ordeal awaited top managers.

First, what united the executives in a period of growth was to become their Achilles' heel. Instead of learning to debate which direction to take, they had mainly learned to give each other mutual support. They had not learned to reconcile their differences and had never dealt with them. In a crisis situation, instead of dealing with their significantly divergent opinions together, they voiced them separately to representatives from their countries and close professionals. This was meant to indirectly influence a president who was difficult to reach, and it considerably politicized management of the bank.

An effort to professionalize management, with the launching of strategic planning and management training for professionals, only accentuated tensions. With better management training, the professionals had the impression that they understood the situation as well as or better than top management. They were more adamant in asking for the right to participate in strategic choices, including CDB's structural choices. On the other hand, the executives, fearing chaos, considered this unacceptable and actually became more authoritarian.

The CDB, jewel of the Caribbean, lost its aura and a good part of its talented professionals. Without the sacred fire and the will to contribute to the struggle against underdevelopment in the region, it became an ordinary financial organization. It can now be considered more an appendix of the major institutions for development assistance than a creative center serving the region. Its politicization has weakened it considerably and taken away its margins for maneuver and its influence in the region's countries and on the most important donors.

So, CDB's strategic management was easier and generally more cohesive in a situation of growth and prosperity. The professionals worked hard to take actions that will concretely facilitate development. They felt as if they were on a mission rather than working for an employer. The relationships between them were close and familial. Top management did not have to specify what direction to take. It was often obvious to everybody. However, they did set out day-to-day priorities. They also worked to reinforce internal operations by acting on factors of discord, and they usually succeeded. In general, management was simple and completely focused on the top executive's patriarchal role. During growth, CDB's strategic management was comparable to that of a small business.

In a difficult situation, such as a crisis for the bank or its environment, the effects were spectacular. Although in a small business the central power would be reinforced, at CDB the power broke down under pressure when the bank's environment and operations became very politicized. Professionalizing the system, adding more norms and operational rules, only aggravated the situation by pushing a system where affect was crucial toward bureaucracy and impersonal behavior. This led, in reaction, to a greater politicization and the aggravation of internal division. It is only here that one realizes that the bank is complex. This was the moment that its management was decisively affected by the diversity of its environment and internal make-up. Top managers accustomed to an easy situation are often thrown off course under such conditions.

3. The AfDB from 1995 to 1998:
From Politicization to Bureaucratic Centralism

The AfDB belonged to the Africans, which was a source of genuine pride for many of its employees. This ownership meant that in the bank's governance system, Africans were in control.

Until 1982, when non-Africans were admitted as members of the bank, African nationalists were more concerned with political appearances than with the efficiency of the bank. The bank was mainly a political plaything, and although it belonged collectively to Africa, its diffuse shareholding and growing politicization meant that in truth it belonged to no African.

Management of the bank was thus ignored by African politicians for many years. In fact, until the beginning of the 1990s, only political relations between the African countries were considered important. The only thing that interested the bank's governors and most of its administrators was who would be chosen as president. This was sometimes for reasons of patronage, but more often for reasons of regional politics. A president who favored one country or another could influence the bank's decisions to serve the geopolitical interests of that country in its relations with the others. This influence was used as a token in Africa's political games. Of course, these games were complicated by the interests and interventions of world powers.

Such conditions provided fertile ground for corruption, acts of patronage, clan formation, and so forth, and this is what happened. The bank's president was a politician concerned with keeping the approval of African members and was sometimes remarkably talented at doing so. Apparently either excluded or excluding themselves from the intra-African political game, non-regional members were insistent about matters of management and governance and often questioned the style of management generally adopted by the president. This led to a high-tension situation at the beginning of the 1990s.

Relations between the president and the board of directors were particularly unbalanced. The president's dependence considerably weakened his ability to manage the bank. He found himself structurally with a minority government. Not only did he have to please to continue being reelected, but he also had to please to be able to keep operating. This kind of situation is only viable when principals share common objectives or are able to work together. At AfDB, this was not the case. The board of directors was deeply divided, due to personal rivalries and a long history of mutual mistrust among nations that was skillfully maintained and sometimes worsened by the colonial powers.

The leading coalition was thus divided, which was of no help in clarifying the rules of the game. As a result, the most common behavior was partisan (Hafsi & Toulouse 1996), with groups pulling in all directions, unrestricted by rules. In a "chaotic partisan system," one after another, the presidents felt obliged to play politics in order to survive. Thus, the bank and its African members championed the major slogans in favor of political independence for Africa in order to prevent non-African members from restoring a minimum of order. Emotional resistance to a reasonable system of governance was considerable. The only management action taken by the president at the beginning of the 1990s, a sanction against one of his vice-presidents who was no longer obeying his orders, was interpreted as a political act and generated a strong reaction from the board, which nearly suspended him.

Decisive actions were taken by the non-African members, the principal donors to the African Development Fund. This fund was not renewed in

1994, and the bank's activities began to slow down until they reached levels that were considered intolerable. Under pressure, the bank's board of governors decided that the entire management structure should be reviewed. An advisory committee was formed. It proposed a reform of the governance structures, giving back a real leadership role to the president and clarifying his relations with the board of governors and board of directors. He would now be authorized to name his vice-presidents. In order to avoid past problems, members of the board of directors could not be elected for more than three two-year mandates, or a total of six years. The board of governors approved all the propositions and in 1995 the president, newly elected after five rounds of voting, was in charge of a demoralized bank, weakened but with new rules.

The president was in charge of renewing the bank by banishing the former practices of nepotism and corruption. He needed to replace his managers and professionals or persuade them to completely change their mentality. It was decided to fire all the managers and replace them using a very formalized, impersonal process of selection. Everyone was tested on his or her management skills. Eighty percent of the former professionals and managers were rehired, but many of them were obliged to accept either a transfer or a demotion if they wanted to stay at the bank. The rest were encouraged to take a rather generous early-retirement offer. About three hundred professionals and managers were thus let go. The president went outside the bank for three new vice-presidents (including, for the first time, a non-African)[5] and chose a new secretary-general from among the former executives. In no time at all, beginning in 1996, he had a new bank in his hands.

A new bank did not mean one that would be able to meet the needs and accomplish the objectives of integrity, internal efficiency, and customer service. It was starting over at zero. The new president kept tight control over decisions to avoid past ethical problems. First he wanted to create a mode of operation that was clean and effective before modifying the management structure. This resulted in very strong centralization.

The professionals and managers were enthusiastic about the changes, resulting in a new work ethic. The general feeling in 1997–98 was that the morale of the bank was again that of its early years. Newcomers were recruited carefully and were sensitive to the problems of Africa, untainted by the bank's history, and had a more modern vision of how an international organization operates. Moreover, many had been recruited among the professionals and executives of the World Bank and the International Monetary Fund.

The AfDB once again appeared a beehive of activity. The professionals were there evenings and weekends again. The board of directors and, particularly, the non-regional members were once more confident and happy to be part of the institution. Madeleine Albright, U.S. Secretary of State, declared that it was "the turnaround of the decade."

However, there were still many problems to resolve. The rules of governance had been clarified, but governance was constantly affected by the way internal operations were being carried out. In 1998, it was pointed out by an administrator that the president had been exercising unshared power since being elected in 1995. Order had been greatly restored, but it was time to give back more space to the managers and professionals.

This was confirmed through a series of interviews with all the managers, the principal officers, and a few important actors (e.g., union representatives, the president of the internal tribunal, and the ombudsman). At the end of this study, it seemed that AfDB was too formalized, too hierarchical, and too rigid in its processes (Hafsi & Le-Louarn 1999). It was also suffering from a lack of coordination, initiative, and innovation. All this resulted in highly-educated troops who were cynical, overloaded, fearful, and felt unappreciated. Once again, the bank was in trouble. It needed a major reform and mobilization of personnel that would reinforce the quality of governance, by giving shareholders an example of an open, dynamic organization.

It would appear that this diversified and structurally global organization was fragile and constantly being questioned. Paradoxically, this was perhaps its guarantee of long-term survival.

4. Discussion: The Intense Life of a Structurally Global Organization

CDB and AfDB are organizations that are structurally global. Their professionals, shareholders, and clients come from a multitude of countries, whether from the entire world or from an entire region. The sensitivities and interests of the many actors are quite divergent. The way the institutions operate is very important to them, and they pay a considerable amount of attention to it. As summarized in Table 1, the fear that one or other of the groups could monopolize the institution favors politicization. The fear of disorder and economic obsolescence favors neutral, bureaucratic management. Both these extremes are intolerable and somewhat pathological for a complex organization that is trying to adapt. When concern about a power monopoly is low and is accompanied by a low fear of disorder and obsolescence (generally a situation where resources are abundant), we have a situation that is perhaps ideal, but rare and not very realistic. In the end, the best situation is one where both fear of a power monopoly and fear of disorder and economic obsolescence are high. These fears stimulate management action. They result in a lively, energetic organization, as described below.

It must be emphasized first that a development bank's actions are carried out by professionals in their everyday life. They are constantly interacting with economic and social actors in the client countries, and they work to generate promising development projects. Top management cannot really evaluate the quality of this work until long after decisions concerning the allocation of resources have been made. In many cases, executives manage in the classic manner, setting up a process that protects the organization's integrity and protects it against embezzlement and criminal deviance. They are less concerned about generating development than they are about generating projects while respecting professional norms. The hope is that this will eventually generate economic development for the member countries.

TABLE 1.   Dynamics of Operating a Structurally Global Organization

		Fear of disorder and economic obsolescence	
		High	*Low*
Fear of partisan domination	*High*	1. Incremental, disjointed management, in a state of flux	2. Politicization of relationships and informal management
	Low	3. Accent on professional management that is neutral, bureaucratic, and centralized	4. Ideal situation, but not very realistic. Management style is of little importance.

This way of operating is generally explained by the uncertainty of development actions. Many factors influence economic development. Moreover, the needs are so great that most solutions proposed by top economists have proved disappointing. Thus, there is a tendency to think that each project should be examined with regard for its potential, even though this may be local and difficult to link to overall economic development. The entrepreneurial nature of each project dominates the operation and pertinence of management actions. In development banks, the entrepreneurs are often the professionals themselves. Their interest in the country, their devotion, analytical and interpersonal skills, and creativity contribute more to a project's success than a classic evaluation of the project. There might even be projects that are difficult to justify in the classic way, but which have a very good chance for success if the right people are associated with them. This requires the professional to take initiatives that are not in his or her job description.

Success requires entrepreneurship, risk-taking, and hence acceptance of a certain probability of failure. But such initiatives are seen as intolerable, because they give much too much power to the professionals and encourage politicization. The search for equilibrium often leads to a dominant management style that is bureaucratic, which is the safest for the professionals and management.

However, as shown by Braybrooke and Lindblom (1963), the wisest thing to do is maintain this tension between freedom of action and risk of monopoly. The relationship between cause and effect is very uncertain, and this justifies constant experimentation and constant questioning of the experiments. The debate forces incremental decisions in which many actors participate in a disjointed, disorderly manner. But these decisions have a better chance of generating suitable results as long as they are conceived and implemented under the watchful eye of internal and external criticism, and as long as their shortcomings are constantly brought out into the open and debated.

Managing a structurally global organization is not an easy thing. If a safe operating style is sought, entrepreneurial creativity and development will be stifled. If operations are allowed to run freely without clear guidelines, which is always the case in activities of an exploratory nature, this may generate politicization and endanger the organization's existence. The best kind of management seems obliged to force apparent disorder to avoid real disorder, divergence, and ultimately the end of the organization. This kind of management maintains constant tension, constant adjustment, and constant questioning, which are the only ways to discover the relations of cause and effect, and thus the most appropriate choices (Avenier 1997). When one really thinks about it, the most appropriate management nurtures life to its fullest, always teetering on the edge of chaos (Holland 1975; Brown & Eisenhardt 1998).

A development bank cannot be thought of as simply a bank, although the managers may find such a concept comfortable. If it were, it would be useless or redundant from the shareholders' point of view. It needs to be considered first of all as an instrument of development, subject to the discipline of a constant search for betterment. An instrument of development is closer to an investment company, constantly searching to create value. However, it is a particular kind of investment company, where each entrepreneur must first sell his or her choices and intuitions both internally and externally before putting them into practice. This means that his or her patrimonial wealth and ethnic and cultural diversity must be used to their fullest. In particular, they must allow disjointed analysis and disjointed judgment to come together to generate a qualitative leap forward. The experiences at AfDB and CDB and, we believe, the World Bank, show that doing otherwise generates bureaucracy and resistance to change, and eventually undoes the very *raison d'être* of these institutions. Rejecting the constant struggle between the desire for order and the desire for freedom, on the one hand, and the struggle between personal interest and organizational interest, on the other hand, would at best be unrealistic and at worst destructive.

Managing a structurally global organization falls into the same category as managing a complex organization. Although we have observed only dysfunctions and pathologies, it can still be reasonably held that development banks' most important resources are centered around the know-how of their professionals. Money alone does not create economic growth for an enterprise, and this is even more true in the case of a country. When professionals have a stimulating vision of the organization as a whole and enough freedom of action to use their creativity and make the contributions they want to make, there is certainly more chance of promoting economic growth than when management is mechanical, based on standards and bureaucratic control. Complexity means having to manage paradoxes (Morin 1981). Neither decentralization nor informal management alone will bear fruit, nor will formalization and centralization alone. A way of operating must be imagined in which decentralization is superimposed onto control and is constantly confronting it.

No doubt the top management at CDB would have done well to give more decision room to their professionals. This is assuming, of course, that the executives themselves would have been able to convince their shareholders and financiers. Their fears of internal disorder and deterioration of economic performance were so strong that they were unable to offer a convincing vision to their shareholders. Contrary to past practice, they stopped being proactive and dynamic in promoting development. It is this very fact that transformed them into an ordinary financial institution and took away the competence that distinguished them, that is, their understanding of and sensitivity toward their milieu and their ability to come up with original and appropriate forms of intervention.

Conversely, the top management at AfDB felt that nothing could undermine the institution. On the other hand, they were vigilant in protecting themselves from possible political actions by their board of directors, thus paradoxically facilitating the fragmentation of ideas and practices, as well as politicization. This situation also nearly led to the breakup of the institution. The modifications made in 1995 radically challenged the previous mode of operation. Actions were taken to counterbalance intense politicization. But actions have their own dynamics. This readjustment put the organization back on a trajectory that again threw it off balance by pushing it toward bureaucratization. Interviews with the bank's managers and professionals confirmed that centralization, first considered necessary to settle the crisis, is today largely experienced as a barrier to modern management and, ultimately, to the resolution of development problems. In short, concern about disorder and the performance of the bank, as well as about the dangers of politicization, should have led to management that was open, democratic, and incremental. Instead, the bank slipped into bureaucratic management, as if the danger of partisan domination by one group was gone forever. It could be predicted that continuing such a style of management would facilitate the return of partisan behavior and add politicization to bureaucratization.

5. Conclusion and Implications for Managing Complex Organizations

Our study of structurally global organizations suggests that the fear of disorder and of its corollary, economic obsolescence, as well as the fear of domination by specific groups within an organization, is at the root of the dynamics of how a global organization operates. These two types of fear can generate four operational styles. The first is an unrealistic operational style that is free of these fears and that we consider to be a textbook example worth forgetting. The second is an unstable operational style that maintains tension between these two fears, requiring constant attention and managing. The third is a politicized operational style with principles of informal management. Finally, there is an operational style of bureaucratic and centralized management. The last two are poorly suited to development and are sources of dysfunction. Like mobiles, complex organizations often swing from the one to the other.

Consequently, managing this type of organization can be successful only if a sort of controlled chaos, nonsensical in appearance, is generated—a paradox. These organizations are "multiple," not only through their specific activities, but also through the groups of clients that they serve and the employees and shareholders that they sustain. In particular, the ethnic and geographic multiplicity of their employees can be used to maintain the organization in a dynamic flux. Freedom of creation must be controlled, not by a structure and systems that are rigid, but through general regulation of the relations between groups and individuals. In a way, the creations are free, but they can only affect the organization if the multiple groups "buy" them. This implies a constant, open struggle between different ideas and interests.

The management of such an organization should be concerned not about the decisions that are made (these would be the product of interactions), but rather about the permanent regulation of relations between groups and individuals. This regulation should watch over maintaining the equilibrium between the need for economic efficiency and the need for groups to express their opinions and positions. It should constantly be adjusted, sometimes in favor of one group, sometimes in favor of another, with the objective of keeping them in tension.

We believe that this applies as much to development banks as to transnational organizations like the European Commission, the United Nations, the Catholic Church, and, of course, the major transnational companies. This general principle remains to be clarified and demonstrated through other studies and research. These organizations, more and more numerous, are without a doubt representative of the new difficulties brought about by today's global management, with a diversity of actors, a diversity of technologies, a diversity of markets, and a growing democratization of companies. Further research should emphasize observations and, eventually, theoretical developments, to allow later for large sample testing and a more convincing generalization.

NOTES

1. Descriptions and analyses in this section are drawn from field studies and the resulting cases, written by Hafsi and Noël (1990) for CDB; and Hafsi and Le-Louarn (1999) for AfDB (see list of references).

2. United Nations Development Program.

3. These systems are often described as composed of agents who have a lot of discretion. They may have multiple levels of organization and structure. They are subject to entropy, so they disappear if they do not get enough energy. Finally, they are able to recognize the forerunners of periodic change and adapt. Many systems and particularly many organizations are complex but nonadaptive. Often, because they cannot adapt, they weaken and die.

4. The terminology here can be misleading. In the theory of complexity, being on the edge of chaos does not mean that chaos reigns. It simply means that both

stable equilibrium and explosive instability are being avoided, giving way to a sort of controlled, creative instability.

5. A high-ranking official from the federal government of Canada who was sent to help manage the bank.

REFERENCES

Avenier, M.-J. *La stratégie chemin faisant*. Paris: Economica, 1997.

Barnard, C. J. *The Functions of the Executive*. 1938. Reprint, Cambridge: Harvard University Press, 1976.

Bartlett, C. A., and S. Ghoshal. *Managing across Borders: The Transnational Solution*. Boston: Business School Press, 1989.

Bower, J. L. *Managing the Resource Allocation Process*. Homewood, Ill.: Irwin, 1970.

Braybrooke, D., and C. E. Lindblom. *A Strategy of Decision*. New York: Free Press, 1963.

Brown, S. L., and K. M. Eisenhardt. *On the Edge of Chaos*. Boston: Harvard Business School Press, 1998.

Chandler, A. D. *Strategy and Structure*. Cambridge: MIT Press, 1962.

Corning Glass Works, HBS International Case Clearing House (ICCH), #9-381-360. Translated at HEC, Montreal, by Christine Laplante, 1987.

Doz, Y. L. *Strategic Management in Multinational Companies*. Oxford: Pergamon, 1986.

Doz, Y. L., and C. K. Prahalad. "Managing DMNCs: A Search for a New Paradigm." *Strategic Management Journal* 12, special issue (Summer 1991).

Hafsi, T. "Management et métamanagement: les subtilités du concept de stratégie." *Gestion* (September 1985).

Hafsi, T., and J.-Y. Le-Louarn. *The African Development Bank: Hope for Africa (A), (B) and (C)*. Centre d'étude en administration internationale, HEC, Montreal, 1999.

Hafsi, T., and A. Noël, *The Caribbean Development Bank (A), (B) and (C)*. Centre d'étude en administration internationale, HEC, Montreal, 1990.

Hafsi, T., and J.-M. Toulouse. *La Stratégie des organisations: Une synthèse*. Montreal: Editions Transcontinental, 1996.

Holland, J. *Adaptation in Natural and Artificial Systems*. Ann Arbor: University of Michigan Press, 1975.

Morin, E. *Mes démons*. Paris: Stock, 1994.

———. *La nature de la nature*. Paris: Stock, 1981.

Porter, M. E. *Competition in Global Industries*. New York: Free Press, 1990.

Vernon, R., and L. Wells. *Economic Environment of International Business*. Englewood Cliffs, N.J.: Prentice Hall, 1976.

Waldrop, M. M. *Complexity: The Emerging Science at the Edge of Order and Chaos*. New York: Simon and Schuster, 1992.

CHAPTER 5

Global Investors and E-Networks: Winners and Losers in the New World Economy

ERNST-MORITZ LIPP

I. The Future of Globalization

What Is Really Driving Globalization?

New trends evolved in the 1990s that are fundamentally changing the global economy:

- During the fifty years of peace-time economy since the end of World War II the entire spectrum of the population in the industrial countries has been able to build up considerable monetary wealth and property, which has attained a high degree of international mobility as a result of the liberalization and globalization of the financial markets. Today, institutional as well as individual investors exercise their investor sovereignty, reallocating their investments rigorously if companies or countries do not live up to their expectations.

Ernst-Moritz Lipp is a financial investor and a partner of a venture capital firm. He has served as a member of the Board of Managing Directors of Dresdner Bank and as Secretary General of the German Council of Economic Advisors. He is a professor at Frankfurt's Goethe University.

- Since the collapse of communism in 1989, formerly closed countries with planned economies and a labor potential of more than a billion people have opened up and begun to integrate themselves in the world economy (Central and Eastern Europe, China, Latin-American countries). The increased regional integration—the European Union (EU), North Atlantic Free Trade Association (NAFTA), and Southern Common Market (Mercosur)—has propelled the deregulation of large economic areas and forced them to open up their markets.
- New information technology such as mobile phones and the Internet has globalized sales channels and marketplaces; the Internet has given consumer sovereignty a whole new dimension. In many industrial sectors, business models are undergoing a sweeping change.

Heterogeneous Developments in the World Economy

The world economy of the 1990s was marked by the unexpectedly long American upswing. By comparison, following the boom at the start of the 1990s fueled by German reunification, the German and the European economy ran into a stabilization crisis that coincided with a monetary crisis and came to a peak when the United Kingdom left the European Monetary System (EMS). Nevertheless, European economic monetary union was achieved. However, Europe is still waiting for a strong upswing and has yet to embark on any noteworthy action toward solving its unemployment problems. As a result of the creation of a single currency and a single capital market in Europe, of the deregulation of large industrial sectors such as the power industry, telecommunications, and transport, and of the growing popularity of shares among issuers and investors, the European economy is becoming more dynamic. Cross-border shareholding links are on the rise, and large and midsize companies are giving their operations an increasingly European slant. Two-thirds of all mergers and acquisitions are carried out in three industries: power, telecommunications, and financial services. Companies are amalgamating or breaking up, are concentrating on new markets and technologies, and are changing from national into European market players. Particularly in telecommunications, deregulation has opened up the market for new suppliers. There are new providers in mobile communications services and the fixed line network in all European regions, and developments in the linkage of mobile phone and Internet are surging ahead as a result. With regard to the Internet in particular, Europe is still several years behind the United States. There, the conditions for the arrival of this industry were more favorable: it is easier to establish new companies and mobilize new talents in America. More venture capital is available in the United States, and access to the stock market through a stock market flotation is simpler. Particularly the last two factors are improving in Europe. The number of stock market flotations of technology shares on the respective new markets rose by leaps and bounds in 1998 and 1999. And finally, the practice of building up old-age provisions on stocks is gradually gaining impetus. What we have yet to see, however, are reforms enabling better access to the labor market.

Developments in the emerging countries in the 1990s were a very mixed bag. Central and Eastern Europe underwent a severe transformation crisis, from which only Poland and Hungary have so far emerged as true success stories. The NAFTA integration process suffered a setback with the Tequila Crisis of 1995 but has developed successfully since then. In Asia the unparalleled rise of almost all the economies was followed by a dramatic fall. Governments and corporations worldwide were collectively guilty of utterly overestimating Asia's potential for development. Over the course of a decade the Asian economies had surged ahead, in some cases at double-digit rates. Objective limits to an economic development of this kind existed in the form of bottlenecks in human capital, weak infrastructure, political mismanagement, and the decay of the social fabric. These limits were also ignored by international companies. The long-running over-investment crisis was ultimately brought to a head by a financial crisis resulting from an ill-advised exchange rate policy and the influx of short-term speculative funds.

How might the broad-based trends look in future?

The Contrasting Future of the Major Regions

Stabilization crises as a consequence of inflation and subsequent high interest rates pushed by the Federal Reserve or the European Central Bank, such as those witnessed in the 1980s, are not on the cards. More probable are growth cycles similar to those in the 1960s, characterized by an alternation of weaker and stronger investment activity. We are currently going through such a cycle, which was caused by overinvestment and exuberant growth and stock market expectations in the technology sector, media, and telecommunication.

This basic pattern should prevail in Europe as well. Although the globalization and the Euro-induced radical restructuring of large industries is already underway, we are still waiting for a reorientation of economic policy in Europe and a new situation in the world market. As a result, the growth trend and the rise in employment in Europe in the years ahead will be weaker than in America during the last decade.

The prospects for the emerging markets of Asia, Latin America, and the developing states may be considered good, although not exhilarating. The world market players seem to have given up their quest for new stars among the emerging countries, into which they then make excessive investments. The alternating of the financial markets between elation and frustration over investments made in the emerging markets appears to have given way to a more level-headed and realistic appraisal. For all the crises that have struck these countries, they still have access to the capital markets; they can raise funds to finance their development, although these funds will remain expensive for some of them. Yet the markets continue to honor reforms and sound economic policy by applying markedly lower risk premiums.

American Hegemony without Consensus

The 1990s were the American decade. The United States economy was predominant in the world. The American financial markets called the tune for stocks and bonds worldwide. For investors around the globe, investments in America remained highly attractive. America was the undisputed world leader in matters of security and military policy. Even the influence of American culture has found universal acceptance—at least with the younger generation. Unlike empires formed down through history, however, America has not succeeded in uniting the rest of the world in a consensus with American norms and values. Indeed, opposition and a critical stance toward the hegemonic role played by the United States is very evident. Nor is American politics doing very much to bolster its hegemonic role by systematically building up a consensus. In almost all areas, this role has come about by coincidence rather than by design.

2. The Impact of New Technologies: E-commerce and Financial Markets

Profound Changes in Major Industries

One of the foremost traits of globalization is the upheaval in the big industries. The wave of mergers that has swept the world for a number of years has made itself felt in all the major business sectors: oil and gas, public utilities, telecommunications, automobiles, chemicals, pharmaceuticals, retailers, banks, and insurers. The concentration process is driven by a number of factors. For technical reasons, lower costs and lower consumer prices can only be achieved in many industries by means of larger production units and a decrease in cost of production. This applies primarily to oil and gas, the public utility companies, and the car industry. High research and development expenditure has forced the pharmaceuticals industry into concentration. The new technologies in telecommunications—mobile phones and the Internet—as well as the deregulation of national monopolies have given impetus to the restructuring and diversification in the telecom industry. In retailing, business models have been transformed, as a result of the combination of "brick and mortar" and the online distribution of consumer goods, to "click and mortar." New electronic sales channels have also been having an impact on banks and insurance companies, as have the creation of a single currency in Europe and the worldwide "disintermediation," i.e., the replacement of the classical deposit/lending bank by stock and bond markets in which private and institutional investors invest their money on the one hand, and companies, banks, and governments raise capital on the other. The sea-change that has befallen the big industries is creating bigger companies, but also allows new, smaller companies to emerge as a by-product of spin-off, sale, and de-merger.

To understand how, and to what extent, new communication technologies such as the Internet and mobile telephony are globalizing distribution channels and marketplaces and altering business models in many sectors of industry, we need to delve a little deeper into the Internet economy. The number of Internet users worldwide has risen from 100 million in 1987 to 250 million in 2000 and is expected to continue mounting to almost 400 million by the year 2003. Of these, an estimated 120 million each will be in the United States and Europe. Of interest to many branches of industry is how many people are likely to purchase goods and services on the Internet. In 1999 the number was around 50 million. It is expected that by the year 2003, 150 million people all over the world will be purchasing online. Electronic commerce (e-commerce) is divided into three segments: business between companies (B2B), business between companies and consumers (B2C) and business between financial institutions through electronic trading platforms (I2I).

E-commerce Business-to-Business (B2B) and E-commerce
Business-to-Consumer (B2C)

There are some fairly authoritative estimates on future trends in B2B and B2C in particular. By far the biggest segment is that of e-commerce between companies. True, at approximately USD 27 billion in 1998, business between companies was not much larger than business with consumers. But an annual growth rate of more than 50 percent is expected worldwide, which is less than expected two years ago, but still a high growth number compared with traditional industries. E-commerce with consumers will not expand so fast. But here, too, growth rates will average some 30 percent. The main features of e-commerce are direct customer access, geographic independence, low barriers to market entry, the break up of value chains, and the importance of brand names.

The most vivid and economically most significant illustration of how the Internet has revolutionized economic relations and business models is e-commerce between companies (B2B). At the beginning of this process, the strongest incentive for companies to use the Internet comes from the procurement side. Building up Internet portals to invite suppliers to tender orders, obtain quotations, close deals, and settle transactions is the first step. The next step is networking with dealers and customers on the sales side. Another step is connecting what the customer wants directly to production facilities by means of the Internet and, in turn, connecting production facilities directly to suppliers of primary products. An interesting case study is the Spanish textiles and fashion group Inditex, which has expanded Europe-wide under its brand name "Zapa". This networking has massive implications for a company's structure and management. Production must react more flexibly than before to the orders and requests coming in from customers by Internet. This calls for different machinery and manufacturing tools. What is more, employees must be able to work with the new technologies. There is enormous cost-cutting potential here, because a business model of this kind means that stocks of finished products and primary products can be reduced. Internet-based supply chain management thus encompasses the entire chain from supply planning, production planning, and stock management down to procurement. The market for supply chain management technologies encompasses hardware delivery and maintenance, software delivery and maintenance, systems integration with traders and suppliers, staff training, advisory services, and much more besides. This clearly illustrates the fact that retooling a company with traditional technology to Internet-based technology calls for substantial investment, a host of organizational changes, and an alteration in staff mentality. Similar challenges arise with the conversion of client relationship management to the Internet, or when a company begins marketing its products via the Internet. The spread of the Internet in industry and the financial services sector is creating not only new virtual markets between companies, financial institutions, and consumers, but also a new supply industry to make companies Internet-enabled in the first place.

E-commerce between Institutions (I2I)

Practically all financial services, with the exception of complex mergers and acquisitions and asset management consultancy, can be digitalized and hence Internet-enabled. In banking there are three different platforms:

- business to consumer platforms
- business to business platforms
- institutions to institutions platforms

Business to consumer platforms are enormously important for personal banking and individual asset management. As far as this segment is concerned, the link between mobile telephony and the Internet is a technical innovation that will revolutionize the market. The retrieval of account information, payments, online brokerage, and even consumer credit can be realized through this medium. With online brokerage, orders can be placed, status queries made, order information delivered, and the portfolio displayed. Banks are seeking to attract new customers through online providers' trading portals by opening virtual bank branches in their virtual shopping malls. According to market research, in a few years' time up to 25 percent of all personal banking will be transacted exclusively through online channels. In addition to their real bank branch, 65 percent of all retail customers will also want to have an online banking relationship.

In business with corporate customers, online banking may become even more important. This would follow the overall economic trend, in which the Internet is assuming even greater significance in business-to-business relations than in the business-to-consumer sector. Payment systems for online traders in the Internet (cybercash) are under development and will soon come onstream. A growing number of the banks' corporate customers are opening cybershops, and in some cases the banks offer them all-in-one solutions for start-ups of this kind. Banks are also offering customers their own buying platforms in the Internet, e.g., for office supplies. In the future, most cash management will be handled through the Internet. A large proportion of corporate customers, possibly more than half, will no longer need a bank branch at all. They will rely entirely on the banks' financial portals and mobile advisory services. Ultimately, all corporate banking products, such as loans, leasing, factoring, and investment facilities, can be provided through the Internet. In-depth consultancy and analysis will be required only for more complex financing transactions. But even these will not require a bank branch, because services of this kind can be offered by mobile financial experts on the customer's premises.

The third line of business in which the Internet is dramatically impacting business models is that of capital markets, i.e., business from institution to institution (I2I). Here we must make a distinction between three elements of the value chain: the issue of securities, securities trading, and the sale of securities to institutional customers.

The greatest progress has been made with electronic trading. These days, foreign exchange, equities, futures, bonds, commodities, and complex derivatives are traded entirely, or for the most part, on electronic marketplaces. But national platforms are still prevalent. The lack of acceptance for the idea of cross-border integration has given rise to new platform providers, called Electronic Communication Networks (ECNs). ECNs offer a transparent order book and trading after hours, are not subject to any national regulations, are available as cross-frontier platforms, feature an ownership structure consisting of international financial institutions with no national interests, and are highly efficient.

Even the flotation of shares and bonds over the World Wide Web is conceivable and will be practiced more often in future. Technically speaking, it means that all the elements of a stock issue will be made available electronically to institutional investors—the prospectus, analysis of the company, the pricing, and the web format for the bookbuilding procedure under which interested institutions can enter their orders. But investors will still want to experience the management of a company that is going public in person and "live," at meetings or forums where they can put direct questions to the company managers. A host of information can be communicated electronically, but not the overall "feel" for a company. The same applies to bonds, or at least bonds of companies that are not so well known. Finally, the placement of securities with institutional customers by the banks' sales teams will also be conducted more electronically. Some of the direct sales contact over the telephone between the bank lead-managing the issue and institutional investors will be replaced by electronic "conversation." But particularly in the case of shares or bonds with a more complex corporate background, counseling of institutional clients will still take place.

Internet technology will probably assert itself as the key element of business models in practically all industries in the next few years. The question is not whether, but how quickly, this will take place. There are possible risks that could put a brake on developments. The first is a continued economic downswing, during which investment is further shelved. The second is that e-commerce will destroy value chains previously integrated into companies. This will give rise to conflicts in the companies, and we do not know to what extent these can be resolved without friction. The third risk involves the fact that restructuring and modernization of the telecommunications industry is vital to swift creation of the necessary infrastructure for the application of Internet technology. The efficient, economical, and cross-border provision of cable services and mobile telephone services must be put in place as quickly as possible. Just how rapidly these services are made available will depend on structural change in the telecommunications industry. Finally, as the fourth risk, consumer acceptance is a crucial factor. Although use of the Internet is spreading very fast, there is still no broad acceptance of electronic facilities by end-users for purchasing goods and services. Thus, forecasts on development of the individual e-commerce segments vary in their reliability. The safest forecast is the widespread introduction of electronic issuing, trading, and selling of securities. But we must view prognoses on the development of electronic business-to-business commerce as slightly less certain. The greatest element of uncertainty lies in forecasts of electronic business-to-consumer commerce.

3. Winners and Losers

The Division of the Labor Market

The radical change affecting big industries, like everything else in the globalization-driven world, produces winners and losers. This is true of all the parties concerned: investors, employees, management, business locations, and nations. Politics finds itself faced with the fact that three classes of employees are materializing:

- employees in knowledge-based activities: the sciences, research, research services, development, design, technical services, control services, supervision, etc.;
- those engaged in industrial work, primarily the production of basic materials and the manufacture of capital and consumer goods;
- personal service providers: trade, catering, hotels, health-related services, transport services, and household services.

The demand for employees in the first category is extremely high, while the supply is limited by the distribution of skills and training opportunities. The jobs of employees in these industries are not under any great threat as a result of international migration or virtual product offers. The greatest threat to jobs exists in the second category, due to cheaper foreign locations and the migration of companies abroad, as well as to virtual product offers. The demand for workers in the third category will continue to rise, not least due to demographic developments. However, workers in the second category are also moving into these growth sectors as industrial jobs continue to lose ground, and because of migration of workers from abroad. A low-income sector will inevitably emerge here, and economic policy will have to concern itself with the consequences.

The Exposure to Globalization

The process of globalization has yet to embrace all areas of the economy and society. Although the Internet has found its way into the smallest of villages and into every language and dialect, traditions and regional identity continue to determine important aspects of European societies. To make globalization acceptable, the local and regional identity must be strengthened. Regions and municipalities must be allowed to decide for themselves what range of public services should be made available, what cultural aspects are to be emphasized, and what towns and municipalities should be developed. Although globalization has not entered all economic areas and all walks of life, its implications are more far-reaching than might appear at first glance. When low-wage sectors develop, local authorities come under pressure to cushion the social consequences. Just as globalization creates winners and losers among companies, it also produces winners and losers among the municipalities in which these companies are located. And so it becomes obvious in this context that economy and society are inseparably linked with one another. Ultimately, not only the companies but also the municipalities have to cope with changes that have their origins in the global market: specifically, this means the immigration and emigration of people, the provision of services by the local authority, and the development of the city or town and its region as well as its cultural appeal. Just as the sea-changes of our times demand that companies come up with new business models and bring new pressures to bear on the balance of interests between consumers, investors, and workers, similarly, these changes call for new ideas with respect to the development of regions and municipalities.

The Challenges for the Democratic Model

Globalization is not a zero-sum game in which some lose just as much as others gain. The world economy as a whole, including individual countries and societies, wins. The sum of all individual advantages is greater than that of all individual disadvantages. But one cannot tell that to the losers. At the heart of the debate on globalization lies growing inequality. The disparity between incomes from "simple" labor and incomes from "intelligent" labor is on the rise. If one already has wealth, one can increase it more readily when borders are open than when they are closed.

Democratic communities are distinguished by the principle of the equality of rights and duties. Essential prerequisites for a well-functioning democracy are the protection and fostering of these rights and principles, equal opportunity, and the avoidance of structural inequalities that threaten the individual citizens as free members of the community. That is why the fundamental understanding of a democracy also includes the idea that power and systems of the economic and political kind must be controlled, regulated, or eliminated as soon as they restrict the citizens' possibilities of free personal development, of taking part in public life, and of self-determination.

In principle, globalization and global competition have a power-limiting, power-destroying effect. For they prevent the domination of a market, force boundaries to open up, and smash national and regional monopolies. They are vital if investor and consumer sovereignty is to fully assert itself. But at the same time globalization is also what causes the inequalities and injustices I have just described, since they create winners and losers on a large scale. This dynamic process can destabilize democratic communities when they are modeled—as in Europe—on the principle of equal and homogeneous conditions between citizens. Whereas, in the past, the threat to European democracies was usually found in the manifestation of political or economic positions of power that lacked due legitimacy, future destabilization risks are more likely to be found in the appearance of a new economic class society that benefits by globalization. Better schooling and training, better access to new communications technology, greater mobility, better earnings opportunities, and more possibilities to increase personal wealth are the foundations of the new class distinctions.

The Capitalist Model under Criticism

The upshot of the consequences of the extensive political and economic changes in the 1990s was that the international world order and the market economy system in general came under fire. The seemingly uncontrollable international capital flows triggered crises. The emergence of a new economic class society destroyed cohesion in democratic societies. The global wave of mergers in major industrial countries produced fears of dominance by big corporate companies. The term "predatory capital" began doing the rounds. Is the globalized economy really synonymous with a rampaging market economy, a train without brakes that wreaks havoc? Studies have shown that ultimately, globalization was born out of a coincidence of highly different trends: the rise in internationally mobile investments, the integration of emerging countries into the world economy, the integration of regional economic areas, the revolution in communications, and with it the formation of virtual marketplaces. Can we or do we want to reverse these trends? Hardly anyone today would want to restrict investor sovereignty, which is to say, the investor's right to invest his assets—however large or small—wherever in the world he chooses. This applies just as much, if not more, to consumer sovereignty, i.e., the consumer's right to shop and travel wherever in the world he chooses. There is less of a consensus over the question whether the emerging and developing countries should, with their goods, be given full access to the markets of the industrial countries and whether their workers should be granted access to the labor market. Yet a far-reaching exclusion from the international market, and with that an exclusion from the international division of labor and from the possibility of achieving a higher standard of living, can scarcely be kept up indefinitely. And ultimately, it is just as impossible to hold back the electronic revolution in communications and subsequently in the marketplaces. The conclusion is that globalization is here to stay, and it will continue to have a mighty impact.

4. Strategic Answers

The current debate has produced three strategies in response to globalization.

The Strategy of Adapting

The strategy of adapting involves the removal of trade barriers and exchange controls, freedom of capital movements, a lean and adaptable welfare state, a labor market that is regulated as little as possible, low inflation, and balanced budgets. The more competitive the economy and the community are, the better this is for jobs and income. On this, the industrial nations and many emerging countries are agreed. But they have not yet found a way of coping with the problem of growing disparities of incomes and wealth.

The Nationalist Strategy of Intervention

The nationalist and interventionist strategy entails erecting trade barriers to shield one's own economy from the negative effects of international competition. Endeavors of this kind are evident in America, Europe, and Asia. Further features of this strategy are the efforts made to keep the wage disparities in one's own country as low as possible, either by forcing low-income countries to fix higher minimum wages or by restricting the migration of workers.

Strategy of Evolution

The third strategic response is to see economic globalization not as a *fait accompli* but as a process that can be influenced and changed. This viewpoint calls, first of all, for the international regulation of child labor, union activities, social concerns, and environmental protection. It also includes introducing international social standards. Second, new forms of economic coordination are deemed necessary. The fragmented international organizations (the International Monetary Fund, the World Bank, and the Organization for Economic Cooperation and Development) must be united to help economic countries in emergencies, monitor the momentum of the international capital markets, and, if need be, take appropriate action to curb volatility. Steps toward this end include a program to ease the debt burden of developing and emerging countries. Third, international institutions must be "democratized" more vigorously. The European Union has to correct democratic deficiencies in its institutions, the developing countries should be more strongly represented within international organizations, and human rights should be pushed through more forcefully by imposing sanctions. This line of thought pursues objectives with which many feel they can identify. But there is a lack of practicable proposals, in particular, proposals that maintain a balance between the desirable efficiency of the international economic system and the removal of undesirable features.

In outlining these three strategies we have come closer to identifying what in international debate is often referred to as the "third way." Depending on one's point of view, it could be either the first or the third strategy. Tony Blair's "third way" is more along the lines of the first strategy, and advocates that the national economy should remain open to the world and market-oriented. The state's task is to compensate for the inequality caused by globalization by implementing appropriate reforms to the welfare state and by promoting education and the training of poorly qualified workers. But the champions of the third strategy, who seek to change the global economic order and the order of the regional integration areas, also speak of a "third way." Their aim is not to check the impact of globalization, however, but to subject the global economic system itself to a new regime.

5. A New Debate on Responsibility and Values

Economic Responsibility and Values

Future debate on the limits to globalization will center not only on questions of economic efficiency, but also on responsibility and values. Because of the diffusive nature of labor in a society, the individual is not fully aware of the consequences of the economic decisions he makes. And even if he were aware, that would not change his decisions because he does not know how others are behaving. The individual finds himself with many parts to play: shareholder, customer, employee, and citizen subject to taxes and in receipt of state benefits. He wants the best possible value for money from the products he demands, he wants to make the highest possible return on his investments, and he does not want to lose his job. Experience shows that customer sovereignty is the highest consideration. No consumer changes his decisions on what he buys in order to save others' jobs. Next in priority is investor sovereignty. No investor foregoes a yield in order to save jobs, because he needs the return on his investments, be it for his old age, to improve his standard of living, or to put his children through an apprenticeship or university. Stock prices are important not only to big shareholders but also to members of a disability and pension insurance that is invested in shares, and to small individual shareholders who have invested their money in shares. Volatility, instability, heavy demands on personal flexibility or on flexibility in the family or at work, are the other side of the coin. The new freedoms enjoyed as a consumer and saver/investor are paid for by a tougher situation as employee.

The management of a company bears particular responsibility in this respect. It has the task of finding the right balance between consumer interests, shareholders' interests, and workers' interests. Yet there is little scope for maneuver where the interests of consumers are concerned. The company must supply its customers with products that are competitive in terms of price and quality. Nor is there much room for compromise on the shareholders' side. The shareholders will sell the shares if a company fails to match the increases in value to be expected for the industry as a whole. But when share prices fall the funding costs rise and the development of the company is harmed; perhaps even a takeover of the company may ensue, which is then followed by a restructuring. The management cannot act in accordance with the workers' interests at the expense of the shareholders' and consumers' interests. The employers' interests are best served when the company, compared with its peers, can offer particularly innovative products and has particularly efficient production and organizational structures in place. The more flexibility the employers have with regard to the structuring of the company and the more they channel their talents into product development and sales, the greater the degree of their freedom will be.

Social and Political Responsibility and Values

Globalization gives rise to new social responsibilities. Borders give way, people move, competition manifests itself through virtual channels. This competition creates losers who need images of "the enemy" as an excuse for their own perceived failings. This makes the demands in dealing with otherwise-minded persons, with foreigners, and with the poor not smaller but greater. More is being asked for in terms of tolerance and solidarity.

Globalization, competition, and the dramatic shifts in the risks of falling down the social ladder and in possibilities of advancement have touched off discussion on individual values. Complaints have been voiced that values such as doing one's duty, bearing responsibility, and acting from a sense of public spirit have been lost at the expense of self-interest, self-realization, and hedonistic materialism. Yet this debate about individual values does not help us in dealing with globalization. The consumer and investor who has his own set of objectives and preferences is, basically speaking, not immoral or lacking in values. Insurance fraud, tax fraud, the falsification of balance sheets—these may testify to a loss of moral values. The phenomena of global competition, of consumer and investor sovereignty, and the resultant shift of winning and losing positions between sectors of the population, professions, and national groups cannot be grasped in terms of individual values.

Politics concentrates not least on questions of equitable coexistence. It follows that the tasks to be fulfilled are also to be defined in these terms.

Taking their cue from the three strategic options outlined above, policy-makers can try to bring influence to bear on the framework of the international order. So far, however, there is absolutely no concrete idea of the direction in which the framework of the international order might be changed without jeopardizing the benefits of the free exchange of goods and the freedom of capital markets. National or regional economic policy offers more scope for action. For example, social security systems can be adapted to provide, in particular, insurance protection for those who lose out to globalization instead of sticking to a one-size-fits-all social insurance scheme for the entire population. Particular thought ought to be given to a system of social assistance for individuals who have to switch to the low-wage sector. Yet such a system must also include rules on how entrepreneurs who have lost their livelihood in the throes of structural change might be given a fair chance to make a new start. A further political task is to promote both basic and advanced education and vocational training. This is where it is decided, for example, with what quality and in what numbers the new generation for knowledge-based services is cultivated, and how much our understanding of economic change as a consequence of globalization is improved. Seen in this light, the task of education is also a task of political leadership. Only if these tasks are taken seriously can the worst option, namely, a return to a national protectionist policy, be prevented.

REFERENCES

Cohen, D. *Fehldiagnose Globalisierung*. Frankfurt: Campus Verlag, 1998.

Kennedy, P. *Preparing for the Twenty-First Century*. Westminster: New York Times Book Review, 1993.

Organization for Economic Cooperation and Development (OECD). *The Economic and Social Impact of Electronic Commerce*. Edited by A. Wyckoff, R. D. Wyckoff, and A. Colecchia. Paris: Brookings Institution Press, 1994.

Picot, A. *Die Internet-Ökonomie*. Munich: Springer Verlag, 1998.

Thurow, L. C. *The Future of Capitalism*. New York: William Morrow & Co., 1996.

Wood, A. *North-South Trade, Employment and Inequality: Changing Fortunes in a Skill-Driven World*. Oxford: Clarendon Press, 1994.

CHAPTER 6

Managing the Multinational Enterprise in a World of Different Cultures: Some Fundamental Remarks on the Pluralism of Cultures and Its Managerial Consequences

HORST STEINMANN AND
ANDREAS GEORG SCHERER

I. Relevance of the Subject to the Present Situation

In the course of globalization one problem is becoming increasingly important for the management of many multinational enterprises (MNEs): How should managers treat different cultures and legal environments? And how should *conflicts* be handled that result from fundamental differences concerning legal regulations, worldviews, value systems, and fundamental principles of life? The solution to this problem as proposed in this essay will

Horst Steinmann is professor emeritus at the Friedrich Alexander University of Erlangen and Nuremberg. His main fields of interest are corporate strategy and international management. He is chairman of the German Business Ethics Network.

Andreas Georg Scherer is a professor at the University of Constance in the Faculty of Administration Sciences.

require a fundamental change in the behavior of MNEs. It will result in modifications concerning all five classical managerial functions: planning, organizing, staffing, directing, and controlling.

One can often read reports in the business press about MNEs and their business partners that are involved in human rights abuses or bribery practices, that do not comply with international social and labor standards, and that do not care much about health protection or the preservation of an intact natural environment. Such problems often emerge as side effects during the process of strategy implementation, when multinational enterprises act in different countries where such issues are not sufficiently regulated by positive law or enforced by legal institutions, as is the case, e.g., in many developing countries. In modern societies these issues are usually treated by the formal rules of positive law and a more or less common concept of "the good life" which forms the basis for the ethical responsiveness of business firms. Here, conflict resolution is based on the rational acceptance of generalized rules which are enforced by the executing institutions of the respective nation-state and which are eventually accompanied by the self-voluntary ethical behavior of the firm. In such a way, both law and ethics contribute to the peaceful stabilization of modern societies.

However, the above-mentioned problems are becoming more prevalent in a globalized world where the conditions of modernity no longer apply. Rather, we see an emerging postmodern world which has, not only multiple power centers, but also different and competing conceptions of "the good life." In such a situation powerful institutions such as the MNEs are becoming responsible for the development of new forms of government. Not only the governments and the public in many industrialized countries, but also the big international organizations (such as the UN) call with increasing frequency for MNEs to do more about the solution of cultural conflicts.[1] In addition, MNEs are asked to provide solutions to problems which the traditional nation-state has become unable to solve (e.g., the enforcement of worldwide social and environmental standards). As such, the *normative* dimension of corporate responsibility is addressed: The company should act "as a good citizen," i.e., it should not only observe the law in the respective country—as it frequently claimed to do in the past—but it should also contribute actively to the peaceful settlement of the cultural conflicts which arise from the globalization of economy.

Two measures are to be applied to reach this aim. On the one hand, the MNE's management should help to avoid or successfully settle conflicts which develop as a result of its own business strategy. This would be a *direct* contribution to the internal and external peace in the respective enterprise. On the other hand, however, there is also a demand for the MNE to become *indirectly* involved in peacemaking by playing a part in the development of an international (global) set of rules for the handling of conflicts, and thus cooperating with other organizations such as the UN, the WTO, the ILO, and, apart from these, with national governments and nongovernmental organizations. Together they form a *network* of private and public actors that creates a new world order.[2]

In this essay we focus on the first aspect, the direct contribution of responsible management to resolve or prevent conflicts resulting from its own behavior. The solution to this problem requires a clarification of two basic questions:

1) How should management organize the interaction with different cultures? Should management accept the proclamation of Western values (*proclamation approach*) or start an unprejudiced mutual process of learning between cultures (*learning approach*)?
2) What are the implications for the design of the management process, i.e., the above-mentioned managerial functions and their relations to each other, resulting from the answer to this question?

As is well known, the first question is the subject of controversial dispute. It is not at all the case—as one might guess—that of the two approaches, the learning approach is the one generally favored. In 1995 the U.S. president Bill Clinton, for example, put forward the "Model Business Principles" with the following statement:

> Recognizing the positive role of U.S. business in upholding and promoting adherence to universal standards of human rights, the Administration encourages all business to adopt and implement voluntary codes of conduct for doing business around the world. . . .[3]

In this formulation the universal validity of human rights is explicitly assumed; the text of the document calls for management to create and establish a suitable code of ethics in order to implement the document's aims. This demand, which is particularly addressed to multinational enterprises, clearly corresponds to a *proclamation approach*. Contrary to this approach, the present essay gives arguments for the appropriateness of a *learning approach* in intercultural management (section 2). The characteristics of this strategy thus have implications for the design of the management process (section 3).

Yet, before continuing, we should note that the *normative basis* of global economic activities is not undisputed. Radical defenders of free trade and free markets strictly object to the (political) establishment and harmonization of social and labor standards and of environmental standards, which are bound to become valid worldwide.[4] We cannot go into this discussion in detail;[5] however, the argument in section 2 also provides, at least implicitly, reasons for the necessity of greater harmonization of the normative foundations of economic behavior in the course of globalization, i.e., through legislation and effective execution. However, as long as there is no supranational institution able not only to formulate but also to execute the rules of the global economy, we are currently living in an interregnum, where such rules are defined and executed by the joint activities of private and public actors.

2. Pleading the Case for the Learning Approach in Intercultural Management

In this section we give reasons for the thesis that the chances of peaceful settlement of intercultural conflicts are significantly improved if all parties involved in the conflict, i.e., including the MNE, agree to a learning approach.

Conflicts between cultures become economically relevant if they affect the peaceful coordination of the economic process. At this stage, at the latest, one must think about the causes of this type of disturbance. As already suggested, they lie in a difference of worldviews, of deeply rooted value systems and principles of life, or, in short, of "normative orientation." The philosophical and crucial question that follows immediately is whether such differences in normative orientations and the conflicts resulting from them can be addressed by a reasonable treatment or not. Those who think that a reasonable handling of conflicts is in principle impossible inevitably have to return to the use of power in its manifold forms—should it be necessary for the coordination of actions in a given situation. The proclamation approach would be such a manifestation of power because by definition it does not aim at explaining reasons, but rather aims exclusively at enforcing values about which a decision has already been made. Conversely, a learning approach is possible to the same extent to which cultural conflicts can be solved in a reasonable way. The problem addressed here has been discussed profoundly and in detail in philosophical discussions of recent years.[6] In the following paragraph we outline the basic ideas of a way of solving problems as it results from the philosophy of methodological constructivism.[7]

A reasonable solution of cultural conflicts must finally depend on justifications and arguments which can be accepted as "good reasons" by all concerned—because of *insight*. Such a solution of conflicts, based on insight and good reasons, is appropriate for *peacemaking* in the sense of a general and free consensus. In this sense, it is possible to reconcile the freedom of the individual with the unity (order) that is necessary for all members of the society to work together. Considered in this light, peace is a work of reason.[8]

We know from the philosophy of science that claims for the validity of normative claims cannot be justified using deductive techniques. This would lead to the trilemma of infinite regress, a logical circle, and the dogmatic breaking off of the process of justification.[9] A solution of cultural conflicts that is peaceful and not arbitrary therefore depends on the existence of a *nondeductive concept of reasoning* which nevertheless can claim reason for itself. The structure of the problematic situation observed in the case where different cultures interact and produce a certain potential for conflict, corresponds with what philosophers recently have been discussing with particular intensity—a "problem of incommensurability."[10] As in the case of cultural conflicts, the problem here is how the (strict) incompatibility of theories, but also of normative orientations, can be overcome, i.e., whether there is in principle a solution for this problem. Geert-Lueke Lueken has suggested how the problem could be handled successfully.[11] He shows the possibility of a solution and at the same time makes clear that a definite abstract (theoretical) solution to the problem cannot be expected from science itself. According to Lueken, precisely those people who represent incommensurable positions, whether it be in academic science or in practice, are forced to repeatedly seek solutions for the task of overcoming incommensurability. To put it differently, the perspective of the observer, i.e., of an uninvolved third party, must be changed—methodologically—to the perspective of those who are directly involved. This will be discussed further below.

Referring to the objections of Paul Feyerabend,[12] Lueken demonstrates that the insolubility of the problem of incommensurability is a consequence of the understanding of rationality based on rules and an axiomatic or deductive concept of reasoning. Thus, reasoning is regarded merely as the operation of logical deduction formed from rules. This is based on two premises, namely, (1) that reasoning is a *method* (of logical operation) and (2) that this method is standardized by a certain set of rules. Logically, it follows that when one doubts these scientific and theoretical methods and rules on a philosophical level, one must critically consider these two premises about the concept of reasoning in order to find a way out of the dilemma. However, in order to do so, one needs a distinctly different *approach* in the methodological structuring of argumentation in order to avoid the impending regressum ad infinitum.

With respect to the first of these two premises, Lueken suggests a concept of argumentation which avoids a priori decisions concerning methodology. Argumentation should be understood as a *practical concept* that precedes all other methods. With regard to the second premise, he suggests giving up the idea of a connection between a concept of argumentation and the preliminary decision about rules. Instead, argumentation should simply be oriented toward the *purpose* of consensus. This suggestion will therefore question and open up for discussion what was previously withheld from criticism in the discussion about incommensurability—i.e., the concept of reasoning and the rules of argumentation themselves.

The reasonability of this new concept depends centrally on whether or not the concept of argumentation can itself be reasonably introduced. Lueken suggests the following definition: "Argumentation is a symbolic action performed to overcome a controversy and aiming at consensus."[13]

Obviously, this definition has been designed in such a manner that it includes the *potential* for solving the problem of incommensurability in a rational way. Argumentation is perceived as *(symbolic) action* and, from the beginning, is therefore not restricted to a certain method of reasoning. Moreover, no reference to a predefined set of rules of argumentation is included in the definition. On the contrary, it rather considers *consensus* as the aim of argumentation. The distinction between Lueken's definition and the decisionistic and power-induced so-called solutions of incommensurable positions consists of exactly this aim. Furthermore, the rational core of this suggestion is guaranteed by the aim of consensus, because consensus is oriented toward free agreement through insight into the arguments put forward.

The central question of how this concept of argumentation can be made comprehensible as a nonarbitrary form affects the correct[14] beginning of the construction of a concept of argumentation. We will show below that this is, however, exactly the question about the correct understanding of the *relationship between theory and praxis*.

Based on a deductive concept of reasoning, praxis always means the *use* of explicit or implicit theories;[15] as a method, theory precedes praxis and has an axiomatic beginning (a "top-down" beginning), as shown in fig. 1:

Figure 1: The Relationship between Theory and Praxis in the Deductive Reasoning Model (from Steinmann and Scherer 1994, modified)

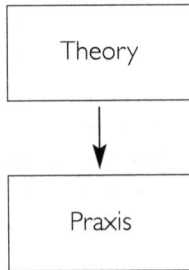

```
        ┌─────────────┐
        │   Theory    │
        └─────────────┘
               │
               ▼
        ┌─────────────┐
        │   Praxis    │
        └─────────────┘
```

The relationship between theory and praxis is reversed in the philosophy of methodological constructivism to which Lueken adheres here, and is developed in detail as shown by fig. 2.[16]

Figure 2: The Relationship between Theory and Praxis in the Constructive Reasoning Model (from Steinmann and Scherer 1994, modified)

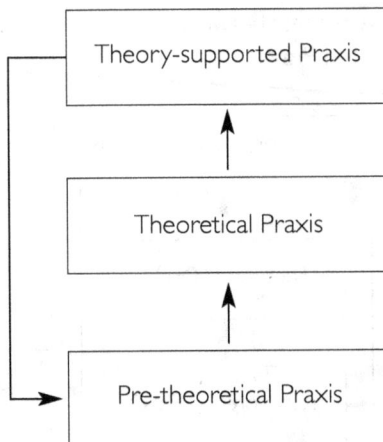

```
     ┌──────────────────────────────┐
  ┌──│   Theory-supported Praxis    │
  │  └──────────────────────────────┘
  │                 ▲
  │                 │
  │  ┌──────────────────────────────┐
  │  │     Theoretical Praxis       │
  │  └──────────────────────────────┘
  │                 ▲
  │                 │
  │  ┌──────────────────────────────┐
  └─▶│    Pre-theoretical Praxis    │
     └──────────────────────────────┘
```

Lueken draws a distinction between pre-theoretical and theoretical praxis. *Pre-theoretical praxis* is regarded as "part of everyday life in which people are engaged and are familiar with control over activities and occurrences without any special theoretical considerations or reflections."[17] This practical "know-how" constitutes the difference between pre-theoretical and theoretical praxis. *Theoretical praxis* in this context is oriented toward the construction of (new) knowledge. Only when the practical know-how of everyday life is no longer sufficient will the change to theoretical praxis become necessary for finding solutions to existing or new problems. In this case, practical know-how must be expounded in order to question precisely those validity claims that had been accepted without questioning in pre-theoretical praxis, or that could be assumed without further reflection because the action had turned out to be successful, without provoking any problems. With regard to our initial problem, theoretical praxis generating knowledge for the clarification of validity claims only needs to get under way when the pre-theoretical knowledge no longer suffices to cope with everyday life. The results of theoretical praxis support the use of theoretical instructions as solutions to problematical actions (*theory-supported praxis*). When these results are successfully and repeatedly accomplished, they will turn into a habit in time and become an unproblematic part of the pre-theoretical practical know-how, up to the point when new problems appear at this advanced development stage of pre-theoretical praxis—problems which call for the creation of new knowledge in theoretical praxis (see fig. 3).

Figure 3. The Interactive Process between Pre-theoretical Praxis, Theoretical Praxis, and Theory-supported Praxis

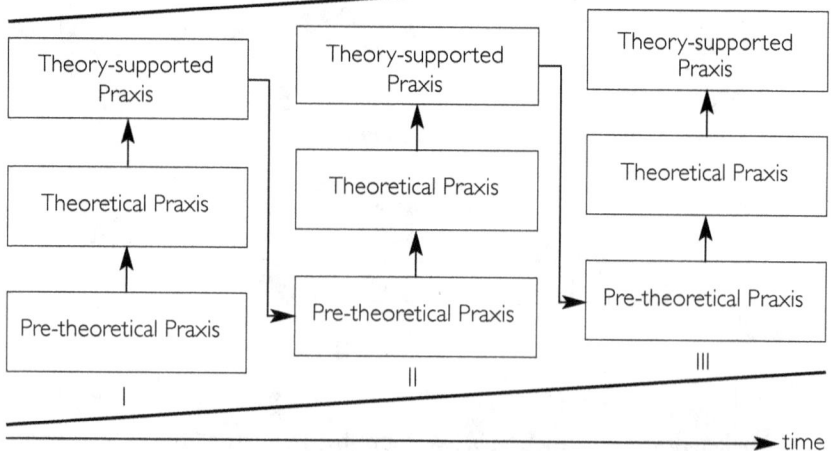

Two points are particularly important in understanding the relationship between theory and praxis.

First, *theoretical praxis is not identical with science*. Theoretical praxis always emerges where a greater distance from everyday practical know-how is necessary, because this know-how has become problematic and the relevant validity claims have to be (re)considered. Thus, theoretical praxis is applied wherever validity claims emerge and we attempt to solve them. This can be the case both in everyday action and in companies or in scientific institutions. Conversely, theoretical praxis, i.e., the verification of validity claims, always requires pre-theoretical practical aptitude. This is achieved by using craftsmanship and the ability to create, as we learn in everyday life in the manual creation of objects ("poiesis"), e.g., within scientific experiments.[18] In the case of elementary social actions, such as the choice of purposes and appropriate means in human interactions ("praxis"), including peacemaking routines for the solution of conflicts relating to a certain purpose, people can rely on social routines practiced in everyday life.[19] In this sense, and with respect to our initial problem, pre-theoretical praxis is the *cause* and the *methodological starting point* of theoretical praxis. Consequently, "science" is merely a special institutionalized type of theoretical praxis that was established in our culture to allow "scientists" to reflect methodologically about problems and solutions of general concern without having to deal with immediate solutions to singular cases.

Second, with regard to the common objection made by defenders of an (axiomatic) deductive paradigm, i.e., that pre-theoretical praxis has always been influenced by theories and that thus a clear beginning in pre-theoretical praxis is impossible, we support Lueken's hint at the following reply.[20] Of course, it remains undisputed that all actions are at least partly influenced by knowledge, since it is the purpose of theoretical praxis to *improve* practical know-how through theoretical knowledge. However, what is crucial is the role of this knowledge in the particular situation where action is required.

The crucial point is that for this situative actualization of practical know-how, no previous actualization of knowledge is needed. It is not necessary for the actor to understand his/her practical know-how as the following of a rule or the using of a theory and to verbalize this rule or theory (depending on the situation). It is also crucial that knowledge does not enter into the situation as knowledge with a claim to validity. As long as we are in the area of pre-theoretical praxis, claims to validity are not discussed. The success of a pre-theoretical situation cannot be seen as confirmation, nor can a failure, as such, be seen as its refutation. Success and failure as well as guidance by knowledge are simply contingent features of the historical situation.[21]

In view of this interpretation of the relationship between praxis and theory, the following becomes clear. The concept of argumentation as suggested by Lueken begins on a level of pre-theoretical practical know-how; that is exactly where it, at the same time, has its origin. The word "reasoning" can then be reserved for argumentation about validity claims on the level of theoretical praxis.[22] As Lueken shows, "reasoning" can be reconstructed as *(speech-)action*. As such, the operation of deductive reasoning is only one category among others within this concept of reasoning.

A controversy cannot be classified from the start in terms of whether it is a conflict between incommensurable positions or not. If the opponents agree to argumentation at all, they will first try to mutually justify the validity claims questioned through reasoning. Only in the course of this game of reasoning will they notice that their positions are incommensurable, namely, when they repeatedly demand new reasoning and do not find a commonly accepted basis for reasoning (reductive-oriented reasoning).[23] They also cannot establish a commonly accepted point of departure on which to base their reasoning attempts (productive-oriented reasoning), since by definition such a beginning does not exist in the case of incommensurable positions.

In such a situation, the opponents can choose either to decide the conflict by the use of power, or else to abandon to reasoning (but not argumentation) in order to first *produce* a common basis for reasoning. The creation of such a common basis for reasoning implies abandoning the method-oriented concept of reasoning supported by rules, i.e., a scientifically oriented concept of reasoning. In light of the previous discussion, this process of abandoning can now more accurately be reconstructed as doing without claims to validity, and that means the *return* from theoretical to pre-theoretical praxis. There, in pre-theoretical praxis, argumentation no longer serves to create and solve validity claims according to methodological knowledge guided by rules, but rather attempts at first to simply understand the contrary positions through joined action, which means creating a common understanding.[24] Based on a (possibly) successful achievement of understanding, the opponents should then have the intention to build a consensus to overcome the incommensurable positions, i.e., to establish agreement. This means that, in this context, argumentation as symbolic action corresponds to pre-theoretical know-how and serves the *construction* of a common language basis and, starting from there, the *reconstruction of instruments of speech*. Such a basis, however, is not available with incommensurable positions, e.g., with fundamental value conflicts between cultures. While the deductive concept of reasoning is only geared to the application of existing rules of argumentation without being able to question their reasoning, the concept of argumentation as suggested here allows for those symbolic actions which serve the construction and constitution of common rules which are understood as argumentative and rational.[25]

When returning to pre-theoretical praxis in order to overcome incommensurable positions, the parties involved must exchange their observer perspective for a participant perspective. Only this perspective of direct involvement in a conflict offers the possibility of mutual understanding, without any need to refer to rules. One can therefore also anticipate that the chance to overcome incommensurable positions is principally linked to changing from the observer to the participant perspective. A more distant observer perspective remains dependent on the application of fixed rules and criteria. Incidentally, this results from the concept of action as an intentional deed. Since only the actor has a privileged access to his or her intentions, intentions can never be deduced with sufficient certainty through simple observation.[26] One has to go one step further, to pragmatic interaction in the form of argumentation between those concerned.

In summary, in Lueken's concept of argumentation four main characteristics can be regarded as a precondition for the possibility of solving the problem of incommensurability. Consequently, these are of central importance in major conflicts involving the normative orders of different cultures:

1) The concept of argumentation is *not defined by a set of rules* and therefore is "open for differing, or even incommensurable ideas of what actions constitute an argument."

2) The concept of argumentation is developed from a *participant perspective* and understands itself as a contribution to "argumentation about argumentation" as it is carried out, not only in the theory of argumentation, but also, partly implicitly and partly explicitly, in the diverse daily practice of argumentation.

3) Furthermore, "argumentation is seen as *concrete action* and is therefore pragmatic."

4) The reference to the *concept of reasoned validity* remains in the concept of argumentation that was put forward so that argumentative rationality can assert itself against the criticism of rationality that is supported by the thesis of incommensurability.[27]

Defining argumentation as "consensus-oriented action" does not merely mark—as mentioned—its difference from power-induced (or decisionistic) solutions of conflicts. It also shows that, as a goal of argumentation, consensus is to be preferred over dissent. In other words, we need not deal with the choice between consensus or dissent as central concepts of the theory of argumentation.[28] Such a choice is completely superfluous when looking at the relationship between the two concepts. Lueken explains:

> It should be noticed that aiming at consensus presupposes controversy, i.e., dissent. Neither consensus nor dissent is a value in itself. The tendency toward consensus is inherent in the argumentative treatment of dissent. Usually different points of view agree in some respects and disagree in others. It depends on the situation, the purposes, and the respective SO ["systems of orientation," Steinmann and Scherer] which of them should be actually pointed out. Sometimes disagreement does not require particular problem-solving activities. But in other cases something has to be done, for the disagreeing parties cannot coexist as long as their opinions conflict. Just cases of incommensurability are of this kind.[29]

In addition:

> Although argumentation may sometimes be necessary to uncover or clarify real dissents obscured by superficial or pretended consensus, we do not need argument to produce dissent. There is a lot of disagreement in our world anyhow. Some people may even prefer disagreement and use argument or different means to produce more of it. But, how shall we decide if decision between dissenting parties is needed? There are probably lots of ways to come to decisions. Argumentation is not needed if one has got the power to bring about one's decisions by more striking means. But in order to clarify points of disagreement, to convince others, to make decisions a common matter, we need argument. There is an essential difference between decisions grounded on power and decisions resting upon reasonable insight of all participants concerned. And argumentation is an outstanding way to come to the latter ones.[30]

In connection with the relevant suggestion that one should return to pre-theoretical praxis in order to find solutions to problems of incommensurability, Lueken eventually takes up a number of objections.[31] In the context of our reflections, the most interesting objection is that, in incommensurable systems of orientation, each of the participants ultimately lives "in another world" in which different things are normal, and because of that, each participant has his or her own pre-theoretical praxis. Indeed, Lueken's suggestion presupposes that where incommensurable positions occur, one cannot assume that the pre-theoretical praxis is already a common one. Therefore, it is important not to "find" a common basis which is already present, but to *create* a new pre-theoretical praxis through practically joined action and a joined process of learning.

> Returning to pre-theoretical praxis does not mean returning to types of action that have always been considered unproblematic but rather researching and learning new unknown forms of action and speech using the pre-theoretical means of practicing and joining in.[32]

It must be emphasized that the *existence* of a mutual basis is not presupposed. The presupposition is simply that the incommensurable systems of orientation are not completely blocked off from each other. Recognizing incommensurable positions implies at least the perception of the *borders* of the differing positions, i.e., the difference between them.

> If the participants mutually seek out the pre-theoretical spot on which the controversy broke out, the borders of their particular pre-theoretical worlds are thereby exposed and the transition into theoretical praxis takes place, and if they also refrain from questions of validity and attempt to move these borders and enter the pre-theoretical praxis of the other person, in other words to explore the other's background, then they do not simply return to their previous pre-theoretical world, but produce a new pre-theoretical praxis by working together and attempting to learn while relying entirely on their elementary ability to act.[33]

Learning in this pragmatic sense does not only mean practicing schematic skills and routines. What is important beyond that is to consciously design and make experience. Education in particular has to contribute to the formation of corresponding abilities.[34]

These basic considerations (which can only be laid out here in a very general way) show that there is, in principle, an alternative to the power-induced proclamation approach. This alternative exists as a practical way of living that is oriented toward a peaceful solution of cultural conflicts based on mutual learning. In the most unfortunate case, should there not even be a common *language* as a starting point for the process of learning, this learning approach has to start with the praxis of life, i.e., by working together in order to build up a common basis of language. This would then be the source for communicating on the basis of reason and argument and for solving cultural conflicts step by step. Once a general free consensus has been reached, one can speak of a status of peace—as suggested above. If peace is understood in this sense (as a general free consensus), it always remains, however, only a *regulative idea,* i.e., an orientation for action. There is no guarantee (even a scientific one) that such a status can be reached. The most interesting issue, the question of the rationality of such a proceeding, is stressed by Lueken as follows:

> Argumentative action is already rational insofar as it is an outstanding way to overcome conflicts and peacefully solve problems. Whenever the rationality of actions is called into question, in addition to our judgment [or "practical wisdom" as it is called in the Aristotelian tradition], we only have the possibility of argumentative action through which the rationality of actions can be and is shown. The rationality of the means for the pursuit of ends must be shown in argumentation about theoretical knowledge. The rationality of purposes and good intentions must be demonstrated through ethical-political argumentation. It can be considered as rational insofar as it is comprehensive or appropriate to bring about comprehensibility, and furthermore, insofar as it aims at agreement to the validity claims of theoretical and political knowledge.[35]

It is possible to demonstrate that this solution of (cultural) conflicts as suggested by methodological constructivism is not relativistic; that moreover it can be distinguished from postmodern positions; and that it is also not founded on transcendentalism. It therefore avoids the problems of those approaches.[36]

3. The Learning Approach and the Management Process

If it is true that a learning approach as outlined above can only be established by the parties involved, in their particular circumstances of living and acting, and that it cannot be developed by "external" scientists, this must have direct effects on the management of a company that is exposed to a plurality of incommensurable cultures. Although it is impossible here to go into the details of this problem, our central thesis is that a learning approach cannot be combined with the classic management philosophy of F. W. Taylor, which is constituted by the division of thought and action. On the contrary, it is necessary to create management structures which promote the learning process described above (for all members of the organization) when different cultures meet. Today, this kind of structure is already increasingly being implemented in the praxis of management. We are therefore not aiming at a revolutionary change in all of management philosophy; on the contrary, the following reflections are meant to at least hint at the fact that a rapprochement can be observed between the demands that economic rationality makes on the management structures of MNEs, and the demands of intercultural management designed to provide a peaceful solution of cultural conflicts in MNEs by practicing a learning strategy.

We can directly conclude from our scientific and theoretical reflections and the resulting concept of learning that a peaceful solution of cultural conflicts requires a company culture and an organizational structure within the MNE that *supports argumentation*. Basically, every manager and every member of the staff must have the chance to initiate processes of argumentation with the goal of identifying developing cultural conflicts "on the spot" and in time. The aim is to evaluate the normative and economic importance and consequences of these conflicts and to contribute creative suggestions for problem-solving to the MNE's decision-making process. The final objectives are solutions based on consensus. All phases of the process of gaining and using information (for the management of companies) must be influenced by the demands on the MNE to solve cultural conflicts peacefully, whenever possible. As we will discuss in more detail below, these phases consist of identification of a problem, evaluation of a problem, creative design of options for action, evaluation of these options, and their authorization—authorization meaning that decisions that have been made are regarded as valid and obligatory for the entire organization. In concrete terms, the peaceful handling of conflicts implies a management model that is *dialogue* oriented rather than monologue oriented, a model that prefers *decentralization* of decision making and responsibility over centralization, and finally a model that is *multipersonal,* in the sense that the process of gaining and using information should involve the thought of as many members of the organization as possible.

It is clear that this approach is exactly the opposite of classic Tayloristic management philosophy.[37] Three attributes are characteristic of this philosophy's concept of the division between thought and action: (1) a rationality defined by monologue that is meant to guarantee correct planning (as a basis for carrying out the plans); (2) the centralization of decision making and responsibility within top management; and (3) the direction of staff via external incentives.[38] The crisis of this traditional management model today is in reality a crisis of these three prerequisites.

The Tayloristic model is based on the idea of rationality defined by monologue and the assumption that it is in principle possible to establish correct plans. This model presupposes that the top management is able to generate ample and correct knowledge about the external and internal environment by rational means, e.g., through prognoses and scenarios. However, as environmental ambiguity (the complexity of cause and effect in the internal and external environment and uncertainty about the future) increases—and this is characteristic of strategic management—such an assumption becomes less and less applicable.[39]

In extreme cases, namely, if uncertainty and complexity have increased in such a way that plans are already outdated before they are set up, planning becomes completely pointless. The management functions of organizing, staffing, and directing must then provide *potentials of flexibility* so that the company can continuously adapt to changing conditions. In such a situation, however, any kind of structure, of predefined roles, i.e., of order, is dysfunctional from the very start. Company management degenerates to a mere "reaction," and if we apply the strict criteria of active development, management is no longer even possible. To put it differently, company management becomes mere evolution.[40]

Modern management concepts that have a certain importance in practice are situated between these two extremes, of total planning on the one hand, and the evolutionary perspective on the other. As a prerequisite, management must be able to develop and form company politics, i.e., there must be a chance of *pro-active* action. This also means that planning can develop a reasonable orientation for action, although without any absolute claim on correctness. Despite a medium level of complexity and uncertainty, it is still possible to give arguments in advance that a selected program of strategic action has a *better* chance of success than the alternatives.[41] The new sense that is thus assigned to strategic planning is important because—as we will show later—it points to the necessity of reviewing the management model with regard to the three attributes mentioned above.

Under the conditions of medium complexity and uncertainty, strategic planning should be understood as an activity that selects the tentatively most promising strategic program of action from the options offered by the future. This activity is based on more or less reasonable suppositions of relevance concerning the development of the internal and external environment. The task of strategic planning is to bridge the gap between the ambiguity of the environment and the unambiguity of orientation that is necessary for action.

A high risk when making selections is necessarily connected with this "bridging function:" Everything can turn out differently than it was planned. Therefore, the strategy *always* has to be open for basic review. For this to be possible, the company needs an additional management potential as a counterweight to planning, and this potential must be designed to compensate for the selectivity of planning and the implied risk, by permanently supervising the chosen strategy. This compensatory function requires a new management function—strategic control.[42] *Strategic control* is to be understood as a process of gaining and using information from the internal and external company environment, information by which threats to the company's strategic course can be identified on time (an "early warning system"). Therefore, strategic control must be able to supply more information than is generated in planning and manifested in the plans themselves. This point is crucial for our argument. In its structural pattern, strategic control therefore cannot be oriented toward the predefined selective functions of strategic planning—as in the Tayloristic management process—in the sense of a plain control of feedback. In other words, it may not simply direct its attention toward objects of control, preselected by planning, and thus *close* its field of problems from the beginning. The very opposite applies. Strategic control must be designed as an answer to the basic inability to separate the internal and external environment and must be an open, non-directed, company wide, and multipersonal activity. Thus, in a way, it becomes a "feed-forward control."

As the following more detailed explanation of the informational process within strategic control will show, this new management function at the same time has the effect that the majority of the conflicts, contradictions, and other dilemmas in the company return to their origins in line management and do not remain at the level of the central staff position for planning. This applies to situations where such problems have left their original positions in line management in the course of the introduction of Tayloristic management models. There, at the line level, their handling and solution must be based on information. The loss of the function of planning (which can be proven empirically)[43] therefore also affects competence of planning to provide measures for regulating and avoiding conflicts, and is thus directly relevant to the problem of intercultural conflict management treated in this essay.

In support of these claims, let us describe the *five steps of the information process* in the context of strategic control. It will then become clear that a broad involvement of all management levels and all staff into the argumentation is a necessary prerequisite for the success of strategic management.[44]

The first step consists of the preliminary *identification of problems*. It is necessary to recognize signals from the external and internal environment, in the sense of both the "objective" and the "social" world.[45] Then, in a first evaluating step, it must be decided whether they are possibly relevant to a change of company strategy. Regarding the objective world, this first step must transform *signals* into *information* with the goal of critically rating the strategy. Accurate local knowledge is imperative at this stage. Even this first step must be dealt with continuously by all members of the organization. It cannot be successfully handled by a central staff unit removed from everyday events. Of course, one cannot always expect unanimous interpretation of the signals. Different perceptions, e.g., of marketing signals such as the behavior of competitors and the interpretation[46] of this behavior, must be taken into account as well as different estimates concerning the future impacts of events. Thus, this first step of gaining information already creates problems and will normally create conflicts and contradictions that need to be solved. This is even more the case where conflicts of interest in the social world are concerned. It is then necessary to adopt the perspective of those directly involved in order to be able to understand the underlying points of reasoning of the parties in conflict.[47]

The second step consists of *evaluating the problems*. A sufficiently reasonable decision must be made as to whether there is in fact a serious strategic threat. The judgment must be based on the information available. Hence, information and expertise from the functionally most different departments of a company must be mobilized and combined in order to evaluate cause-and-effect connections in the objective world. At this second step, top management therefore has to rely on various preparative work that cannot be taken over by a central staff position. In this situation, too, conflicts and contradictions are part of the daily management job. However, the evaluation of problems in cases of social conflicts cannot be carried out merely from the observational perspective of top management.

The evaluation of problems initiates the third and fourth steps, i.e., the *creation* and the *evaluation of new options for action:* Which alternatives for action are available in view of the new situation or which completely new alternatives should be created? Which of them are most promising? In this *innovative* phase, which refers not only to the objective world but also to the social world, it is again important to use the situative knowledge, expertise, and creativity of many members of the organization. New alternative future scenarios must be designed and evaluated with a view to changed conditions. Programs of action for these scenarios must be created, structured, and evaluated. In these phases in particular, difficult dilemmas are possible or even likely to occur because options for action often have to be developed and evaluated with regard to performance criteria that are in a state of mutual conflict.

The fifth step of the information process is the *authorization* of a chosen (changed) strategy, i.e., the fact that decisions have become *obligatory* for the whole organization completes the strategy reviewing process. At this point the company's formally leading executive bodies and their decision-making competence come into play. Their task is to legitimize decisions in terms of the actual corporate legal structure.

The *implementation* of the strategy follows its authorization. In this phase, again, new strategic and critical information must be generated, and this renewed identification of problems initiates the next cycle for gaining and using information. At the same time, however, the organizational members must solve the permanent dilemma between questioning the strategy and carrying it out. Therefore, together with their superiors, they must continuously pay attention to the question of when it is critical to *open up* in order to work with information generated by new problems, and when unrestricted identification with the given strategy (the closing of problems) becomes necessary.[48]

This also demonstrates that a style of management by incentives that relies only on extrinsic motivation, as in the Tayloristic management model, is a problem for strategic management when considering the changed general conditions. Although the Tayloristic model structures the finalized plans without conflicts and in such a way that the objectives and necessary steps for fulfilling them are sufficiently concrete, the process of gaining and using information, as described above, particularly aims at the possibility of a strategic revision within the framework of strategic control. The process must therefore necessarily be *open* and *not directed,* i.e., it cannot exclude anything at the outset. Since objectives cannot be given *ex ante,* extrinsic management by incentives cannot work, and in addition will be dysfunctional. This point is important because we are considering the functionality of a process in the course of which questions of truth in the objective and the social world must be dealt with and, if possible, clarified. Accomplishing this requires an environment that promotes attitudes and methods of action which contribute positively to critical argumentation. As mentioned above, *understanding* is essential rather than power. Understanding, however, cannot be manipulatively created from the outside. Apart from expertise, it relies on impartiality, absence of force, informality, and seriousness concerning the exchange and evaluation of *reasons*.[49] A company culture with a positive attitude toward argumentation can only enable such processes or their prerequisites. Those processes must be supported and brought about by the employees themselves. To do so, the organization's members must have an intrinsic motivation, i.e., they must act for the sake of the case itself (the truth).

This brief abstract of the processes of gaining and using information within strategic control has attempted to show that the functional loss of strategic planning, together with an increased complexity of the environment, requires a change of logic in future management. Instead of assuming the presence of correct and complete plans from the beginning, which are generated by top management without further dialogue and put into practice using external incentives for staff members, successful strategic management of the future must count on the vigilance of all members of the organization. This is necessary to compensate for the high risk of strategic planning. Rationality based on dialogue, decentralization, and intrinsic motivation of organizational members is imperative to achieve this aim. Simons has recently put forward some remarkable suggestions concerning the realization of these basic ideas.[50] The point of our present considerations is that a learning approach, as characterized above, must count on exactly such a management model in order to handle intercultural conflicts successfully. Given the aim of peaceful handling of cultural conflicts, the learning approach is also dependent on organizational structures and cultures that encourage processes of argumentation within the organization rather than the exertion of power.[51] Dialogue, decentralization, and multipersonal organization: these are the central ideas that must inform the management of organizations in the future—in the interest of both effectiveness and efficiency as well as a peaceful solution of intercultural conflicts.

4. Conclusions

We have tried to gain a fundamental orientation for the handling of intercultural conflicts by management based on recent philosophical reflections. The case for a learning approach in dealing with foreign cultures is based on the insight that despite the fundamental differences in the normative orientation of various cultures, a *possibility* exists of settling conflicts peacefully by the use of argument. Seizing this chance to solve conflicts is the task of those people who are directly involved. In other words, peace as a general free consensus cannot be manipulatively created from the observational perspective of scientists; it requires the insight of those who are acting directly within a situation. This result provoked the question of how management processes in MNEs would have to be designed in order to enable and support such a learning strategy in intercultural management. The conclusion is that the classic Tayloristic management model must be replaced by company structures and organizational cultures that tend to count on dialogue and rationality, decentralization of responsibility and decision making, and the involvement of managers and organizational members in the management processes throughout the whole company. There are good reasons for thinking that such a management model is not utopian, but rather is already becoming a reality in the praxis of management, due to the model's successful strategic concept. However, this result weakens the claim that the requirements of intercultural management will necessarily conflict with the goals of economic rationality (efficiency and effectiveness). On the contrary, a perspective of harmonization can be recognized. Then again, this is a demand on an MNE's management to take a serious interest in creating such a perspective, i.e., changing the status quo in the direction of the new company structure and organizational culture. Of course, the demand on *human resource management* is now particularly high: employees must be put in a position and motivated in such a way that they can both start the necessary changes, together with management, and support them permanently. The management of human resources is thus visibly turning into a central factor of success in intercultural management. The traditional "crash courses" to prepare staff for working in a foreign country are no longer adequate.

NOTES

1. See Vernon (1998).

2. See Held/McGrew/Goldblatt/Perraton (1999), p. 444ff.; Reinicke/Witte (2000).

3. United States Department of Commerce, Model Business Principles, Washington, D.C., 1995, printed in the *New York Times,* May 27, 1995, p. 17. For an overview see Scherer/Smid (2000).

4. See, e.g., Krauss (1997), Lal (1998).

5. See, e.g., Bhagwati/Hudec (1996a), (1996b).

6. See Apel/Kettner (1996), Habermas (1992), Lütterfelds/Mohrs (1997), Rorty (1991), Steinmann/Scherer (1998a), (1998b).

7. See Kambartel (1989), Lorenzen (1987a), (1987b), Mittelstrass (1985). This philosophical theory should not be confused with "Radical Constructivism." For differentiation see Janich (1992).

8. For more details see Lorenzen (1991), p. 61.

9. With basic reference to this see Albert (1985).

10. For an overview see Scherer/Steinmann (1999).

11. See Lueken (1991), (1992). For an overview see Scherer/Dowling (1995), Scherer/Steinmann (1999).

12. See Feyerabend (1980).

13. Lueken (1992), p. 218. Translations of Lueken throughout are by the authors of this essay.

14. Introducing the word "correct," Kambartel writes: "With all reasoning and understanding of reasoning we deal at first with the correctness or incorrectness of our actions, especially of our linguistic actions. By gaining actions we learn as it were a use of the terms "right" and "wrong" . . . The practical agreement that should be created or ensured here generally uses statements such as ". . . is right . . .", ". . . is correct . . .", ". . . is wrong . . .", ". . . is not correct . . ." (Kambartel [1998], p. 107ff., translation by the authors).

15. See, e.g., Popper (1959), p. 377, (1969), p. 23, (1972), p. 85ff.

16. For the relation of theory and praxis see esp. Lueken (1992), p. 174ff., Mittelstrass (1977), (1985), Scherer/Dowling (1995), p. 218ff., Scherer/Steinmann (1999), p. 526ff.

17. Lueken (1992), p. 176.

18. See Mittelstrass (1977), (1985), Janich (1988).

19. See Lorenzen (1987b), (1991), Kambartel (1989); for the important differentiation between "poiesis" and "praxis" particularly, compare Gethmann (1992).

20. See Lueken (1992), p. 176ff.

21. Lueken (1992), p. 177. Only after the application of new theoretic knowledge is successful (or fails) in sufficiently many situations can one say that the theory has proven itself (or the converse). See recent publications of Janich (1999).

22. See Lueken (1992), p. 237ff.

23. Gethmann (1979) suggested the relevant concepts of "reductive" and "productive" reasoning.

24. See the explanations of Kambartel (1991).

25. See Lueken (1991), (1992), p. 215ff.

26. See Beck (1975), Lueken (1992), p. 190ff. Therefore even in theoretical praxis the privileged nature of the participant perspective is more valid than the observer perspective. For the problem of understanding in the participant perspective, see Kambartel (1991).

27. See Lueken (1992), p. 218.

28. E.g., Lyotard (1984) and Willard (1987) demanded the replacement of the idea of consensus by the idea of dissensus, and Cannella/Paetzold (1994) have argued

that science would be threatened by stagnation if it were too much oriented toward consensus. Instead, especially dissensus would promote scientific progress.

29. Lueken (1991), p. 248.

30. Ibid.

31. See Lueken (1992), p. 285ff.

32. Ibid.

33. Lueken (1992), p. 287.

34. Lueken (1998), p. 316.

35. Lueken (1992), p. 208.

36. See Lueken (1998) for more detail, esp. p. 292ff. Lueken makes remarks concerning the relationship of our position to American Pragmatism.

37. See Spender (1996).

38. See Steinmann/Kustermann (1999).

39. Mintzberg (1994), p. 227ff.

40. See Malik (1993), Kirsch (1992), and for an overview, Kieser (1994).

41. See Steinmann/Schreyögg (1997), p. 135.

42. See Schreyögg/Steinmann (1987).

43. See Brews/Hunt (1999).

44. Identical with Simons (1995), p. 91ff.

45. For this distinction see Habermas (1987).

46. See Porter (1980), p. 47ff.

47. In relation to this, see also Osterloh (1993).

48. We would like to remark that this decentralized and multipersonal design of gaining and using information in the course of strategic control is compatible with Mintzberg's suggestion (1978, p. 945ff.; 1994, p. 23ff.) to distinguish between "intended" and "emerging" strategies. His suggestion explains how intended and emerging strategies follow each other and thus proves again the inadequacy of the classic Tayloristic management model. On the basis of more up-to-date and more accurate information, strategic control must critically question the (necessarily) long-term and therefore abstract plans of strategic planning, i.e., the "intended" plans which are based on average estimations. Thus, strategic control enables the emergence of new and improved strategies "bottom up."

49. Concerning the significance of these "dialogue criteria," see Habermas (1990) and Kambartel (1974) as well as Kambartel (1989), p. 42ff.

50. See Simons (1995).

51. Concerning such processes of learning in international management, see Kumar/Hoffmann (1999), Steinmann/Scherer (1998b).

REFERENCES

Albert, H. *Treatise on Critical Reason*. Princeton: Princeton University Press, 1985.

Apel, K.-O. and M. Kettner, eds. *Die eine Vernunft und die vielen Rationalitäten*. Frankfurt am Main: Suhrkamp, 1996.

Beck, L. W. *The Actor and the Spectator*. Clinton, Mass.: Colonial Press, 1975.

Bhagwati, J., and R. E. Hudec, eds. *Fair Trade and Harmonization: Prerequisites for Free Trade?* Vol. 1, *Economic Analysis*. Cambridge, Mass.: MIT Press, 1996a.

———, eds. *Fair Trade and Harmonization: Prerequisites for Free Trade?* Vol. 2, *Legal Analysis*. Cambridge, Mass.: MIT Press, 1996b.

Brews, P. J., and M. R. Hunt. "Learning to Plan and Planning to Learn: Resolving the Planning School/Learning School Debate." *Strategic Management Journal* 20 (1999): pp. 889–913.

Cannella, A. A., Jr., and R. L. Paetzold. "Pfeffer's Barriers to the Advance of Organizational Science: A Rejoinder." *Academy of Management Review* 19 (1994): pp. 331–341.

Feyerabend, P. *Erkenntnis für freie Menschen*. Frankfurt am Main: Suhrkamp, 1980.

Gethmann, C. F. "Zur formalen Pragmatik der Normenbegründung." In *Methodenprobleme der Wissenschaften vom gesellschaftlichen Handeln*, edited by J. Mittelstrass, pp. 46–76 Frankfurt am Main: Suhrkamp, 1979.

———. "Universelle praktische Geltungsansprüche. Zur philosophischen Bedeutung der kulturellen Genese moralischer Überzeugungen." In *Entwicklungen der methodischen Philosophie*, edited by P. Janich, pp. 148–175. Frankfurt am Main: Suhrkamp, 1992.

Habermas, J. *The Theory of Communicative Action*. Vol. 2. Translated by T. McCarthy. Cambridge, England: Polity Press, 1987.

———. "Discourse Ethics: Notes on a Program of Philosophical Justification." In *Moral Consciousness and Communicative Action,* translated by C. Lenhardt and S. W. Nicholsen, pp. 43–115. Cambridge, Mass.: MIT Press, 1990.

———. "The Unity of Reason in the Diversity of Its Voices." In *Postmetaphysical Thinking,* translated by W. M. Hohengarten, pp. 115–148. Cambridge, Mass.: MIT Press, 1992.

Held, D., A. McGrew, D. Goldblatt, and J. Perraton. *Global Transformations: Politics, Economics and Culture*. Stanford, Calif.: Stanford University Press, 1999.

Janich, P. "Truth as the Success of Action: The Constructive Approach in the Philosophy of Science." In *Scientific Knowledge Socialized,* edited by I. Hronszky, M. Fehér, and B. Dajka, pp. 313–326. Dordrecht: Kluwer, 1988.

———. "Die methodische Ordnung von Konstruktionen. Der Radikale Konstruktivismus aus der Sicht des Erlanger Konstruktivismus." In *Kognition und Gesellschaft: Der Diskurs des Radikalen Konstruktivismus II,* edited by S. G. Schmidt, pp. 24–41. Frankfurt am Main: Suhrkamp, 1992.

———. "Kulturhöhe und prädiskursiver Konsens: Zur lebensweltlichen Konstitution von Wahrnehmungsgegenständen." In *Wechselwirkungen: Zum Verhältnis von Kulturalismus, Phänomenologie und Methode,* edited by P. Janich, pp. 187–205. Würzburg: Königshausen & Neumann, 1999.

Kambartel, F. "Moralisches Argumentieren—Methodische Analysen zur Ethik." In *Praktische Philosophie und konstruktive Wissenschaftstheorie,* edited by F. Kambartel, pp. 54–72. Frankfurt am Main: Suhrkamp, 1974.

———. *Philosophie der humanen Welt*. Frankfurt am Main: Suhrkamp, 1989.

———. "Versuch über das Verstehen." In *"Der Löwe spricht . . . und wir können ihn nicht verstehen." Ein Symposium an der Universität Frankfurt anläßlich des hundertsten Geburtstags von Ludwig Wittgenstein. Mit Beiträgen von Brian McGuiness et al.*, pp. 121–137. Frankfurt am Main: Suhrkamp, 1991.

———. "Zur Grammatik von Wahrheit und Begründung." In *Zwischen Universalismus und Relativismus: Philosophische Grundlagenprobleme des interkulturellen Managements*, edited by H. Steinmann and A. G. Scherer, pp. 106–125. Frankfurt am Main: Suhrkamp, 1998.

Kieser, A. "Fremdorganization, Selbstorganization und evolutionäres Management." *Zeitschrift für betriebswirtschaftliche Forschung* 46 (1994): pp. 199–228.

Kirsch, W. *Kommunikatives Handeln, Autopoiese, Rationalität: Sondierungen zu einer evolutionären Führungslehre*. München, n.p., 1992.

Krauss, M. *How Nations Grow Rich: The Case For Free Trade*. New York: Oxford University Press, 1997.

Kumar, B. N. and K. Hoffmann. "Cross-cultural Understanding and International Management: Some Considerations on a Conceptual Framework for Conflict Resolution in Management in Foreign Cultures." In *Unternehmensethik und die Transformation des Wettbewerbs: Shareholder-Value, Globalisierung, Hyper-Wettbewerb. Festschrift für Horst Steinmann zum 65. Geburtstag*, edited by B. N. Kumar, M. Osterloh, and G. Schreyögg. Stuttgart: Schäffer-Poeschel, 1999, pp. 343–363.

Lal, D. "Social Standards and Social Dumping." In *Merits and Limits of Markets*, edited by H. Giersch, pp. 255–274. Heidelberg: Springer, 1998.

Lorenzen, P. *Constructive Philosophy*. Translated by K. R. Pavlovic. Amherst: University of Massachusetts Press, 1987a.

———. *Lehrbuch der konstruktiven Wissenschaftstheorie*. Mannheim: BI-Wissenschaftsverlag, 1987b.

———. "Philosophische Fundierungsprobleme einer Wirtschafts- und Unternehmensethik." In *Unternehmensethik*, edited by H. Steinmann and A. Löhr, pp. 35–67. 3rd ed. Stuttgart: Poeschel, 1991.

Lueken, G.-L. "Incommensurability, Rules of Argumentation, and Anticipation." In *Proceedings of the Second International Conference on Argumentation*, edited by F. H. van Eemeren et al., pp. 244–252. Amsterdam: SicSat, 1991.

———. *Inkommensurabilität als Problem rationalen Argumentierens*. Stuttgart–Bad-Cannstatt: Frommann-Holzboog, 1992.

———. "Relativität ohne Relativismus? Amerikanischer Pragmatismus und die Überwindung irreführender Alternativen." In *Zwischen Universalismus und Relativismus: Philosophische Grundlagenprobleme des interkulturellen Managements*, edited by H. Steinmann and A. G. Scherer, pp. 291–321. Frankfurt am Main: Suhrkamp, 1998.

Lütterfelds, W., and T. Mohrs, eds. *Eine Welt—eine Moral?* Darmstadt: Wissenschaftliche Buchgesellschaft, 1997.

Lyotard, J.-F. *The Postmodern Condition*. Translated by G. Bennington and B. Massumi. Manchester: Manchester University Press, 1984.

Malik, F. *Systemisches Management, Evolution, Selbstorganization. Grundprobleme, Funktionsmechanismen und Lösungsansätze für komplexe Systeme*. Bern: Haupt, 1993.

Mintzberg, H. "Patterns in Strategy Formation." *Management Science* 24 (1978): pp. 934–948.

———. *The Rise and Fall of Strategic Planning.* New York: Free Press, 1994.

Mittelstrass, J. "Changing Concepts of the A Priori." In *Historical and Philosophical Dimensions of Logic, Methodology and Philosophy of Science,* edited by R. E. Butts and J. Hintikka, pp. 113–128. Dordrecht: Reidel, 1977.

Mittelstrass, J. "Scientific Rationality and its Reconstruction." In *Reason and Rationality in Natural Science,* edited by N. Rescher, pp. 83–102. Lanham, Md.: University Press of America, 1985.

Osterloh, M. *Interpretative Organizations- und Mitbestimmungsforschung.* Stuttgart: Poeschel, 1993.

Popper, K. R. *The Logic of Scientific Discovery.* London: Hutchinson, 1959.

———. *Conjectures and Refutations: The Growth of Scientific Knowledge.* London: Routledge, 1969.

———. *Objective Knowledge.* Oxford: Oxford University Press, 1972.

Porter, M. E. *Competitive Strategy: Techniques for Analysing Industries and Competitors.* New York: Free Press, 1980.

Reinicke, W. H., and J. M. Witte. "Interdependence, Globalization, and Sovereignty: The Role of Non-Binding International Legal Accords." In *Commitment and Compliance: The Role of Non-Binding Norms in the International Legal System,* edited by the American Society of International Law. Oxford: Oxford University Press, 2000.

Rorty, R. "Solidarity or Objectivity." In *Objectivity, Relativism, and Truth, Philosophical Papers.* Vol. 1, pp. 21–45. New York: Cambridge University Press, 1991.

Scherer, A. G., and M. J. Dowling. "Towards a Reconciliation of the Theory-Pluralism in Strategic Management—Incommensurability and the Constructivist Approach of the Erlangen School." *Advances in Strategic Management* 12A (1995): pp. 195–247.

Scherer, A. G., and M. Smid. "The Downward Spiral and the U.S. Model Business Principles: Why MNEs Should Take Responsibility for the Improvement of World-Wide Social and Environmental Conditions." *Management International Review* 40 (2000), no. 4.

Scherer, A. G., and H. Steinmann. "Some Remarks on the Problem of Incommensurability in Organization Studies." *Organization Studies* 20 (1999): pp. 519–544.

Schreyögg, G., and H. Steinmann. "Strategic Control: A New Perspective." *Academy of Management Review* 12 (1987): pp. 91–103.

Simons, R. *Levers of Control—How Managers Use Innovative Control Systems to Drive Strategic Renewal.* Boston: Harvard Business School Press, 1995.

Spender, J.-C. "Villain, Victim or Visionary? The Insights and Flaws in F. W. Taylor's Ideas." In *Scientific Management: Frederick Winslaw Taylor's Gift to the World?* edited by J.-C. Spender, and H. J. Kijne, pp. 1–31. Boston: Kluwer, 1996.

Steinmann, H., and B. Kustermann. "Die Managementlehre auf dem Weg zu einem neuen Steuerungsparadigma." *Journal für Betriebswirtschaft* 46 (1999): pp. 265–281.

Steinmann, H., and A. G. Scherer. "Lernen durch Argumentieren: Theoretische Probleme konsensorientierten Handelns." In *Globale Soziale Marktwirtschaft: Ziele—Wege—Akteure. Festschrift für Santiago Garcia Ecchevaria,* edited by H. Albach, pp. 263–285. Wiesbaden: Gabler, 1994.

———. *Zwischen Universalismus und Relativismus: Philosophische Grundlagenprobleme des Interkulturellen Managements.* Frankfurt am Main: Suhrkamp, 1998a.

———. "Corporate Ethics and Global Business: Philosophical Considerations on Intercultural Management." In *Ethics in International Business,* edited by B. N. Kumar and H. Steinmann, pp. 13–46. Berlin and New York: Walter de Gruyter, 1998b.

Steinmann, H., and G. Schreyögg. *Management, Grundlagen der Unternehmensführung.* 4th ed. Wiesbaden: Gabler, 1997.

Vernon, R. *In the Hurricane's Eye: The Troubled Prospects of Multinational Enterprises.* Cambridge, Mass.: Harvard University Press, 1998.

Willard, C. A. "Valuing Dissensus." In *Argumentation: Across the Lines of Discipline.* Edited by F. H. van Eemeren, R. Grootendorst, J. A. Blair, and C. A Willard, pp. 313–320. Dordrecht: Foris Publications, 1987.

CHAPTER 7

Governance in a Border-Free World: Economy and Currency

DARIO VELO

I. The Historical Role of Currency and Finance

Historically, finance, particularly significant movements of capital, has played a key role in the internationalization process. However, its effects cannot be said to fit a homogeneous model. Rather, relations between the "real economic" (concerning the production of goods and services) and the financial aspects of the internationalization process have varied according to both time and the different economic systems involved.

These aspects can be best illustrated using a schematic historical approach. The period from 1870 to 1914 can be considered a turning point in economic history, with the advent of the internationalization of *production,* a process that can be regarded as the culmination of a sustained period of expansion in international trade.[1] There was a marked increase in the number of companies developing industrial production outside their countries of origin; the organization of working processes across national boundaries,

Dario Velo is dean of economic sciences at Pavia University, president of the European Community Studies Association, head of the Masters Programs in International Finance and in Bank and Finance, and guest professor at the University of Bordeaux and the Université Robert Schuman (Strasbourg).

rather than being based exclusively on political, financial, or business factors, began to be determined by production logistics. Naturally, corporate economic behavior continued to be affected by the political, financial, and business framework in which companies were expanding, but new and specific decision-making variables were being introduced, which were to have extremely significant consequences in the years that followed.

The expansion of corporate productive internationalization suffered a period of stagnation between the two world wars. Following the Second World War, however, a phase of strong expansion began, one that is still underway more than half a century later. It can be divided into many stages, each of which features the predominant nature of the strategic internationalization variables introduced by companies.

The First Contemporary Expansion Stage: From 1945 to the 1960s

The first stage of expansion following the end of the Second World War was characterized by the leadership of the United States, with North American companies gaining footholds in international markets, mainly through direct investments.[2] These investment flows were directed mainly toward the American continent and, to a lesser although increasing extent, toward Europe.

The main strength of North American companies was their openness to innovation, more specifically their ability to create new products boasting cutting-edge technology. Initially, companies at the forefront of the internationalization process followed *market-seeking* strategies. Their strategic target was to gain growing market shares in the countries where companies were in the process of becoming established. On-the-spot production also allowed companies to overcome the protectionist barriers that continued to split the world market at that time.

Consolidation of the Internationalization Process: The 1970s and 1980s

Widespread economic expansion occurred during the 1960s. A growing number of countries were able to become part of the internationalization process. The result was an increase in the phenomenon of internationalization, alongside increasingly extended differentiation between the strategic expansion strategies employed. By the 1970s the stock of direct investments abroad was between 4 and 5 percent of world Gross Domestic Product (GDP), a value that reached an average of 5 percent during the 1980s and as high as 7 percent by the end of the decade.[3]

The leadership in direct investment passed to Germany, the European Community's economic leader, and to Japan. United States supremacy decreased, at least according to official statistics. This was not due to a real decline, however, but rather to the fact that American companies had by then matured to the stage of being able to use local finance to back the companies they had established abroad over previous years. The United States also became the liveliest hub for direct investments abroad, in terms of investments from the rest of the world.

It is equally important to stress that new internationalization models[4] were successfully established during this period. Japanese companies led the way in using a model based on productive factors—labor and raw materials—at the lowest market prices. Investments were concentrated on mature, standardized production market segments. Moreover, Japanese experience exploited the drive of small to medium-sized firms, whereas earlier models, such as those followed by the United States, had relied on large-sized companies. Finally, Japanese strategy featured the establishment of collaborative relations with local partners, with or without capital participation, to consolidate their own roots in the local market. In the Japanese model, the relation between the relative significance of financial and real economic aspects to be found in a productive internationalization process changes in favor of real economic aspects.

European firms, on the other hand, exploited specific domestic features. A clearly European model emerged, particularly with respect to Central Europe. While more peripheral countries continued to be swayed by local historical and cultural influences, Central European firms tended to follow an eclectic model, halfway between those of the United States and Japan. The European experience was closest to the American, in terms of the significance given to the expansion of productive internationalization in sectors with strong technological features. At the same time, it resembled the Japanese experience in the important role played by small to medium-sized firms, which have backed up real network dynamics.

The Single European Market and the Globalization Process

At the end of the 1980s, the creation of a single European market, closely followed by the expansion of globalization, gave a decisive boost to the productive internationalization process. In fact it is difficult to distinguish between the impact of the single market and that of globalization, since the two phenomena expanded simultaneously, each encouraging the other's growth.

The stock of direct investments abroad as a proportion of world GDP continued to grow apace to above 8 percent during the 1980s. This figure assumes even greater significance when one considers that this ratio increasingly understates the importance of the productive internationalization process.

The globalization process profoundly influenced corporate strategies, which tended toward the management of each factor in the production line, including companies' foreign branches: international optimization of production value became a priority.[5] Within this framework, small to medium-sized firms, particularly those in Europe and Japan, found new opportunities in certain market segments for international expansion and the furtherance of the globalization process.

At the same time, another innovation resulting from globalization was the expansion of the internationalization process to the service sector. This is evident in the spread of productive internationalization to the banking and financial sectors, where previously, international activity had been largely limited to the standard transfer of capital.

Today, increased significance is given to an activity's taking root locally, by establishing companies or by underwriting strategic alliances, with or without capital participation. A decisive boost in this direction was given by the increasing momentum of deregulation, which abolished technical barriers and policies that had been splitting the world services market, especially in the banking, financial, insurance, telecommunications, and transport sectors.

2. Governance of the Globalization Process: An Evolution Led by the United States

The above observations imply a framework that would appear to be in conflict with the dominant image of internationalization and globalization processes. In fact, I have emphasized the growing significance of small to medium-sized firms, the increasing momentum of productive internationalization in new geographical areas, and an increase in the relative significance of real economic aspects, as compared to financial aspects. The results of this analysis are not in line with the preconceived idea that globalization is a process dominated by big multinational companies (North American companies in the first place) and by international financial speculation. This apparent contradiction can be better understood by taking a central aspect of globalization into consideration, namely, the governance of the process.

In the push toward a global market free from trade barriers, procedures typical of federal systems have been adopted, involving inter-system competition. Today, both individual economic operators and the systems to which they belong must reckon with international competition. Competition between systems encourages research into competitiveness in all factors forming the systems, public and private, at both the regulatory and the operative levels.[6]

The existence of a radical gap in the rules of competition logic between organized federations on the one hand, and the global market on the other, must be stressed. Within federal states, competition between systems is structured by essential rules of a constitutional, legislative, and regulatory nature, affecting the federation as a whole. This is also true within the European Union, which can be regarded as a federal state in the making: competition between systems is controlled by the framework of European Union law and regulations.

On a global level, competition between systems has grown without a consolidated legal and regulatory framework. International institutions pursue this target, but the effectiveness of their work cannot, at least at present, be compared to the effectiveness of federal states, including Europe (a federation in the making). Today, on a world level, relations between states can be established and in the most advanced cases can have characteristics of a federation. Federal experiences do not at present extend beyond continental dimensions.

The occasionally anarchic nature of the globalization process has been successfully dealt with by the regulatory abilities of the major industrialized players, who perform a substitute role for world authorities, the latter not yet being sufficiently organized. The first power to perform this function was the United States, which was able to influence international order on the basis of its own internal, legal, and economic order.

The global market is currently in a state of transition, and choices must be made about its direction. Restrictions on and reasons for these choices can be analyzed and assessed in different ways. Undoubtedly, there is a problem of transition from an old to a future international order, requiring the establishment of an international legal framework by new democratic procedures. It is highly likely that this transition will be a major innovation in developments over the next few decades.

An emerging problem is how far the international community is able to manage problems of international dimensions; this also brings domestic systems into discussion, to the extent that they have an international impact, directly or indirectly affecting other domestic systems, within the rules of competition logic between systems.[7]

Each transition phase leaves ample space for action to those possessing higher bargaining leverage, who are thus less in need of the protection of law and regulation. From a long-term perspective, transition can be analyzed by using the targets toward which the process is projected as criteria of success. The choice of values takes on an essential role in this kind of analysis, projected toward the future, in the same way as in the historical analysis of the past. The issue is to propose principles for the interpretation of the present, with a consistent vision of the future as their underpinnings.

The governance of globalization can be examined from various aspects. I shall concentrate on reconstructing the decision-making process which led to globalization; government alternatives within the process; institutional choices already made to back up the globalization process (in particular, fiscal federalism and the autonomy of central banks); and the prospects for backing up balanced development of globalization.

The Acceleration of Globalization

Globalization is the outcome of the historical process of market expansion, alongside the expansion of state organizations. Europe can be considered as the place where this process has been most clearly displayed, insofar as, over the centuries, Europe has established some of the most developed forms of political and social organization, from the local dimensions of the Middle Ages to the current dimensions of the European Community.

The historical process shows that market expansion has often preceded expansion of the state itself. With globalization, we may well be witnessing a new aspect of this phenomenon.[8] On each occasion, those promoting the process have had to face up to the necessity of interpreting the requirements of society, searching for new forms of organization consistent with the current maturity of the process of social and economic development.[9]

If this is true, what has greater significance is the development process of phenomena, in which a series of specific problems are to be found which must relate to the process itself. The immediate deduction from this statement is that visibility of the process and its ensuing problems depend on its degree of development. This approach does not underestimate the wealth of alternatives available and the significance of tensions that are typical when taking action on a social level; these aspects take on special significance when analysis covers a more restricted time span.

Within this perspective, globalization's takeoff does not represent the beginning of the process, but rather a particular phase of the overall process, a phase that imposes the adoption of political, economic, and institutional measures, so as to adjust the process to governance. In this sense, we can legitimately place globalization's development as a characteristic of the 1990s, whereas the origins of the globalization process are most certainly to be found in earlier decades.[10]

The Promoting Role of the United States

In the wake of the Second World War, the international economy was redirected toward growing interdependence, in direct connection with the historical defeat of the National Socialist economic and social model of organization.[11] More generally speaking, the Second World War marked the irreversible crisis of a closed national state, of which National Socialism was the extreme expression. Seen from this perspective, the leadership of the United States performed an essential role in backing up international economic integration.

The international community developed the process of opening borders, thus beginning to break down the barriers dividing the world into protected areas. The outcome was the gradual increase of interdependence between economies, starting with the most advanced. From the outset, the opening up of economies was handled in such a way as to enable developing countries also to benefit from the advantages ensuing from the construction of a world market.

The basic structural condition which enabled this process to begin was the United States' ability both to offer its partners goods and services, and to apply the required monetary instruments to finance imports of the aforesaid goods and services from the rest of the world.

In the 1980s the United States found itself starting a new, more advanced phase in the internationalization process without, however, being able to claim economic supremacy as it had during the postwar period, and without having the instruments to direct the process. There is continuity in the role performed by the United States; nevertheless, the difference in availability of governance instruments has a crucial importance on which it is important to concentrate attention. The extent of internal debate in the United States that preceded the decision to support the globalization process, including an assessment of connected new forms of governance, must also be stressed.

During the 1980s the United States took the lead in the debate on international order and new relations between state and society, which then took on global dimensions, involving an ever-growing number of countries. Themes involved in this debate have included globalization[12] and neo-federalism. Both words describe processes undergoing definition, rather than fixed reference models.

3. The Debate on the International Order

The Different Scenarios of Globalization

A rough outline of globalization can be based on a comparison between two alternative scenarios, or possible directions, for the international community. The first scenario consists of building an international, multipolar, and organized economic order based on cooperation between areas, partly closed to international competition. The second scenario consists of going ahead with the building of a single world market. This second possibility more explicitly implies the need to devise controls for the market.

In examining these two alternative scenarios, the forces favoring one or the other in the United States, as well as in Europe and the rest of the world, must be analyzed. This is fundamental in order to understand choices made and to find the right direction in forecasting the path of future developments.

We must base the initial analysis on factors deemed to be particularly reliable indicators. This does not mean that other phenomena have less importance. Their exclusion from an interpretive framework results from the current limitations in our ability to understand them.

The first area for consideration is the governance of the international community. The United States, to the extent to which it forms a competitive economic system and a consolidated political system, finds itself in the position of being able to control its participation, including its ability to control either of the alternative scenarios described above. It is able, far more than other areas, to support the globalization process.

A second area for reflection concerns the social and economic aspects (governance of the social balance within systems, to the extent in which the said balance has suitable fluidity). From this viewpoint too, the United States possesses the ability to control its participation far more easily than other industrialized countries (especially European industrialized countries), including its ability to control either of the alternative scenarios and, in particular, the globalization process.

The different degree of regulation over the economy and social relations gives direction to various countries in the globalization process, which, in its turn, creates debate about the desirable level of regulation.[13] Globalization and neo-federalism are in fact so interdependent as to make the search for a connection between cause and effect of the two phenomena futile: they develop in parallel.

If it is true that neo-federalism does not form a finished model, as I believe, the decision-making process assumes greater significance. It affects assessment of resources on all levels and in all sectors. The main point is to establish the connections between neo-federalism and the globalization process, rather than to seek for a causal relationship.

Neo-federalism, not overlooking the historical exception achieved in the United States, has privileged the market's role as an instrument to allocate resources in a way more compatible with the globalization process. The role of the state has been changed, not only in the sense of re-qualifying its activity, but also in the sense of curbing expenditure for purposes of solidarity.

Neo-federalism and the Principle of Subsidiarity

Neo-federalism can best be assessed by comparing it to its "European alternative," formed by the principle of subsidiarity. The basic and substantial difference between the neo-federalism of the United States and the European principle of subsidiarity is the different emphasis given to changing the relations between state and market.

The principle of subsidiarity questions how both the market and the state are governed, searching for advances in both sectors of society. Subsidiarity requires redistribution of public powers with greater federal flexibility, including a decrease in the area of public jurisdiction. Likewise, subsidiarity requires redistribution of private powers, by means of action against powers of concentration. Subsidiarity requires redefining the welfare state, so as to raise the level of solidarity to be on a par with resources used or to preserve equivalent levels of solidarity in the face of decreases in available resources.[14]

The globalization process provides another opportunity for societies to exercise choice over the different procedures—albeit with the same targets—through which they can be organized. Experience seems to prove that the globalization process does not impose homogeneous solutions on various social systems: societies can organize themselves consistently with their own traditions by putting resources into action using different procedures.

The heterogeneity of the European experience, as compared to the experience in the United States, should perhaps be researched at the level of solutions put into action so as to implement principles of solidarity, rather than purely at the level of abstract principles.[15]

The problem of the degree of freedom with which societies can organize themselves stands out significantly.

Choices of a Constitutional Nature for the Governance of Globalization

The acceleration of the globalization process is accompanied by the assumption in the United States of an economic policy hinged on fiscal federalism, the pursuit of a balanced national budget, and an orthodox monetary policy.

This new economic policy has directed the actions of international institutions (starting with the IMF), and was then asserted in industrialized countries. The areas that first made a move in this direction can be singled out by systems that are organized according to federal models.

Analysis of this process, taken as a whole, is beyond the scope of this essay. From our perspective, the significant aspect is the constitutional extent of these options, which directly link up with the definition of the governance of the global economy.

At the center of the new constitutional management of the economy is orthodox control of monetary policy, which involves the assertion of the central bank's autonomy.

Within a federal system, powers controlling monetary policy are ascribed to the highest institutional level, whereas the jurisdiction of intermediate and basic institutional levels is mainly over control of tax policy.[16] This means that it is always in the interest of lower institutional levels (national and local authorities) that powers to control currency should not be used by the central authority with the purpose of draining resources, thereby depreciating the currency's value. In countries with a federal structure, the central bank enjoys a high degree of autonomy: it can balance the distribution of powers among the various institutional levels by guaranteeing local powers against powers of concentration pursued through discretionary use of the monetary policy.

To the extent to which the globalization process brings the problem of world government to the surface, it also reveals the problem of the relation between monetary and tax policies at the world level, even though political and institutional mechanisms are currently lacking at this level to ensure an effective federal order.

On a continental level, within organized areas or areas which are in the process of becoming organized by using federal solutions (primarily, the United States and the European Union), the autonomy of the central bank as the keystone of balanced development of tax federalism becomes a problem at the core of federal constitutional planning.[17]

The time is not yet ripe for a world central bank.[18] The same rules of logic which support the central bank's autonomy at the continental level also support orthodox control by the IMF (International Monetary Fund) at a global level, as well as a trend toward fixed exchange rates between the large continental federal areas and, from a broader viewpoint, the counterbalancing of monetary policy as a control instrument for economy. The global economy tends to privilege tax federalism as a governance instrument rather than the use of currency as a redistribution instrument for buying power.

Obviously, these considerations bring the vision of a long-term trend to the surface, which could be contradicted over a short-term period by a series of negative events leading back to the uneven distribution of power in the world. This is typical of historical processes, which rarely develop with neat linearity. Nonetheless, these considerations direct thought toward grasping the connection, of a constitutional nature, between fixed exchange rates, central bank autonomy, orthodox monetary policy, and fiscal federalism. In the last analysis, the constitutional logic of globalization's governance is thus outlined, within a long-term perspective, toward international democracy.

4. Globalization's Governance and Domestic Policies: A Growing Interdependence

The development of globalization's governance toward international democracy is a process that will inevitably face the uneven distribution of power in the world. The power of globalization can have a profound effect on domestic policies, making them increasingly consistent with support for globalization's development. This connection is likely to become more binding, to the extent to which it will deepen interdependence between regional development and that of globalization.

In this sense, the European experience allows us to forecast equally successful trends in other areas as a direct consequence of Europe's greater openness and, therefore, its greater obligations regarding domestic choices with their influence on the globalization process. One has only to consider the European economic and monetary policy, including relations between euro exchange rates, as compared to other currencies, notably that of the United States dollar.

The considerations outlined above suggest what is at stake for Europe when planning an orthodox monetary policy and when pursuing the establishment of steady exchange rates, potentially fixed, with the dollar. The two targets are interdependent and correspond to interdependence between domestic economic expansion and globalization. At the same time, this policy is consistent with a long-term plan, aimed at backing up neutralization of monetary policy as a governance instrument.

Within this framework, a specific problem emerges—that of the less-developed areas, which are behind in developing regional organization following federal models, and now need to catch up within a very short space of time so as to be able to participate in the globalization process on an equal footing. This problem highlights the conflict between the need for balanced international development and options for a development that is unbalanced but swifter—features of the currently developing globalization process. This divergence applies to all areas, Europe included, but is much more marked for those areas that lag further behind the front runner, the United States.

These considerations direct thought toward the assessment of developments underway in United States policy, which seem directed toward the decreasing use of the dollar as an international governance instrument in favor of alternative instruments of an economic and real nature. These developments, should they be confirmed, will form the basis of a new international order, in which globalization would have a multiplying effect.

5. Governance of Globalization: Going from Currency's Preeminence to Reasserting the Priority of the Real Economy

History demonstrates that state power has rested on two main foundations: arms and finance. These could be exerted by states (thanks to the consent expressed by society) in different ways over time and within different systems. The historical phenomenon we are witnessing is the redefinition of the state and the progressive neutralization of these powers.

At the European level, the central bank's autonomy has been consolidated by the transfer of power from national states to that of a functional authority. At the world level, increasingly steady exchange rates between lead currencies can be envisaged, in future supporting a system of fixed exchange rates; this long-term prospect is no more than a transfer of currency's sovereignty to a functional international authority. This point is of utmost importance, since it *apparently* corresponds to the view held by Keynes when the international monetary system was reestablished at Bretton Woods. In fact, however, the international order that is in the process of taking shape is totally different from that conceived by Keynes and his followers in subsequent decades.

The process of currency neutralization implies taking away monetary power from states without handing over this power to a higher political authority; it is reallocated to a functional authority, strictly bound by its own operational capacities.

The new concept of the state that is taking shape can be analyzed from different viewpoints. A phenomenon with a historical range cannot be interpreted by laying aside the complexity of the energies involved. It is also unrealistic to suppose that developments will proceed in a linear fashion. During the development stages, various core problems can be expected to arise, distinguishing each stage of the process. These are not abstract considerations. Historically, the development of the process of European integration is proof that this formulation for analysis is required to direct thought, particularly when faced with an innovative process which goes far beyond the traditional outlines of a concept—traditional outlines which were functional for an order that is now in the process of becoming obsolete.

A theory for interpretation can be proposed to deal with the relationship between globalization, the process of governance, and the development of new forms of state. It can be summarized, in a perhaps oversimplified form, as follows:

1) the United States stage of globalization
2) the neo-Atlantic stage of globalization, centered around relations between the United States and the European Union
3) the global Atlantic stage, centered on relations between the American continents and the European continent

The points proposed are no more than a theory on globalization's development process, as related to areas leading the process. The proposed theory for interpretation also needs to be assessed by singling out the core problem at each stage.

The sketchiness of this formulation is obvious; we only need to refer to world powers that are not directly covered within these points. Moreover, the rationale for this formulation is essentially an attempt to single out the core problem at each stage, as a key for interpreting the complexity of developing phenomena underway.

The United States Stage of Globalization

This is a stage that is underway: the globalization process is supported and directed by the country at the system's very core. The key problem during this stage, from our interpretive viewpoint, is the assertion of competition between systems and within systems. Competitiveness assumes a pivotal role in governance.

The real economic aspects become more important than monetary aspects, which are being neutralized as economic policy instruments. For Europe, taking part in the process implies renouncing the monetary sovereignty of states and transferring this power to a functional authority. For the United States, the conditions of retaining leadership of the process involve writing off its federal deficit and reasserting the autonomy of its central bank (which is starting to become a functional authority, as in Europe).

The Neo-Atlantic Stage of Globalization

This forms the logical outcome of the first stage. Once the process of globalization has become established, the key problem is ensuring closer control. The responsibility for this will fall initially on the United States and the European Union, in their capacities both as the main international economic leaders, and as possessors of the economic systems undergoing the most rapid and radical changes to adapt to and encourage globalization.

The problem distinguishing this stage is anticipated to be the control of competition. Globalization will bring all systems closer, and, in particular, the United States and European systems will move to the threshold of a single Atlantic market. This will set the problem of controlling the process over and beyond competitiveness. Controlled competition implies coordination of policies, i.e., assertion of a "positive" constitutional process. During the neo-Atlantic stage, the central point of debate will be the establishment of common regulations and constitutional amendments required to ensure their control.

The United States and the European Union will have to tackle a "Monnetian" problem [i.e., Jean Monnet] of singling out new constitutional solutions to give suitable and realistic replies to the historical problem of starting up political integration between systems and creating a standardized economic system.

These considerations are not intended to play down the role of Japan and other developed countries. All OECD countries can be expected to develop growing integration. The power of action of individual countries and large integrated areas will inevitably vary, at least in the medium term.

The Global Atlantic Stage

The globalization process involves all world-level systems. The attention we have given to the role played by the United States and the European Union corresponds, from our point of view, to the central responsibility these two systems have, systems that will implement decisions that are bound to have repercussions in the remaining areas. Around the neo-Atlantic core of the process, we can realistically suppose that some systems will have the opportunity of exerting a certain degree of influence on the decision-making process and that other systems will have less of this power. At the European level, a system formed of concentric circles has been outlined: we may expect to see at least a partially similar system develop at the world level.

Analysis of the above would require definition from at least two viewpoints: the estimated time required for the process to become effective, and assessment of enforceable alternatives. Both aspects require in-depth research beyond the scope of this essay.

The geographical area that can be expected to represent the claims of transiting economies and most likely to affect global Atlantic governance is Central and Southern America. This forecast is based on a structural datum, consisting of the fact that these countries are able to integrate their economies with those of both the United States and the European Union. This supposes that multiple relations between these three large areas will increase. Should the above prove true, the countries in this area will have the opportunity to define a new stage in the globalization process and bring the problem of balanced development to the forefront.

Integration between the United States and Europe sets the problem of controlled competition. The historical differences between the two areas and the different features of social policies are such as to make shared control of competition crucial.[19]

The introduction within this framework of Latin American countries, with their different degree of economic and social development, is bound to create problems as regards the suitability of solutions—solutions that undoubtedly will be outlined by the two most large and developed areas of the world. The central problem formed by the need to ensure greater balance for international development is bound to translate into pressure for different economic policies. Institutional solutions, which the United States and the European Union must be the first to work out for the control of their own integration, could prove unsuitable for a more balanced development at a broader international level.

We can legitimately outline a scenario for the stage we have called neo-Atlantic, in which a circuit of growing integration between the United States and the European Union can be triggered, including controlled competition and institutional innovations. We can also outline a scenario for the stage we have called global-Atlantic, in which a circuit of growing integration between South America, the United States of America, and European Union can be triggered, including controlled competition, institutional innovations, and readjustment of policies.

6. Comprehension and Assessment of the Globalization Process

In the social sciences, making value judgments is part of the interpretive process. The concepts outlined in this essay are the expression of an evolutionary vision of history with subsidiarity and universalism as essential reference points.

The conceptual systems described above can be used either as interpretive criteria or with the intent of formulating provisions; the alternative is anything but neutral. We have chosen to use them as interpretive criteria, and it is with this in mind that they have been put forward. Furthermore, being simultaneously interpretive and predictive, the systems postulated can be considered as frameworks within which a variety of future alternatives may develop.

Comprehension of the existing order is essential if we are to identify opportunities for amending it. Any attempt aimed at changing an existing order must first identify the key problems. The neo-federalism of the United States, European subsidiarity, solidarity-oriented federalism: all of these are potential interpretive systems which should be considered for their own merits, or as seedbeds for new ideologies.

NOTES

1. For analysis of this period, as regards the corporate internationalization process, see the complete collection of essays by G. Jones, *Transnational Corporations: A Historical Perspective. A Library on Transnational Corporations* (London: Routledge, 1994).

2. Direct investments are a measure of the process of a company's establishment abroad. At first, these direct investments abroad were usually financed by risk capital transfer, covering the basic amount of the investment. Recently, expansion of these internationalized companies has been financed by the reinvestment of local profit as well as by resorting to local or international financial markets. However, the above leads back to the observation that investment flows abroad form a good indicator of how important the investment made at the very start is.

3. See J. H. Dunning, *Multinational Enterprises and the Global Economy* (Aldershot: Edward Elgar, 1992); United Nations, *World Investment Report 1998: Trends and Determinants* (New York and Geneva, 1998).

4. For overall analysis of the different territorial models, as regards internationalization, see S. Vaccà and E. Rullani, "Oltre il classico modello di impresa multinazionale: nuovi comportamenti nel processo di internazionalizzazione delle imprese," *Finanza Marketing e Produzione* nos. 1–2 (1983): pp. 133–174, and no. 3 (1983): pp. 139–160. For more specific analysis of the Japanese model, see the great number of works by T. Ozawa, including *Multinationalism Japanese Style: The Political Economy of Outward Dependency* (Princeton, N.J.: Princeton University Press, 1979), and "Japan in a New Phase of Multinationalism and Industrial Upgrading: Functional Integration of Trade Growth and FDI," *Journal of Trade World* 25, no. 1 (1991): pp. 43–60. As regards analysis of the European model, see J. Cantwell, *Multinational Investment in Modern Europe* (Aldershot: Edward Elgar, 1992), and S. Urban and S. Vendemini, *European Strategic Alliances, Co-operative Corporate Strategies in the New Europe* (Oxford: Blackwell Business, 1992).

5. For more in-depth examination of this topic, see C. A. Bartlett and S. Ghoshall, *Managing across Borders* (Boston: Harvard Business School Press, 1989).

6. For in-depth analysis, see G. Usai and D. Velo, *Le imprese e il mercato unico europeo* (Milan: Pirola, 1990).

7. To explain this aspect, we can make reference to the expansion of financial derivatives, which could become instruments of destabilization on an international level. In the first place, their expansion leads back to internal choices developed by the economic and financial system of the United States, choices then followed by other industrialized countries, according to the mechanisms of competition between systems. An international regulatory problem certainly arises at the level of basic phenomena which lead to the intense use of financial derivatives. See Bank of International Settlements (BIS), *Recent Innovations in International Banking,* Basel, 1986.

8. See K. Ohmae, *The End of Nation State—The Rise of Regional Economies* (New York: The Free Press, 1995).

9. Obviously, the historical process did not develop coherently. Any analysis of these dimensions must consider the relative autonomy of the political dimension of human action. On this last point, see M. Albertini, *Il Federalismo* (Bologna: Il Mulino, 1993).

10. See P. Bairoch, "Globalization, Myths and Realities: One Century of External Trade and Foreign Investment," in *States against Markets: The Limits of Globalization,* ed. R. Boyer and D. Drache (London: Routledge, 1996).

11. Jean Monnet and Jean Moulin were among the spokesmen who made this contradiction their essential reason for thought and action. For historical recon-

struction of the environment within which action was taken, in particular by the latter, see D. Cordier, *Jean Moulin*, vols. 1-3 (Paris: Editions J.-C. Lattes, 1989–1993).

12. For a critical synthesis as regards this debate, see the collection of essays by P. Krugman, *Pop Internationalism* (Cambridge, Mass., and London: MIT Press, 1996). Also see M. E. Porter, *Competition in Global Industries* (Boston: Harvard Business School Press, 1986) and L. Thurow, *Head to Head: The Coming Battle among Japan, Europe and America* (New York: W. Morrow & Company, 1992).

13. See L. Thurow, *The Future of Capitalism* (London: Breasley, 1996).

14. Commissione Diocesana "Giustizia e Pace" della Diocesi di Milano, *Autonomia Regionale e Federalismo Solidale* (Milan: Centro Ambrosiano, 1996).

15. A. Quadrio Curzio, "European Union and Italian Federalism: Is There a Catholic Thought?" *The European Union Review* no. 1 (March 1997): pp. 7–29.

16. A. Jozzo and D. Velo, "L'Autonomia della Banca Centrale in Italia e in Europa," *Moneta e Credito* no. 134 (1981): pp. 191–204.

17. Regional monetary reform, in particular European reform, from the viewpoint of the required world reform, is analysed by Triffin in a number of his essays. In particular, see R. Triffin, "The World Monetary Scandal: Sources and Cures?" *Economic Notes* 10, no. 2 (1982): pp. 3–19.

18. Theoretically, on whether a world central bank is desirable, a number of economists have stated their opinions: e.g., see R. N. Cooper, *The International Monetary System* (Cambridge: MIT Press, 1987).

19. See *The Economist*, 13–19 March 1999, and S. Micossi, "La nuova agenda transatlantica: Una prospettiva europea," *Il Mulino* (February 1997): pp. 85–94.

REFERENCES

Albertini, M. *Il Federalismo*. Bologna: Il Mulino, 1993.

Bairoch, P. "Globalization, Myths and Realities: One Century of External Trade and Foreign Investment." In *States against Markets. The Limits of Globalization*, edited by R. Boyer and D. Drache. London: Routledge, 1996.

Bartlett, C.A., and S. Ghoshall. *Managing Across Borders*. Boston: Harvard Business School, 1989

Bank of International Settlements (BIS). *Recent Innovations in International Banking*. Basel, 1986.

Cantwell, J. *Multinational Investment in Modern Europe*. Aldershot: Edward Elgar, 1992.

Cooper, R. N. *The International Monetary System*. Cambridge, Mass.: The MIT Press, 1987.

Commissione Diocesana "Giustizia e Pace" della Diocesi di Milano. *Autonomia regionale e federalismo solidale*. Milan: Centro Ambrosiano, 1996.

Cordier, D. *Jean Moulin*. Vols. 1–3. Paris: Editions J.-C. Lattes, 1989–1993.

Dunning, J. H. *Multinational Enterprises and the Global Economy*. Aldershot: Edward Elgar, 1992.

The Economist, 13–19 March 1999.

Jones, G. *Transnational Corporations: A Historical Perspective. A Library on Trans-national Corporations*. London: Routledge, 1994.

Jozzo, A., and D. Velo. "L'Autonomia della Banca Centrale in Italia e in Europa." *Moneta e Credito* no. 134 (1981): pp. 191–204.

Krugman, P. *Pop Internationalism*. Cambridge, Mass., and London: The MIT Press, 1996.

Micossi, S. "La nuova agenda transatlantica: Una prospettiva europea." *Il Mulino*, February 1997, pp. 85–94.

Ohmae, K. *The End of Nation State—The Rise of Regional Economies*. New York: The Free Press, 1995.

Ozawa, T. *Multinationalism Japanese Style: The Political Economy of Outward Dependency*. Princeton, N.J.: Princeton University Press, 1979.

———. "Japan in a New Phase of Multinationalism and Industrial Upgrading: Functional Integration of Trade Growth and FDI." *Journal of Trade World* 25, no. 1 (1991): pp. 43–60.

Porter, M. E. *Competition in Global Industries*. Boston: Harvard Business School Press, 1986.

Quadrio Curzio, A. "European Union and Italian Federalism. Is there a Catholic Thought?" *The European Union Review* no. 1 (March 1997): pp. 7–29.

Thurow, L. *Head to Head: The Coming Battle among Japan, Europe and America*. New York: W. Morrow & Company, 1992.

———. *The Future of Capitalism*. London: Breasley, 1996.

Triffin, R. "The World Monetary Scandal: Sources and Cures?" *Economic Notes* 10, no. 2 (1982): pp. 3–19.

United Nations. *World Investment Report 1998: Trends and Determinants*. New York and Geneva, 1998.

Urban, S., and S. Vendemini. *European Strategic Alliances, Co-operative Corporate Strategies in the New Europe*. Oxford: Blackwell Business, 1992.

Usai, G., and D. Velo. *Le imprese e il mercato unico europeo*. Milan: Pirola, 1990.

Vaccà, S., and E. Rullani. "Oltre il classico modello di impresa multinazionale: nuovi comportamenti nel processo di internazionalizzazione delle imprese." *Finanza Marketing e Produzione* no. 1–2 (1983): pp. 133–174, and no. 3 (1983): pp. 139–160.

CHAPTER 8

The Ambiguities of Globalization

PHILIPPE DE WOOT

I. Ambiguous Dynamics

The Race for Competitiveness and Performance

The opening up of markets, deregulation, and privatization are creating an economic and financial space that is growing without bounds. Information technologies are continuously progressing and are providing us with globalized and flexible communications networks which, in turn, give human society a highly sensitive "nervous system," facilitating ever-faster reactions and an increasing number of interactions. These developments are well known. They contribute to the globalization of the economy while leaving the field free for enterprising and innovative players: businesses and financiers.

Through the vigorous stimulus of those players, globalization is accelerating and impacting more and broader fields of activity. The most effective global player today is the business enterprise (in industry, service, and finance), because it is best suited to this type of evolution. It has very quickly developed an effective and successful international savoir faire.

Philippe de Woot is professor emeritus at the Université Catholique de Louvain and has been a guest professor at INSEAD for the Avira program. His research and teaching focus on business strategies and their consequences for the global society. He has taught business ethics. He is a member of the Belgian Académie Royale, the International Academy of Management, and the European Academy of Arts and Sciences. He holds an honorary doctorate from the University of Bologna.

In reality, business enterprises are the only organizations that have succeeded in simultaneously crossing every threshold of globalization:

- the threshold of *magnitude:* many of them are "multinationals" and transcend the borders of nation-states;
- the threshold of the *temporal horizon:* they pursue long-term strategies in a manner unlike those in the worlds of politics, administration, or education;
- the threshold of *complexity:* they are becoming capable of effectively managing diversities, multiple ways of thinking, risk, and resource development; thus they are able to change and adapt rapidly;
- the threshold of *information* and *communications* that allow them to "hook up" with the world and act promptly and efficiently.

Due to their competitive dynamics and enterprising spirit, businesses have adapted to globalization more rapidly than have most of our political, social, and educational institutions. Their competitive logic has been the subject of many studies and is beginning to be widely acknowledged. It is based on several interdependent elements:

- the development of strong *strategic ability:* development of key resources such as management, technologies, networks, information, partnerships, etc.;
- *continuous innovation* and the creative destruction that makes it possible to replace the old with the new;
- the race for *productivity* that aims to reduce costs, especially social costs;
- *outward growth* through mergers and acquisitions: these strengthen a business's power over resources and markets.

To these developments we must add the growing strength of financial capitalism. The free circulation of capital makes it more readily available for business undertakings. This facilitates international investments,[1] as well as short-term speculation that can create instability and even generate crises.

Large pension funds also have a great influence on economic decisions, by generalizing the criterion of shareholder value.

These market dynamics have made an enormous contribution to the creation of wealth. If we merely consider the economic viewpoint, world production today is fifty times greater than it was in 1820 for a population that is only six times larger. Later we shall see that the distribution of this prosperity, however, is becoming increasingly unequal.

This economic performance has created an ideology that tends to confuse the market economy, modernity, and democracy. Today, we are reviving the doctrine of laissez-faire: market forces—Adam Smith's "invisible hand"—will allocate resources in the most effective manner, and therefore, we must intervene as little as possible in the workings of these forces and limit ourselves to promoting competition.

The Ambivalences of the System

Despite the economic and technical effectiveness of this system, we hear many voices raised in protest against it, by those who want to limit it or place more controls on it. The demonstrators outside the World Trade Organization meeting (WTO) in Seattle in 1999, or those who caused the Multilateral Agreements on Investments (MAI) to collapse, are but the more visible elements of a growing resistance movement. What is the reason for such opposition when economic performance continues to grow, thereby creating value? The answer is that the ambiguities and injustices of the system are becoming increasingly obvious, and citizens are growing more acutely aware of them.

The Rise of Private Powers

A new feature of the phenomenon of globalization is that it is gradually escaping the control and the laws of nation-states. The global economic arena is filled with businesses and financiers, but no new rules to govern the economic game have been firmly established. In this situation, individual players use their own decision-making criteria—economic, commercial, and financial. Such criteria are indeed important for economic efficiency, but they do not encompass the full meaning of the *common good*. Thus, without any political debate, private powers impose upon us the pace of change; they impose their guidelines for economic and technical progress, and they invade non-business areas as well.

The speed of economic and technological change is accelerating from the effects of global competition. We have entered a race where the pace is set by the dynamism of businesses and competitive games. This pace is often faster than that of political, civil, and institutional society. Our administrative, educational, and social systems are having a great deal of difficulty adapting. Such a shift is creating the danger of increasing inequalities, exclusion, unemployment, and social ruptures. We are beginning to run the risk that the system will crush the people.[2]

If the logic of technological and economic innovation is that of creative destruction (following Joseph Schumpeter), we might ask ourselves whether the destructive effects today outweigh the beneficial effects of creation for some people. In other words, isn't the human cost of such rapid change too high?

The *guidelines of technological progress* are increasingly provided by private players and by the invisible hand of market forces. Businesses are appropriating and taking over even greater portions of the world's resources and knowledge, thanks to their enormous efforts in research and development, and they are deciding the type of research to be undertaken and thus the types of products and services that will be sold. Businesses function this way, it is true, on the basis of input from the market, and we might believe that this is the best way to direct resources. But, this is only partly true: the invisible hand only serves what or who can pay. It is clear that its criteria are exclusively financial and commercial.

Let us look, for example, at pharmaceutical research: the lack of a market that will pay in poor countries means that drug companies do not promote the development of certain drugs intended to treat diseases in these countries ("orphan drugs"). They invest much more money in studies on treating obesity and impotence in rich countries.

Another example is the installation of the equipment of the digital revolution. Up to now the information society was developed almost exclusively in response to the needs of the market or of ratings. Resorting to a caricature, we might say that a major technological advancement, television, rather than responding to educational needs, for example, has led us into a short-term, "zapping" consumer culture that is highly influenced by, and bears the strong mark of, the United States.

It is true that the Internet will give citizens a broader range of choices. They will be able to manage interactivity by using criteria other than those of the commercial networks. This shows, once again, that technological progress is neutral, and that we can make use of it for better or for worse.

The invasion of non-business areas by private powers raises an even more serious political problem. Let us recall the recent developments of multimedia groups and their influence on culture and education. They have already invaded the world of leisure and entertainment, and they are gradually guiding it toward what they consider *entertainment*. If we allow the

American multimedia conglomerates to dominate the scene, our grand-children will run the risk of being introduced to the *Iliad* and the *Odyssey* by Mickey Mouse and Donald Duck. Some may argue that the Web will make it possible to avoid this, but are we not underestimating the power of the conglomerates, which obviously will be very active in all networks? The same type of problem arises for films. In spite of the Internet, there is a real danger of reducing cultural diversity through the influence and sheer weight of the dominant cultures.

Another unsettling example is the takeover of the life sciences by private powers. The fact that certain sequences of the human genome can be patented and can cease to be a collective asset, or to belong to the public domain, raises a real political issue. One need only mention here that the Patent Institute in Great Britain has agreed to patent not only the process of human cloning developed by the inventor of Dolly the sheep, but also the human embryos cloned by this method. This means that a developing human embryo can become the property of an individual or of a business. This decision was made without much political or ethical debate.

The Rise of Inequalities

While multiplying wealth, the market and the "invisible hand" are incapable of ensuring that it will be distributed equitably. Mechanisms for redistribution that are implemented by states are practically nonexistent on the global level, and inequalities continue to grow. The gap between rich and poor countries increased from 1 to 3 in 1820 to 10 in 1900, 30 in 1960, 60 in 1990, and 74 in 1999.[3] Of the world's six billion inhabitants, 1.3 billion live below the absolute poverty line (earning less than one dollar per day), and 2.8 billion survive on the edge of poverty (earning less than two dollars per day).

To this we must add the crises of unemployment and exclusion in rich countries. Some people believe that a freer economy will remedy this. Others, and I belong to this group, think that these facts are a sad illustration of a rate of change that is too fast to allow our societies to adapt without excessive suffering. One of the greatest challenges we must face is that of reconciling the dynamism of the market economy with social justice.

A Political Void

Globalization is rapidly escaping the control of nation-states, which are becoming "too small for the big problems, and too big for the small ones" (as Raymond Aron put it). This is creating a sort of impotence in the guidance of strategies for development. Major economic decisions often extend beyond a country's borders, and have consequences that are difficult, if not impossible, to control. It is as if globalization were imposing itself on states without leaving them the freedom to choose the most suitable type of market economy. Thus, the Anglo-Saxon model (a more financial and less social model) is gaining ground every day over a more human model (the social market economy, or the Rhenish model).

Since there is little European or world "governance," citizens are losing their political landmarks. They are beginning to feel that their lifestyles, their social security systems, and their cultural identities are threatened.

2. Toward a New Control of Developments

The Return of Politics

What can we do in the face of an exclusively economic and financial globalization? Are we condemned to submit to the laws of a new empire of markets and pension fund investments? Or can we conceive of political, social, and cultural change that will reestablish checks and balances and will ensure that the economy serves the general interest? In other words, will we succeed in maintaining all the dynamism and creativity of the current phenomenon of globalization while suppressing the negative aspects of this evolution, and take charge of the issues that it cannot handle? There are urgent problems today, such as pollution and poverty that require a global approach.

The idea of the common good for the planet must be discussed democratically (via debate) and politically (beyond economics). For the first time in history, thanks to globalization, to technical progress, and to the ability of businesses and citizens to take action, we can deal seriously with the problems of a human society that by 2050 will comprise nine billion people. Henceforth the common good includes a common fight against poverty, disease, and lack of education. It calls for new forms of governance. Thierry de Montbrial explains this quite clearly:

> The idea of government as an organization exclusively in charge of public affairs within a state seems more and more inappropriate, because the growth and complexity of interdependence are stripping the word

"guidance" of its customary meaning. This is also due to the increasing takeover of the public good by civil society, a phenomenon that is—albeit slowly—spreading throughout the planet in spite of some pockets of resistance.

The concept of governance, like the regulation of complex networks of all kinds (the question has been raised in relation to the Internet), vaguely refers to all the mechanisms of regulation at work in human systems (businesses or other organizations, states, groups of states . . .) that are not understood in terms of a central decision-making unit, but that bring into play coordinating arrangements that are both ad hoc and of varying dimensions in both time and space.

As a principle of organization, governance is opposed to the idea of hierarchy. It can be readily related to the idea of subsidiarity.[4]

To mention governance is to mention *debates* and the confrontation of different points of view. Major economic players are beginning to participate in these debates. They are actually beginning to *listen* to opinions that differ from their own.

Governance also implies a certain degree of *common action*. Is it not possible to envision combining cooperative actions with the competitive mechanisms that are effective for earning profits, in order to put all the know-how and strategic abilities of businesses in the service of global causes (involving water, health, pollution, etc.)?[5] Solidarity is a value that we must gradually extend to the needs of the entire world.

One of the most important political tasks is to create forms of governance (institutions or networks) that can link tasks of global interest to local politics, while leaving the world as open as possible.

The Business Enterprise and Its Purpose

If we wish to control the current evolution toward a global world, it seems important to rethink the purpose of economic progress and of its principal players.

Purpose

No one argues with the fact that the business enterprise is a phenomenon of today's society. As a catalyst for development, the competitive enterprise assumes the risks and obligations inherent in economic and technical progress. It does not limit itself to the production and distribution of goods and services: under the banner of competition, it cannot survive without constantly renewing its products, its procedures, its markets, and its methods. It could easily adopt the motto of the Hanseatic League: "navigare necesse est." Innovation is at the heart of its activities. The enterprise is an essentially dynamic organization. Its specific function is that of assuring our society's economic and technical creativity. To define its purpose in purely financial terms (as *shareholder value*) is to diminish it considerably and to cut short any political, social, or cultural discussions concerning its activities.

We might defend the thesis that among the great civilizations, Western civilization has continuously valued this type of progress and elevated its pursuits to the level of fundamental and admirable activities. And if we look at the great founding myths of our culture, we quickly see that they grant an important place to economic and technical creativity. This is the essence of the myth of Prometheus, who took the risk of progress by stealing the gods' fire, the dominant force of all the arts, the infinite road opened for mankind. Prometheus symbolizes the qualities and the spirit of the entrepreneur. He ensures this type of human progress:

> . . . but listen to the tale
> Of human sufferings, and how at first
> Senseless as beasts I gave men sense, possessed them
> Of mind . . .
> In the beginning, seeing they saw amiss,
> And hearing heard not, but, like phantoms huddled
> In dreams, the perplexed story of their days
> Confounded; knowing neither timber-work
> Nor brick-built dwellings basking in the light,
> But dug for themselves holes, wherein like ants,
> That hardly may contend against a breath,
> They dwelt in burrows of their unsunned caves.
> Neither of winter's cold had they fixed sign,
> Nor the spring when she comes decked with flowers,
> Nor yet of summer's heat with melting fruits
> . . . But utterly without knowledge
> Moiled, until I the rising of the stars
> Showed them and when they set, though much obscure.
> Moreover, number, the most excellent

Of all inventions, I for them devised,
And gave them writing that retaineth all,
The serviceable mother of the Muse.
I was the first that yoked unmanaged beasts,
To serve as slaves with collar and with pack,
And take upon themselves, to man's relief,
The heaviest labor of his hands: and I
Tamed to the rein and drove in wheeléd carts
The horse, of sumptuous pride the ornament.
And those sea-wanderers with the wings of cloth,
The shipman's wagons, none but I contrived.
These manifold inventions for mankind
I perfected. . . .
But hear the sequel and the more admire
What arts, what aids I cleverly evolved.
The chiefest that, if any man fell sick,
There was no help for him, comestible,
Lotion or potion; but for lack of drugs,
They dwindled quite away; . . .
. . . and I purged
The glancing eye of fire, dim before,
And made its meaning plain. These are my works.
Then, things beneath the earth, aids hid from man,
Brass, iron, silver, gold, who dares to say
He was before me in discovering? . . .
And in a single word to sum the whole—
All manner of arts men from Prometheus learned.[7]

There were other gods and heroes around this central figure, gods who incarnated the role of progress: Hephaestus, who forged tools, weapons, and jewels; Odysseus and Jason, the great voyager-traders who set up shop around the Mediterranean and Black Sea, and even Icarus, the hero of poorly calculated risk and aborted progress.

Step by step, the West has maintained and developed this belief in potential and useful material progress, whether it be in our admiration of great discoveries and adventures—of Marco Polo, Christopher Columbus, Magellan—or in our constant desire to define ourselves as an urbane society, inclined toward international trade, open to the sea and all the freedoms it offers. A guiding thread in the development of the West is that of the merchant, of business, and free cities: Athens, Alexandria, Byzantium, Venice, Bruges, Antwerp, Amsterdam, London, New York. This development was one of movement, of a tension toward other things, a constant questioning of the existing order, an adherence to a rapid evolution that we accepted and sometimes believed we were leading. Frédéric Tristan has put it nicely: "The Venetians are [money] changers but what genius does it take to transform dried fish and salt into silks and spices, and these into Tintoretto or Palladio?"[7]

However, even though they are gods and heroes, these mythological figures carry a curse: Prometheus is damned, Icarus dies, Odysseus cannot go home, Jason sees his family exterminated, Hephaestus lives in a cave and is lame. Why? There is a fundamental question at the heart of these myths: What is the purpose of economic and technical progress? They clearly reveal the fundamental ambiguity of the pursuit of material progress that is not completed and is left to run wild, as it were.

Prometheus is bound because he made material progress an end unto itself. He believes that he can find transcendence as he shouts his proud cry: "I took from man the pangs of death." What an illusion! And he ends by recognizing this: to the question put to him by the Chorus, "What medicine found'st thou for this malady?" he replies, "I put a headband on his eyes."

Urged to moderation and submission to the gods (to a moral order), Prometheus persists in his excesses and reveals how far untamed technical progress can go.

> Therefore let lightning leap with smoke and flame,
> And all that is be beat and tossed together,
> With whirl of feathery snowflakes and loud crack
> Of subterranean thunder; none of these
> Shall bend my will . . . .

Today we know that technical progress is neutral and that it can raise or degrade man according to the use he makes of it. As Prometheus says, it can lead to the Apocalypse. The current trends toward globalization, deregulation, and privatization emphasize this ambiguity more than ever before and raise the issue of the meaning and purpose of economic and technical activity.

Aeschylus's loud cry is heard in the words of Moses, who also announces possible catastrophes:

But it shall come to pass, if thou wilt not hearken unto the voice of the
Lord thy God, [if you do not give economic development an ethical
dimension] . . . cursed shalt thou be in the city, and cursed shalt
thou be in the field.
Cursed shall be thy basket and thy store. Cursed shall be the fruit of
thy body and the fruit of thy land, the increase of thy kine and the
flocks of thy sheep . . . .
The Lord shall send upon thee cursing, vexation and rebuke to all that
thou settest thine hand unto for to do, until thou be destroyed,
and until thou perish quickly . . . until he have consumed thee
from off the land, whither thou goest to possess it.
And thy heaven that is over thy head shall be brass, and the earth that
is under thee shall be iron . . . .
The Lord shall cause thee to be smitten before thine enemies . . .
The Lord shall smite thee with madness, and blindness, and astonish-
ment of the heart . . .
If thou shalt hearken diligently unto the voice of the Lord thy God . . .
Blessed shalt thou be in the city and blessed shalt thou be in the
field . . .
Blessed shall be the fruit of thy ground and the fruit of thy cattle, the
increase of thy kine and the flocks of thy sheep . . .
Blessed shall be thy basket and thy store . . .
The Lord shall command the blessing in all that thou settest thine
hand unto."[8]

We know that the market economy and competition promote the creation of wealth. It is not a matter of calling the effectiveness of these mechanisms into question, but of highlighting their ambiguities and limitations.
Specifically, it is a matter of managing problems that are becoming global.
Business and the market economy will not be fully legitimized in this global
world if they do not address the following issues: *economic and technical
progress, what for? for whom? and how?*

These are truly political and moral issues. And it is definitely in this
sense that the concept of the "civic enterprise" finds a meaning.

The Civic Enterprise

Must we change the system of the market economy? No! But we do need to
regulate it, complete it, and open it up to social debate. Must we chain

Prometheus and restrict the real power of the business enterprise? No, but we must civilize it appropriately and guide it toward the great challenges facing the planet.

Do we need more government or bureaucracy? No! We need more policies, more regulation, more debate, more creative imagination and skills to guide the world's affairs.

Cooperation is an essential approach to the problems of the twenty-first century. It need not replace the market's mechanisms, but rather should complete and go beyond them, to aid in all the areas where the "invisible hand" does not reach or does not reach far enough. Debate and dialogue will help raise the basic questions and find the paths toward the common good. These paths will be found more out of the confrontation of several ways of thinking than from the predominance of a single economic or financial logic. We are witnessing the birth of this type of approach today. It is being organized around several players: the public, the private, unions, associations, and universities. The 1992 United Nations conference in Rio on the environment is one interesting example of this.

In this perspective the evolution toward the "civic enterprise" is doubtless the most desirable trend if we wish to bring together the effectiveness of competition and the need for cooperation. Many businesses are beginning to orient themselves in this direction. But are they doing it quickly enough, and are there enough of them?

The civic enterprise would develop new attitudes. It would listen to society and not only to the markets: it would pay more attention to weaker elements, to the whistle-blowers, to the nongovernmental organizations (NGOs), to their cries of alarm or distress. It would participate in society's debates when they touch on its specific function, which is to assure economic and technical progress: each time this type of progress involves the challenges facing society, the civic enterprise would participate actively in discussions. It would increasingly finalize its function by seeking valid responses to the great social and political questions associated with economic and technical progress. It would agree to participate in certain cooperative actions that are not related to the market or to the invisible hand; it would contribute its know-how, its enterprising spirit, its ability to act on a large scale and in an efficient manner; and it would do this in a way that is acceptable to all parties involved.

Several large enterprises have already embarked on this road, especially those in the realms of education, of assistance in the birth of new businesses, of pollution, etc. And in doing so, these enterprises are not simply playing the role of entrepreneur and manager, they are entering into the realm of general noncommercial activity; and thus they are accepting a broader social responsibility (statesmanship) in a quest for the common good.

All of this will increase their legitimacy. In the final analysis, the common good is the purpose of every organization and every manager.

An Ethics of Responsibility

The expansion of purpose and the convictions that lead to it are an important milestone in the evolution of economic and technical action. However, we must incarnate these values in life and in concrete decisions. It is here that the ethics of responsibility obtains its full meaning. It implies attitudes that are strong and vital enough to have a real influence on the actions of the decision makers:

- *attention* and *vigilance* with regard to people. If ethics begins at the first cry of human suffering,[9] every decision that might hurt people or risk dehumanizing them must be handled in an ethical manner, that is, by taking humans into account. Ethics is concern: we must not forget that a lack of concern and vigilance led to the tragedy of AIDS-contaminated blood in France and to that of child victims Julie and Mélissa in Belgium. Concern must be in the heart, as doubt is the heart of intelligence.
- *sufficient humility* to listen to other points of view, to participate in debates, to agree to revise or moderate one's position. We can no longer tolerate the arrogance of certainties or the indifference that led to the catastrophes of Minamata, of Bhopal, of toxic wastes and oil-blackened seas.
- *a spirit of service* rather than of domination. The exercise of power is a revealer of values and purpose. "It is difficult to know the spirit or the heart of a mortal until he has exercised great power. Power reveals the man."[10]

The legitimate manager is the one who serves his organization and the common good. As Erasmus said: "He is not a prince if he is not a man of good."

NOTES

1. Direct foreign investments throughout the world have increased from $24 billion in 1990 to $120 billion in 1999.

2. A. Touraine, *La critique de la modernité* (Paris: Fayard, 1992).

3. The Human Development Report of the United Nations Development Program, 1999.

4. T. de Montbrial, "Le monde au tournant du siècle," *Ramsès 2000* (1999): pp. 16–17.

5. Lisbon Group, *Limits to Competition*. (Cambridge, Mass.: MIT Press, 1995).

6. Aeschylus, *Prometheus Bound,* trans. G. M. Cookson, Encyclopaedia Britannica, Inc., 1980.

7. F. Tristan, *Venise* (Paris: Presses universitaires de France, 1984).

8. Deuteronomy 28:1–8, 15–29, King James Version.

9. G. Fourez, *La construction des sciences: Introduction à la philosophie et à l'éthique des sciences* (Brussels: De Boeck, 1988).

10. Sophocles, *Antigone,* in *The Plays of Sophocles,* trans. Sir Richard C. Jebb, Encyclopaedia Britannica, Inc., 1980.

PART 2

Institutional Designs

Globalization and Cultural Diversity: The Contribution of European Institutions

ROMANO PRODI

I. Introduction

Globalization in the sense of the simultaneous liberalization and acceleration of trade is often deemed incompatible with the coexistence and development of different cultures. As the recent European experience has proved, this idea does not always correspond to reality and such a generalization cannot, in any case, be applied on a global level.

There is no doubt, however, that different "cultures" by nature tend to attribute different value to public goods, so that it may become necessary to provide a "framework" to guarantee respect for different outlooks. The supranational European institutions created as part of the European Union have provided and will continue to provide concrete examples of an appropriate type of "framework" and of the conditions needed for its development.

Romano Prodi has been a professor at the University of Bologna since 1971. He has had a political career in Italy as minister for industry (1978–1979), as chairman of the Istituto per la Ricostruzione Industriale (IRI) from 1982 to 1989 and from 1993 to 1994, and as prime minister (1996–1998). He has been president of the European Commission since 1999.

In this regard, the existence of a viable legal framework has proven to be a fundamental element. These distinctively European institutions, however, are evolving simultaneously through a process of continual learning. Beyond the legal frame of reference, they must develop other elements of legitimization, such as the multiple opportunities for dialogue that are necessary to encourage the contributions of democratic representatives and of civil society.

This learning process has been long: it began with the Treaty of Paris in 1951, followed by the Treaty of Rome, the Acte Unique of Luxembourg, and the Maastricht Treaty; we now have the Treaty of Amsterdam (1997) and the Treaty of Nice (2001). Before Slavic cultures can be added to the constellation of Latin, German, Anglo-Saxon, and Nordic cultures that are already part of the Union, the process will still have to move forward significantly.

Up to what point is it possible to transpose the effective frame of reference that has been created, thanks to the European institutions, to a global level? One indispensable condition for the existence of a world-scale institutional frame of reference is certainly its level of accessibility and transparency.

2. The Nature of the Interaction between Globalization and Cultural Diversity: Basic Considerations and a Few Examples of the Contribution of the European Institutions

When we use the word "globalization" we are affirming a specific vision of the world in which nation-states, with their deep and often ancient cultural roots, whether they want to or not, exercise increasingly limited "control" over their own destinies. From this point of view, nation-states, especially the smaller ones, are habitually represented as passive elements in the globalization process

On the other hand, the European Union, far from being the result of passive acceptance of a general phenomenon, is rather the product of the *active desire of the member states to combine their sovereignties in order to achieve the common objective of bringing peace and stability to the continent.* In the progressive opening of the respective markets of the Union's member states we can see—but only up to a certain point—an analogy on a reduced scale with the liberalization of markets on the global level. We can, however, learn something useful from the experience of the European institutions.

According to a commonly held belief, globalization would endanger the specificity and even survival of cultural "identities." In its most elementary form, this thesis maintains that businesses in a society where a high level of social protection is considered indispensable for cultural reasons would be at a disadvantage in a global market, where their competitors work under less stringent regulations concerning social protection, etc., and hence, incur lower social costs. At first glance this theory is convincing and is often quoted when the unemployment rate is high in societies such as those in Europe. In fact, the "European social model" requires that unavoidable risks must weigh not on individuals but on the collectivity as a whole.

This cultural condition favoring a collective coverage of risk, which we may call "solidarity," is one explanation for the relatively high level of public spending for the social welfare system in European economies. Depending on the methods of coverage, these burdens on our economies could, to a greater or lesser extent, limit our ability to participate in the competition imposed by globalization. As proof of the thesis that contests the benefits of globalization, we usually cite examples from the textile industry or similar industries.

Without wishing to demonize an opinion that is widely held throughout Europe, we should note, however, that in reality—even independently of the by now classic explanations of economists concerning the many imperfections of the global markets—the most formidable competitor of any company is almost always its immediate neighbor. It is usually a company in the same group of advanced countries, subject to the same cost structures imposed by similar cultural factors. That is why the real problem on which businesses must focus, both those that are fully involved in globalization and those that are relatively protected, is different. They must, first of all, determine whether they have the energy and versatility required to sustain, or rather to surpass the rate at which their home-country competitors adapt to technical and managerial changes. In many industrial fields, the most formidable competitors are Japan and the United States; at the same time, they are frequently considered to be the countries that offer the best opportunities abroad for Europeans. This can be interpreted as a proof of the ambivalence revealed when the so-called defects of globalization are examined in more depth.

Globalization, therefore, is as much a source of opportunities as it is of risks, be they real or imaginary. Asking what contribution the European institutions can make actually amounts to asking not only how the different cultures comprising the Union can be protected from the presumed dangers of globalization, but also how they can reap the greatest benefits from it.

We must add that Europe has enormous advantages that allow its businesses to assert themselves in an economy that is becoming global. One of the features of this process, for example, is the transition to a "knowledge-based economy" in which access to information and the speed of that access become exceedingly important in terms of competition. In this regard, promoting investments in research and development, on the one hand, and the development of the Internet, on the other, account for two of the fundamental priorities of the new European Commission's policy plans, especially in the fields of new information and communications technologies. "E-Europe," for example, is the Commission's political initiative for guaranteeing that the European Union profits from current changes due to the information society. For this we will have to adapt the training and education of young people to the needs of the new digital era, facilitate access to the Internet, develop e-commerce, and make greater use of the new technologies in services and government.

We must also place the goal of creating a European arena for research on the same level, by knocking down existing barriers and integrating scientific research and technological activities on a European level. This means that centers for development will exist where there is easy access to information, especially information that is useful in terms of profitability and efficiency for businesses.

The groups of companies and centers of excellence that are developing in this way are useful to neighboring companies in both the local and the global markets. The high level of education of the population, good communications infrastructures, technological skills, and the development of service industries within the economy place Europe in a privileged position.

Economists and politicians, however, will readily agree that the increasingly rapid rate at which new technologies are adopted affects the *structure of the demand for labor in our societies*. The demand is shifting toward higher levels of skills faster than labor can be recycled, leaving behind the unskilled when their productivity, whatever it may be, can no longer keep up with the pace. This undesired effect is real, and is certainly exacerbated by globalization in the sense of the easier, and above all faster, transfer and adoption of new technologies.

European institutions, and especially the European Commission, cannot remain silent or inactive in the face of a problem that threatens the less skilled sector of our labor force. Throughout Europe these people are respected and respectable, and it would go against the cultural traditions of our continent to leave them to their fates. This is why increasingly greater financial resources will have to be earmarked for specific projects based on continuing education and training and on professional redirection. This educational/employment aspect is just one example of the contribution the European institutions can make.

The European Union, especially since 1993, has wanted to promote debate among its member states on countermeasures that might reasonably be implemented to solve this problem. The changes introduced in 1997 by the Treaty of Amsterdam and the Luxembourg summit on employment made it possible to reach an agreement on a European policy for employment, with guidelines on the European level and an effective process for planning measures on the national level. This topic was the object of serious consideration at the special European Council, "Employment, Economic Reform and Social Cohesion—Towards a Europe of Innovation and Knowledge" that was held in Lisbon in March 2000.

The analyses the European Commission has done up to now have revealed the promising ideal of easing non-salary labor costs, specifically for the lower levels of the salary scale, which is the category most at risk. A decrease in non-salary labor costs would protect jobs, and the reduction of compulsory contributions could be compensated for by taxing other activities. In order to remain true to the cultural traditions of our continent and the widespread interest in environmental protection, the targets for this type of taxation could be businesses that pollute or that use large quantities of nonrenewable natural resources.

The debate over these ideas that was launched by the Commission demonstrated the usefulness of European institutions as a forum for discussion and for the development of a consensus on the measures to adopt to ease certain side effects of globalization. The Commission does not claim to have invented the idea of transferring tax burdens from workers onto the "wicked" who harm the environment, but it does deserve the credit for having organized and stimulated the debate on the European level, thereby putting into proper perspective the resistance that could have blocked that idea in many isolated countries, and succeeding in controlling it better. Let us take a closer look at that resistance.

Quite obviously the first source of resistance was the innate caution and traditionally conservative spirit of the fiscal authorities. The European institutions opened the debate on this subject among the authorities so that the most cautious could see the progress achieved by those who experienced fewer difficulties in this area, and thereby allowed these ideas to gain strength, to become accepted, and finally to be gradually implemented.

Another source of resistance, as we might expect, was among the large, energy-consuming industries which, because of intensive exposure to the forces of globalization, demanded compensation or indemnification in the form of stabilizing their fiscal situations. To ensure fair competition among these industries in the European markets, these auxiliary measures should clearly follow a coordinated presentation of the issue, which is something the institutions themselves are best suited to do.

The third source of resistance to the ideas proposed for combating the side effects of globalization on a given sector of labor can be found in the doubts of some economists and scholars, who feared that changing the taxable base would only increase inflationary pressures. They also feared that the opportunistic behavior of the companies and the workers' representatives would wipe out the money saved on non-salary labor costs, transforming it respectively into benefits and advantages for the existing labor force instead of augmenting the possibilities of creating new jobs. In this case, too, the ability of the European institutions to compare and evaluate the experiences of different countries, especially the intensive and continuous exchange of information between the Commission and the academic world, favored the emergence of a realistic view of the issue.

These practical examples of the experiences of the European institutions prove that, thanks to their role as honest intermediary, as a "guiding spirit" and possible coordinator among the member states, they contribute to finding concrete solutions to the negative effects of globalization, whatever they might be.

According to a commonly held belief, globalization could have a destabilizing impact on our culture, due to its effects on our labor markets. Another opinion periodically dusted off by the sensationalist, tabloid media is that market liberalization inevitably goes hand in hand with "cultural enslavement." This, however, is nothing more than the reverse side of a coin, and Europe is well acquainted with the other side in the sense that free markets, especially when combined with greater access to information and communication, multiply the opportunities and possibilities for choice for all concerned. It is the consumer who becomes king, and not the dominant culture.

Furthermore, European institutions have largely proved that they can adapt the rules of market access to the different governments and legal traditions of the Union's member states. The principle of subsidiarity enables the coexistence of different legal and institutional systems and the common need for access to markets that has been augmented by economic globalization. Subsidiarity is the daily bread of European institutions, and in practice it is not limited to determining the best level for lawmaking, as is borne out by the composition of the institutions themselves. Within the Committee of the Regions, for example, the regions of the member states are represented in different ways that reflect the specificities of each country as to the traditional organization of its institutional architecture.

The idea that freeing up markets risks harming consumers and the environments that characterize our European cultures is closer to hypothesis than to reality. The European institutions and the legal framework they apply have had to evolve, but this evolution has indeed gone in the right direction. From attempts at harmonization and sometimes precarious compromises between member states in conditions that sometimes required unanimity, we have progressed to a situation that assumes a mutual, generalized acceptance of the rules. We then moved forward again, giving new member states the possibility of maintaining and protecting standards that were higher than those they generally applied. Today, with the implementation of the Treaty of Amsterdam, Article 95 allows a new option and permits member states to introduce these higher standards as long as their motivation is sincere and they are not acting out of mere protectionism. How this innovation will actually work is something we will see gradually, in the light of the specific cases that arise.

This example illustrates an important aspect of European institutions, that is, their defense of the cultural dimension in conditions of market liberalization. The European institutions and the frameworks they apply are perpetually evolving. They must adapt to the aspirations of an increasingly aware and knowledgeable population, and to the new perspectives introduced with each enlargement of the Union, which guide them. This receptiveness and this ability to adapt on the part of European institutions lead us to ask, more now than in the past, what the significance of their contribution will be in the future.

3. The Evolution of European Institutions toward Better Promotion of Cultural Diversity

At the dawn of the new century, it is appropriate to contemplate European integration from a standpoint that encompasses both our past and our future. There is every reason to believe that in the future, European institutions will evolve even further to maintain an active role in protecting and promoting diversity. Furthermore, we will have to ask ourselves to what extent the lessons learned in Europe can be transposed to institutions that function globally.

We must envision a new form of world government ("governance") to manage the global economy. On the European level this will mean closer integration. Europe is entering a new, decisive phase in its process of integration. The integration that we have known up to now, based primarily on economic considerations and perspectives such as the single market or the single currency, is making way for a phase in which political reform will be the driving element. This is not a choice but a necessity: European political integration must go hand in hand with its geographic enlargement. The new frontiers of European integration are justice and domestic security, foreign policy and that of common security, cooperation in matters of defense, and the critical theme of fundamental political values. These are issues that go to the heart of national sovereignty and that force us to seek an even higher level of political consensus than that which we achieved during the 1980s and 1990s.

The translation of this political dimension into concrete action will consist, first of all, of promoting new forms of government (governance) on a European scale so that through innovation the European institutions may continue to safeguard different cultural dimensions by creating a point of dialogue, an exchange of experiences, and mutual understanding and encouragement.

To this end, the Commission has presented a White Paper, "European Governance," the main objective of which is to raise fundamental questions concerning the policies we will need in a European Union that may comprise thirty members, and the best way to implement them. There will then be the question of which institutions we will need for the twenty-first century and a new distribution of tasks among the Commission, other institutions, the member states, and civil society: in other words, a new and more democratic form of partnership among the various levels of governance in Europe.

Why do we think we have to move in this direction? I will try to explain our point of view. Over the years the European Union has built itself up, so to speak, in successive layers: first the customs union, then the single market, and finally the single currency. Different policies gradually developed in parallel as they became necessary, and as each layer settled.

Up to now there has never been an "overall plan" for formulating and coordinating our policies; thus our attempts at generalizing some of them, such as environmental policy or those of equal opportunity, by incorporating them into all other sectors, have had rather limited success. But the European Union is preparing to face great expansion over the medium and the long term. This will force us to radically rethink a large part of these existing policies and the methods proposed to implement them. We must ask ourselves the following questions:

Are citizens seeing and understanding what we are doing? Are our working methods sufficiently simple and effective? Have we done away with all superfluous bureaucracy? Are our priorities the fruit of in-depth reflection or have they been more or less accidentally dictated by the course of events? To tell the truth, we must carefully review all our policies in the light of our new priorities. Those that are no longer suitable must be entirely reinvented or simply abandoned.

Next, we must ask ourselves what must be done at the European level and what duties the member states, the regions, and civil society, must assume. Rather than claiming a centralizing role for "Brussels," I believe that the time for radical decentralization is upon us. It is time to realize that Europe is not managed solely by the European institutions; it is also managed by national, regional, and local authorities and by civil society.

The challenge, therefore, is not only that of reforming the European Commission, although that may be an important task, nor that of making the institutions function more efficiently, although that, too, is an essential goal. The challenge consists of completely rethinking our method of making Europe, of giving Europe a new project, of inventing a completely new form of governance for the world of tomorrow.

I believe that we must stop thinking in terms of hierarchies of duties and responsibilities that are broken down according to the principle of subsidiarity; we must envision a reticular system in which all levels of governance contribute to formulate, propose, and implement policies and then to verify the results.

For this we must double our efforts to reorganize the treaties and to render the corpus of rules that form the basis of the common actions of the member states clear, coherent, and readily comprehensible. This will significantly raise the level of democracy in Europe and will grant everyone easier access to, and a better understanding of, the basic regulatory principles contained in the treaties.

The project has been defined in the White Paper on European Governance. The procedure of institutional reforms will be moved forward on a par with the Intergovernmental Conference because one of the key points will be that of determining exactly which institutions we will need in the twenty-first century.

Like every parliament we have seen in history, the European Parliament will demand and will obtain a louder voice. It is no accident that the

Parliament has obtained greater powers with each treaty revision. The European Parliament is the guarantor of the expression of diversity within European institutions and even of several types of diversities, all clearly distinct from each other and recognized as such. Political diversity and cultural diversity are both represented, but they do not necessarily move at the same pace and cannot be identified with each other.

Our Parliament has already distinguished itself by encouraging the European institutions, and especially the Community budget, to pay attention to cultural issues and to give natural preference to the protection and the promotion of the extraordinary diversity that exists in Europe. There is no doubt that the European Parliament will continue to support the expression of our cultures in all their richness, and well beyond the boundaries of the Union. Gradually, as globalization creates new and increasingly distant opportunities, Europe—who has always exported her cultures—will no doubt seek to exploit them to the fullest.

4. Conclusion

Thanks to the European institutions, the cultural diversity of the member states has not only survived in the face of market liberalization and globalization, but has obtained a real advantage.

To achieve this result, institutional structures and their working methods have had to evolve in the past and will have to continue to do so in the future. This type of evolution is essential in order to give due weight to the advantages and the bonds that the continuous enlargement of the European Union, its growing maturity, its progress in communications and information technologies, and above all the accessibility of its institutions, will bring.

As these changes take place, the European Union will become a beacon of civilization and will guide other international organizations toward full respect for cultural diversity.

CHAPTER 10

European Unification: A Response to the Challenges of Globalization

EMILIO GABAGLIO

I. Globalization and Regionalization

In the current debates on globalization, we have the impression that we are dealing with a "natural," external force that escapes all forms of regulation by the welfare state. In fact, we must not underestimate the risks of globalization. The astounding international upheavals which in part originate in political decisions (for example, the liberalization of the telecommunications sector) nevertheless also offer perspectives and new potentials for political arrangements that we must consider as such, and on which we must establish our political strategies in Europe. This, however, means, that at the dawn of the twenty-first century, we must set aside our accepted and time-worn modes of behavior. One essential condition, in my opinion, is that the political players, management and unions—but also governments and political parties—must extend their organizational structures and their fields of action beyond national boundaries in order to be able to organize the globalization process effectively and responsibly. At its 9th Ordinary Congress in Helsinki (1999), the European Trade Union Confederation (ETUC)[1] finally explained that it would accept the new challenges in order to organize the

Emilio Gabaglio is general secretary of the European Trade Union Confederation (ETUC).

current pattern of internationalization in the interests of the whole population. According to the ETUC, the European social model is the European response to the risks that globalization poses for individuals.

On the other hand, globalization is not an entirely new phenomenon. The internationalization that took place after World War II was based primarily on an enormous expansion in international trade that contributed to prosperity throughout the industrialized world—often to the detriment of the Third World—and left national sovereignty more or less intact. What is new in today's situation is a set of three parallel developments that have contributed to accelerating globalization.

First, the liberalization of financial and capital markets beginning in the mid-1970s and the progress in the fields of information and communications technologies are among the determining factors in globalization. The open financial markets and the resulting monetary flow have reached a magnitude that is difficult to manage without effective measures on an international scale.

Second, since the 1980s we have also been witnessing new dynamics in direct international investments. When we analyze these trends we see, for example, that 70 percent of direct American investments are made in the extremely attractive market of the European Union. This means that in global competition for plant locations, places for production are not chosen solely on the basis of labor costs. The logic of direct international investments is based primarily on guarantees and the expansion of markets. Direct investments overseas by European groups certainly contribute to a new international distribution of labor, but they also contribute significantly to safeguarding the economic situation and hence employment in Europe.

Third, the collapse of state socialism and the consequent disappearance of competition between the capitalist market economies and the socialist centralized economies have brought about the opening of the central and eastern European markets. The increase in direct investments in central and eastern European countries is, in fact, a necessary condition for the success of the process of economic and political transformation in those nations. Only stable economic conditions will contribute to the success of these young democracies and to the establishment of efficient industrial relations that will, in the end, permit membership in the European Union.

These developments can, however, be contradictory, and cannot be described solely as objective external restrictions that merely limit union and political actions. For example, the possibilities for action and for organization derive from the fact that the importance of regionalization and decentralization increases along with globalization. The creation of regional trade restrictions shows that the opening of the world economy will not occur all at once. These restrictions are a reaction to international competition (a result of decompartmentalization) for markets and plant sites. We can see the margins of political maneuvering by comparing the situation of the North American Free Trade Agreement (NAFTA), which lacks social involvement, with that of the European Union. As opposed to NAFTA, the European Union has political institutions and a network of supranational regulations. At the ETUC Congress in Helsinki it was rightly acknowledged that the European Union has enabled a process of unification and created a social dimension that is still unique in the world.

In addition, in Helsinki the unions once again made it clear that they cannot nor do they want to accept the new challenges using old programs! Just as the European Union member states relinquish their national sovereignty to supranational institutions such as the European Commission, the European Parliament, the European Court of Justice, and recently the European Central Bank, a new European standard that complements the unions' national level of action will be inevitable. The "social dialogue" has already drafted such a standard, and it must be systematically expanded to a European arena of industrial relations. This will give the European labor movement the means to provide new political responses to globalization. Modifying the existing structures will not, however, be sufficient. Globalization and regionalization require a structural transformation of international labor collaboration. In this regard, we are convinced that regional, and in particular European, integration is the sole viable option for a social control of global capitalism that can compensate for the loss of national sovereignty. In spite of a number of shortcomings, the European model is increasingly becoming a clear reference for other regional economic blocs. But everything will depend on the extent to which the European economic and monetary union will evolve toward unification on a social level and in the realm of employment. This means finally laying the bases for the internationalization of the "social Europe" that the unions demand.

2. A European Employment Pact

The struggle against mass unemployment is still Europe's main social problem. Employment policy still has much to do, even more since the creation of the monetary union, because exchange rates can no longer be used as national regulatory instruments.

The ETUC has always come out in favor of economic and monetary union because, without it, there can be no convergence of economic, financial, and social policies. Given the expanding Europeanization of business activities, if there is no European framework the national possibilities for regulation in the legislative and contractual fields will decrease without being replaced by suitable new European regulations. This type of development could, over the long term, threaten the social and economic interests of the workers. The ETUC has, however, always linked its approval of monetary union to the need for modifications to the EU treaty that will broaden the scope of social and employment policy.

For many years the Union's employment policy strategy has been limited to rhetoric. It was only with the addition—as demanded by the unions—of a chapter on employment in the Treaty of Amsterdam that the EU Commission acquired the concrete tools for an employment policy. These tools had already been used before the ratification of the Treaty of Amsterdam. Guidelines for the employment policy had been adopted for the first time at the European Summit on employment in Luxembourg in November 1997. The unions hailed the "Luxembourg process," but at the same time they argued that it was imperative first to establish concrete, qualifying, and binding goals for employment policy. This is the only way to break the endless chain of declarations on employment policy. In addition the ETUC clearly demonstrated that an active policy on the labor market alone will not succeed in eliminating mass unemployment. In its opinion, we must use all the tools of economic policy. Such multifaceted European policy must be implemented with the least possible tension and must promote employment. This is the main task of the European Employment Pact as it was put into effect in June 1999 under the German presidency.[2]

This European Employment Pact is not a single document to which the members affixed their signatures. It is a long process, one that is certainly not free of contradictions, and it will only be successfully consummated when the unemployment rate is below 7 percent and the employment rate in the European Union is steadily over 70 percent. That, as the ETUC congress indicated, is the moment when we will truly be able to talk about a European "plus" for employment.

The European Employment Pact ratified in Cologne is based on the interdependence of the following three factors:

1) a macroeconomic policy mix favorable to growth and employment;
2) a common and coordinated employment strategy including an active labor market and training policy (the pursuit and application of the Luxembourg process);

3) structural reform of the markets for goods, services, and capital (the Cardiff process), which is as necessary for Europe as the modernization of the labor market.

On the qualitative level, macroeconomic coordination is the new element in the European Employment Pact. From the unions' point of view, the long-needed breakthrough for an employment policy depends on the success, within the framework of macroeconomic coordination, of a combination of monetary policy, public investment policy, and salary policy oriented toward production, a combination that would be most favorable to employment. The revalorization of employment policy into a macroeconomic task in the context of the Employment Pact is a new, long-awaited step in the elimination of mass unemployment in Europe. The fact of renouncing the unilateral declaration according to which the European job markets would not be sufficiently flexible is an important element.

The disastrous state of the job market is also due to weak demand. In Cologne, the heads of states and of governments of the European Union acknowledged that the rigidities of the European job market alone do not explain the disparity between the employment rates in the United States and in Europe. Given the limited maneuvering margins for government expenditures, the European Central Bank must use its own maneuvering margin to stimulate demand by lowering interest rates. Thus it could make a concrete contribution within the context of the European Employment Pact. The unions, in turn, are responsible for coordinating their salary policies on a European level, establishing common guidelines based on inflation and productivity increases. In this way they would contribute to guaranteeing current employment and to creating new jobs in Europe.

The European employment alliance must be completed by Europeanizing industrial policy and by harmonizing fiscal tax policy, that is, by working together toward the elimination of fiscal disparities through an agreement on minimum tax rates or "spread goals." Redirecting assessments by taxing rare natural resources (energy, raw materials, etc.) rather than the abundant Labor resource, is part of these measures. According to the European Commission, real taxation of salaries and wages rose from 34.9 percent to 42.1 percent in the EU between 1981 and 1995 while taxes on corporate profits decreased from 45.5 percent to 34.4 percent during the same period. The tendency to overtax labor while favoring capital is true discrimination. This fiscal discrimination of employment is as disastrous as unfair fiscal competition—both must be stopped! We must act quickly, especially in the direction of ecological fiscal reform, coordinating taxation of companies and taxes withheld at the source. High taxation of low incomes is not an incentive to work and is detrimental to employment.

The European alliance for employment grants employment its due place in social policy. If this new impetus of employment policy makes it possible to drastically lower unemployment and markedly increase the employment rates, it will also mean much for a greater equilibrium in the relationship between economic and social policies in Europe. In addition, it will durably reinforce the European social model as a point of reference on the international level.

3. Enlargement of the European Union: Preserving the European Social Model

In the context of the next intergovernmental conference, eastward expansion and the necessary integration of institutional changes that must precede it are the greatest challenge the EU faces.[3] The first hurdles have been overcome. Negotiations were launched in July 1997 with five Central and Eastern European countries (CEEC): the Czech Republic, Hungary, Poland, Estonia and Slovenia, as well as Cyprus. The ETUC immediately pronounced itself in favor of negotiations with all the countries applying for membership; consequently, it was pleased with the decisions the council made in Helsinki, under the Finnish presidency, to begin negotiations quickly with the "second group" of applicant countries. The imminent expansion is not comparable to the previous expansion of the Union because those applicants for membership never had to transform their entire political and economic systems as radically as those of central and eastern Europe will now have to do.

It is equally clear that expansion will not come without consequences, nor will it be easy. On the contrary, alongside all the undisputed political and economic advantages, it will put the social interests of "the two sides" to a hard test. Objectively, central and eastern Europe remains the arena of competition between the "European social model" and the "American way," which is trying to transform the eastern European countries into neoliberal, in situ experimental laboratories. The unions, therefore, are just as eager for the European model of development to take root in these countries. The ETUC had good reasons to begin the process of labor union unification at an early stage and to embrace a whole series of central and eastern European organizations. The ETUC is, in fact, collaborating with its central and eastern European member organizations to draft an expansion policy that takes common interests into account. During this transitional period, the countries applying for membership must adapt their laws to existing European legislation. The "White Paper" behind this process contains a series of provisions and directives that also cover social policy and industrial relations. A gradual adaptation of national laws to European legislation will contribute to establishing the major guidelines of the European social model in central and eastern Europe.

The expansion of the Union is not an "act of grace" but a historic obligation. It is logical from a political standpoint, and it can increase the strength of the European model in competition with other economic regions. The European Union is the sole model of regional integration that goes beyond the market. This model cannot be guaranteed and developed over the long term unless it integrates the central and eastern European states. One essential condition is that an agreement be reached within the framework of the next intergovernmental conference to give to the Union the necessary breadth and scope so that an expanded Europe may indeed have a future as a social reference model within the realm of international competition.

4. The European Social Model: A Reference Model in a Time of Globalization

In spite of the many challenges that the European social model has to face, Europe has become one of the world's most advanced societies. It has managed to overcome the phase of neoliberal hegemony, during which the European social model was brought into considerable question, and we can clearly see an evolution of the current political and social climate, not only in Europe. On the whole, we recognize the need for a balance between economic effectiveness and social justice; even the political players are increasingly convinced that we must make the European social model a reference point for other regions of the world. This means, of course, further social development in Europe. The recent crises in Asia, Russia, and South America have clearly shown the shortcomings of the development models of these countries when they do not take the social dimension into account.

Establishing the European model as a social model also involves the establishment of an international framework of rules and policies capable of limiting the negative effects of free exchange and unregulated markets, and of organizing globalization in the interests of the entire population. In order to accomplish this, Europe must, in view of its economic and political importance, assume its role as a global player. For the European Union this means it must make itself heard in one voice within international institutions—the International Monetary Fund (IMF), the World Bank, and the World Trade Organization (WTO). Within the framework of these institutions we must create a new world order that satisfies the needs of all countries and all people. The ETUC believes that the European Union must strengthen its commitment and solidarity vis-à-vis poorer nations by canceling their debts and increasing aid for cooperation in order to reach the minimum level set by the United Nations, that is, 0.7 percent of the gross national product.

Concerning the social structures of the globalization process, there is also the issue of creating new rules governing the movement of capital. For example, we must support the introduction of a Tobin tax on speculative short-term capital transactions. We also need appropriate tools for monitoring and regulating the activities of multinational corporations, banks, and financial institutions. An effective multinational tool is also needed to regulate the flow of direct international investment capital. The failure of negotiations on the Multilateral Agreement on Investments within the Organization for Economic Cooperation and Development (OECD) clearly showed that agreements that do not take the fundamental rights of workers into account have no chance of succeeding. A multilateral agreement is feasible only if direct international investments go hand in hand with better distribution of economic prosperity and environmental regulations, and promote development on the local level, social participation, and economic democracy.

At the Doha WTO Conference in 2001, the European Union clearly voiced the need for social and environmental standards to be taken into account in the new round of trade negotiations. This move was strongly supported by the European trade unions and despite having failed to deliver concrete results in that context it has confirmed the European Union's commitment to promote labor rights and sustainable development in the international forums.

Using the European model as a reference means that even within the context of globalization, economic and social issues cannot be separated. In the twenty-first century, the ETUC and its member organizations will further pledge to strengthen the social dimension of the European process of integration in order to make a concrete contribution to the indispensable guidance of globalization in the interests of workers and citizens.

NOTES

1. The ETUC comprises seventy-four member organizations from thirty countries and eleven European industry federations.

2. The European Employment Pact contents are now an integral part of the overall growth and employment strategy decided in 2000 by the European Council in Lisbon.

3. The 2001 Nice Treaty determined the enlargement agenda. First accessions are envisaged for 2004. A European Convention is presently meeting in Brussels to propose future reforms in the Union to be decided finally by an intergovernmental conference that will convene in the second half of 2003.

Europe in the Face of Globalization without a Political and/or Historical Program

MIHAIL PAPAYANNAKIS

Globalization and the construction of Europe are two processes of our era in which we are involved in different ways, with prospects that have every possibility of diverging—assuming that at any one time they have converged. The first of these, globalization, falls within the more general process of the growth of capitalism; the second, in the sense of a historical project of political unification, implies voluntary intervention in the "natural course of things," that is to say, our relations at all levels, on both a continental and world scale. Independently of the awareness that the protagonists may have of these processes, over the long term they are contradictory, and we cannot objectively foresee how the contradiction can be overcome.

Mihail Papayannakis is a member of the European Parliament and of the Parliamentary Committees on Environment, Public Health and Consumer Protection; Economic and Monetary affairs; and Fishing. He is a member of the leadership of the European Movement, chairman of the Greek Section; member of the Political Secretariat and Central Committee of the Coalition of the Left Wing and Progress (Synaspismos), Greece; and a former teacher and researcher at Paris, Montpellier, and Athens.

I. Globalization: A New Burst of Power for an Old Historical Trend

The trend toward globalization is as old as capitalism itself in the sense that this system of organizing, operating, and developing production is by definition and hence essentially "free" of all bonds with the land or with one or more groups of consumers to whom its products would be (pre)destined for reasons other than those of the market. In other words, merchandise is by definition destined for those that can purchase it, wherever they may be and whatever their personal or social status. In this sense, the capitalist market has been virtually global since its birth. The attempt to meet or to forge this market is a central element of the system's logic and its unstoppable tendencies.

This tendency has developed historically, passing through distinct phases in a real world organized according to different systems and principles. The social, political, and administrative barriers to the expansion of the market and to the capitalist organization of production tend to disappear, first within the framework of the nation-state, then within the framework of larger groups and finally of the whole world. This means that, starting from a certain point, the nation-state itself and the larger groups that tend to reproduce its interventionist features are considered obstacles to this development.

The initial expansion of capitalism in the pre-capitalist world through trade, the "discoveries," and colonization, generally brought about either a gradual or a brutal destruction of preexisting systems for the organization and development of production, without creating others that could function according to the principles and logic of spreading capitalism. This led to a new contradiction: on the one hand, the world tends to unify through the expansion of the system of capitalism, and on the other, dividing lines develop between developed and underdeveloped parts within the same global space. Explanations for this evolution have been sought in the contradictions, the weaknesses, and the organizational modes of the dominant system (for example, movements of productive capital hindered by internal crises; introversion of the system in which the market and profits could be arranged "in loco," thanks to the contribution of the "social-democratic" compromise favoring wages that increase at the same rate as productivity), as well as in the systemic resistance and weaknesses of the economies and societies that bowed to capitalism's expansionist pressures.

2. Overcoming a "Fatal" Dichotomy

For a long time we believed that these dividing lines created structural inequality, that the distinction between the developed and underdeveloped parts of the world was inherent in the capitalist system, that it was common to all, and that the position of either in this common system was immutable. The "socialist" alternative that was historically inscribed in the world with the emergence of the USSR and the "Eastern Bloc" seemed as much an alternative for the underdeveloped part of the world (also known as the Third World, where the options were open) as an obstacle to the expansion of central capitalism.

In this debate there was a great tendency to forget Marx's famous "prophecy" according to which, in the power relationship initially established by the global expansion of capitalism, a capitalist India would take the place of Great Britain, and vice versa. It was actually much less of a prophecy than an extrapolation of the basic tendencies of the system's expansion that was little, if at all, concerned with the particular countries or their national peculiarities. In this historical period, economic, political, and military power were not forgotten; rather, there was confidence in these powers and in the potential of the national states where capitalism had initially developed, guaranteeing them technological progress and a leading role in the world's political affairs that allowed them to act, to reserve the "advantages" of the common system for themselves, while preventing it from spreading to others. The established geopolitical parameters could also permit them to resist and take a forceful stand against the pressures and needs of the geo-economic evolution inherent in the system.

Now, for the past few years, we have been living in a historical phase in which this "immutable" division is beginning to make less and less sense. The development of "multinational corporations" in the 1970s and 1980s marked the period with new features: a considerable increase in direct investments outside the boundaries of the "developed" world; an orientation toward productive investments that led to the delocalization of industrial and, shortly thereafter, of service activities; the division of work within a network of plants established in a growing number of countries; programming and management of the whole in an increasingly "global" context. This was a new beginning or spurt in the expansion of capitalism on a world scale. It began to resemble a real rush after the opening of China in the 1980s and the breakdown of the "socialist camp" after 1989. It was facilitated by technological developments in the fields of information, communications, and transportation, where advances permitted the unification of markets and global management, as well as by changes in economic policies in many countries—candidates for benefiting from the results of the globalization process—toward neoliberalism and deregulation, which are considered essential conditions of globalization under the aegis of businesses focusing on their own globalization.

3. The Consequences and Mitigated Reactions of the Involved Parties

The consequences of the new phase are barely beginning to be felt. The area of capitalist development has expanded to an unprecedented extent, although it does not yet include the entire world: a "fourth world" is appearing that is comprised of the excluded, especially in Africa. Capitalism, released from regulations and political intervention, which are the results of social compromise in the history of developed capitalism, is producing the inequalities inherent in the system with vigor: they are developing on a global scale as well as in the developed capitalist societies. A sort of "fourth world" is emerging there, too, consisting of the unemployed, the "new poor," the excluded, the stateless. The hierarchy of living standards, of wealth and power, is changing globally: the rich and powerful of the world are being brought closer together, as are the poor. The threats and attacks against ecological equilibrium are assuming truly planetary dimensions. The distances between production and consumption are becoming greater than ever; this increases the opacity of the exchanges and products for the citizens and consumers and accentuates the characteristics of a "society at risk," as shown by the crises of "mad cows," dioxins, GMOs (genetically modified organisms), hormone-treated meats, and nitrates in vegetables—creating an acute problem of "nutritional safety"—as well as by the lesser-known problems of radioactive steel products, dangerous children's toys, etc. The same opacity and the same diffusion of uncontrolled centers of economic activity facilitate the growth of criminality and of a parallel and often "black" economy on a scale that makes the official statistics, the economic policy measures that are based on them, and every other attempt at economic and political regulation barely credible.

These are some of the consequences of globalization that cause growing reactions in public opinion and in large sectors of the political world, especially in developed capitalist countries. And this is an interesting differentiation: we are forced to realize that reactions in the countries that accept the trends toward globalization are attenuated and often different. There is no doubt that we deplore the destruction of traditional manufacturing activities that lead to rural exodus and social upheavals, but we are also demanding an intensification of movements that are essential to globalization, such as the new delocalization of businesses, increased free trade (notably of agricultural products, regarding which we do not hesitate to ally ourselves with the United States against the remnants of European protectionism), the rejection of social or environmental regulations, etc. This is mildly paradoxical: globalization, at least in a considerable number of countries, no longer limits itself to destroying old production systems, it installs new ones; it uproots the farmers, but it creates wage earners; and, as some have said with a touch of sarcasm not lacking in realism, "these people are demanding the right to be exploited." In order to understand the political and ideological difficulties of globalized reactions to this phenomenon, we may recall the fiery words of President Boumedienne of Algeria, who demanded the "right to pollute" when the polluting effects of his brand new petroleum and petrochemical industry were pointed out to him.

4. Is This a Matter of Moral Judgment?

This ambiguity renders moral judgments difficult, assuming they have a place in the analysis of contemporary events. Globalization clashes with many of the benefits acquired by developed societies. At the same time, it brings a large number of previously underdeveloped societies into modern development with all their contradictions, disadvantages, and misfortunes. But we are in a poor position to mention them alongside those who have profited from the misery of the former situation.

In addition, judgments of this type would only make sense if we were able to act and modify or completely change the course of globalization—supposing that this is a process that can be controlled by any political subject. Now, and in spite of the current economic situation, it is not a controllable process. The fact that the governments of the United States and European countries are among the defenders and promoters of globalization, whether it is a matter of an ideology that rationalizes globalization or a matter of practical measures that facilitate it, does not prove that globalization is "American" or "European." Can we imagine that by a political upheaval, for example, the United States or some other government would start to combat globalization and succeed in stopping and reversing the trends? On the contrary, it is obvious that they are attempting to derive the maximum advantage from globalization, and that they are succeeding and will succeed as long as political intervention, especially on the part of the greatest emerging power of the previous period, has meaning in a process that is unfolding essentially without a subject and that is a long-term product of the system. And this doubtless will be the case for a long time.

5. A Need for Policy

The excesses and contradictions of globalization are demanding more and more political direction, a new type of regulation that recalls the debates on liberal capitalism and its shift to the mature and organized capitalism of the twentieth century. The crises and wars, the social battles as well as the existence of a "camp" or faction that sees itself as a radical alternative, generally explain this shift. Might there be factors today of a similar force that can push toward worldwide political regulation of globalization? We can see that the pressure of these factors has been strongly diminished by globalization itself: today's technological wars certainly cost more, but at "zero deaths" they no longer pose the social problems of earlier armed conflicts; natural social battles to a large extent are short-circuited by alternatives of delocalization offered to companies and by the regulatory effects of unemployment; the alternative adversary, to the extent that there was one, no longer exists.

On the other hand, the crises of the system itself, as the brief experience of the new phase shows, are much more threatening because of an unprecedented potential scope, a practically and truly global magnitude, a real-time rate of propagation, and an unpredictable destructive force. These are also the effects of the profound interdependence and globalization of the participating economies. If only for these reasons, the need for political direction becomes increasingly pressing; we need only read the statements and even the vocabularies of the highest officials of international bodies and of the governments of large capitalist countries following the recent crisis in southeast Asia to be convinced of this: exhortations for social cohesion, the need for good governance and balanced development, appeals to end corruption, indeed, a surprising argument in favor of democracy. And despite all the neoliberal and noninterventionist formulas that continue to be in effect at the same time, these officials have taken action and spent hundreds of billions of dollars in interventions aimed at preventing the crisis from expanding.

Along with economic crises (restructuring production, financial or stock-market overinvestments), social upheavals and environmental disasters, amplified by globalization, are assuming unprecedented dimensions and are becoming truly global threats. The accelerated pace of economic destructuring and restructuring, social and political excesses, and the liberalization of trade, which could hardly be expected to limit itself to capital and goods alone, are the undeniable factors behind the growth and acceleration of migratory movements, be they legal or clandestine. Certain ideological and cultural movements such as Islamic fundamentalism, because of their value systems and general visions of the world, cannot be assimilated with globalization (which no longer exports a model as it did in the preceding phases, but, on the contrary propagates a non-ideology). These movements raise unsolvable and frightening enigmas in their own logic. The destruction of tropical rain forests, climate changes, the "holes" in the ozone layer, pollution of the seas and ground waters, etc., are becoming even greater economic menaces alongside those threatening the balance of life and nature. None of these have any self-regulation, nor do they have an "invisible hand" that could reestablish a balance, at least not during an acceptable timeframe on the horizon of human life. A demand, an appeal for intervention against "the normal course of things," is rising in the world.

Moreover, whether from the heritage of the past or attempts to organize the future, infra-political but non-negligible forms of regulation have existed for a long time or have been recently implemented: technical organizations of all sorts regulate the mail and air and sea traffic; they define health standards and vaccines and monitor epidemics; they are concerned with protecting endangered species; they provide monitoring and warnings about climatic phenomena, etc. In addition, organizations are taking strong measures concerning monetary issues and loans for development, and recently they have imposed rules on world trade and indirectly on international investment. However, even when their roles are important, as in the case of the World Trade Organization (which has recently and justly been called "the international tribunal for trade"), the responsibilities of these organizations remain partial and limited, and for this reason it is difficult or impossible to establish their political legitimacy (as we saw seen in 1999 in Seattle). The United Nations is only slightly—if at all—suited to regulatory intervention and political guidance of these phenomena, since it is excluded from the areas where it could play such a role, to the gain of the new North Atlantic Treaty Alliance (NATO). More flexible and ad hoc forms of international coordination such as the G7 (Germany, Canada, the United States, France, Great Britain, Italy, and Japan), which is now the G8 since the inclusion of Russia, are not engaged, at least for the time being, in anything more than exchanging viewpoints and rounds of abstract observation without any desire for or attempts at sustained and global action; and even if that were the case or were its ambition, it would resemble an oligarchic directorate much more than a legitimate democratic government.

6. The Summary of a Hypothetical Analysis

Let us summarize these brief thoughts: globalization is not a surprising, exotic, or satanic phenomenon. It is the phase of a new and rapid burst of capitalist development facilitated by a confluence of political and techno-logical circumstances, whose basic conceptual elements, however, contain nothing strictly new. On the contrary, if it were stripped of its features, its servitude, and its previous phase of development, the system that is devel-oping before our eyes bears an enormous resemblance to what we know from our history books about the period before World War I. The novelty of the phase consists of the shift of emphasis from geopolitics to geo-economics. In other words, we could say that the economic "base" of the system is ex-panding and is tending to encompass the entire earth, whereas the political superstructures corresponding to the new phase are not yet either in place or properly implemented to guarantee, accompany, and promote this devel-opment, to attenuate its crises and reduce the threat of its exploding under the pressure of its contradictions, and to assure the conditions for a con-sensus of those who are living within the framework of the social, economic, political, and cultural relations that comprise the system.

Within the capitalistically developed nation-states, this construction of a consensus has always been, according to Gramsci, the preeminent political movement, the establishment of a hegemony in the social and political sys-tem justified by an ideological structure and a worldview (Weltanschauung).

Can we now assert that the process of a hegemonic construction within a nation-state could, by analogy, be transferred to the level of a globalized system, which will allow us to predict the direction of future evolution? Most probably, yes, but the analogy is limited to the obvious need for a new cor-respondence between the economic and the political. That said, the "negoti-ation" of consensus and access to the hegemonic moment in a globalized system raises new problems: the pairing of leaders-led (managers-managed) within the nation-state cannot be reproduced on the global level, where there are a large number of leaders-led pairs, with each partner participating to unequal and differentiated extents in the new mobile and global hierarchy. A negotiated consensus among the leaders of these states does not guaran-tee an internal consensus, and the news gives us plentiful examples of this.

However, a leaders-led consensus above and beyond the state seems totally unrealistic today: it would presuppose the suppression of nation-states, the unification of leaders on a global scale, and effective economic and political mechanisms for the redistribution of power and revenues on the global level. The response to the appeal for political management and regulation of globalization must absolutely come from the nation-states, with everything that this implies in terms of incertitude and instability.

7. For a Political Management of Globalization: The United States and Others—What Do They Think about It, What Can They Do?

In the United States the debate on the political management of globalization is taking place in a particularly harsh manner. The term "leadership" recurs with obsessive frequency in the great majority of articles on and analyses of international politics. Coupled with marked repugnance for all politicized approaches to the issues of globalization, this gives a very clear indication of how the new period is conceived: in a process of general depoliticization, the United States alone would play a political role in leading world affairs, in the stability and development of globalization. To obtain an idea of this it is sufficient to read the headlines of articles in the *International Herald Tribune*, for example, that reflect global ambition from an American perspective. They are written mostly in the imperative (do, say, remember, do not forget, boycott, etc.) and are clearly addressed to the government and the elite of the United States. They deal with practically all aspects of world politics and give orders to follow necessary courses of action, sometimes bizarrely recalling the style of traditional left-wing newspapers. The American ambition is understandable, and according to many analysts it is justified and founded on real relationships of force that emerged during the preceding phase, that is, the Cold War and bipolarism.

What is the response of the United States' actual policy to these problems? Several writers analyze it as an imperial structure oriented toward the imposition of a new order through direct force or through political intervention on behalf of American businesses and American concepts of world organization and globalization.

8. "Hegemony" and Power: Uncertain Options and Perspectives

Since political management is "hegemonic" by definition, it assumes that along with forceful imposition there is also consensus, and the latter is equivalent to a certain acceptance of the new order on the part of the "led." This acceptance is the result of the realization that the interests of the "led" are taken into account, obviously to a certain extent, and one that they can readily conceive. And it is precisely this extent and its interpretation that raises problems and creates instability. The task becomes even more difficult if we take into account the fact that the sole superpower must be able to satisfy the whole world "to a certain extent" in this effort toward true hegemony; in the words of an American proverb, "when you are the rainmaker you are also responsible for drought!" The current issue of the underlying geopolitical problems and the modern geo-economic problems, such as those of the new geopolitics that is developing on the horizon, offers many examples and impossibilities, including examples of the rainmaker's ineffectiveness and abstentions, all of which contribute to accentuating the uncertainties and shadows of the future.

In fact—and it is hardly provocative to state this—the United States, in order to respond to this dialectic of hegemony, should gradually begin to denationalize itself, which is effectively and eminently contradictory. In any event, aspects of this debate often appear in the classic opposition between isolationists and internationalists in that country.

The alternative of pure violence obviously remains an option, but it is hard to see what problems it can resolve: the problems of globalization are not essentially problems of force, even if we cannot ignore this dimension. In any case, it is hard to see how we can resolve the problems of globalization in a way compatible with the sophisticated technology of "Star Wars." American experts are aware of this when they refer to explosive social and political upheavals which they have the unfortunate tendency to reduce to terrorism and fundamentalism, like the new threats that they feel—and declare—themselves poorly prepared to face on a world level.

The directions that American and world policies will take remain uncertain, all the more so since these directions will be the result of many factors other than American considerations alone. In the context of the new phase and within a reasonably foreseeable time frame, new economic powers are developing; they are difficult to manipulate, both in the traditional geopolitical framework and in the new one that is taking shape. One of these powers is already very present; its choices and its destiny will, to a large extent, prefigure the architecture and operations of tomorrow's world. Europe is an essential element of the current architecture, and it is vitally important to know if it will also be so in the architecture of tomorrow, and with what influence.

9. Europe: Starting from a History and an Ambition

Europe, even at the current level of unfulfilled political unification, seems to have anticipated globalization. But in fact, at least up to the beginning of the 1990s, it has especially been the answer to a series of questions deriving from the contradictions of an earlier period: that of the predominance of the nation-state. Europe expressly aspired to the reconciliation of the two large nation-states on whom the peace of the continent depended. Certainly, through the logic of integration as it was envisioned by its founding fathers, this Europe went beyond the needs of the postwar period and already prefigured a structure of global magnitude, a leading geopolitical role. Today it is faced with existential dilemmas because its ambitions are beginning to clash with the current trends of globalization.

Globalization's trends toward liberalization and deregulation, the equalization of production conditions, and the differentiation of growth levels and rates, are also pushing toward the suppression of political intervention and even of politics, and hence the modification of the essential political European plan and of European integration, among that of other regions in a globalized, free market.

The European Union's initial tendency toward economic unity corresponded in part to the tendencies and challenges of this process: the member states dismantled their tariff, economic, and administrative boundaries. This could have been a step in the right direction. But as the Union gradually moved ahead along the path of common policies and collective political ambitions, it caused reactions by its partners in globalization: from the trade "wars" that were caused by the development of the Common Agricultural Policy (CAP), to the recent political opposition regarding a European identity within NATO. Probably the decisive step was taken with the creation of the single currency and its inevitable institutional and political consequences: the unification of economic policy; a first step toward a real European Policy of Common Security; and the expansion on a continental scale of a plan that amounts to much more than simple geographic expansion, since it encompasses the political sphere and all the European Community's achievements. In both cases, the strengthening of the Union and the expansion of its area of influence, the political element should theoretically tend to be strengthened, at least potentially. This is a source of mounting contradictions with the spontaneous trends of globalization defined, for the time being, only on the economic level. European unification is finding itself more and more openly in conflict with the imperatives of globalization as it is occurring today. The examples of the battles that it wages within the World Trade Organization are extremely telling.

10. Scenarios of Resignation or Illusion

In Europe we do not generally discuss these problems in terms of leadership. We tend to deal with them in defensive terms, i.e., of survival. This seems to correspond to the real situation: Europe is becoming "smaller and smaller" in globalized economics and politics. The purely European political domain is not yet large enough to produce a debate and a decision-making process with purely European criteria and objectives. The intergovernmental and the community come together in unwieldy and ineffective syntheses. Europe is still continuing to chase events and changes that it has difficulty grasping, mastering, and influencing. One need only observe how quickly revisions of treaties follow one another, each one announced just when the previous one has been ratified, and the reforms that provide responses to challenges (economic in the case of the WTO, geopolitical in the case of the war against Yugoslavia, and in launching the new NATO and excluding the United Nations) which have already created *faits accomplis.*

Given these rather pessimistic comments, the scenario of resignation, albeit unacknowledged, seems to be making headway. It does not openly reveal the necessary sacrifices and expected "advantages," but more and more often it is coming up in concrete debates on European institutions, on legislation, or on foreign policy. In general this slows down the unification process (if it is not making it move backwards), and in one way or another, it is tearing down the European political structure, abandoning attempts or possibilities for intervention in the evolution of things. The advantages will be flexibility in adapting to globalization conceived as a one-way street; growth released from political, social, and ecological bonds, mutually defined, and hence stronger and more effective; cooperation and a more harmonious and fruitful alliance with the sole superpower of this era. And with what consequences for the other elements of European unification, which are probably incorrectly considered obvious and given? Could a level of European integration that is certainly lower than what has been achieved to date and that could be "tolerated" by this scenario be maintained if the project of unification which justifies the partial and progressive, yet not always satisfactory, transfer of sovereignty were abandoned? It is highly unlikely, and on the contrary, another historical movement would develop toward a recovery of these transfers. We would probably have no more than a Europe of a dozen nation-states weakened by globalization, which could be multiplied by armed interventions creating micro-states as a non-response to the complicated issues that demand new and daring European responses (as is currently the case in the Balkans, a real "black hole" of Europe which is expanding). Instead, we would have a geopolitical and geo-economic landscape that bears a strong resemblance to a large-scale Jurassic Park.

And yet, the trends that seem to support this scenario are not inevitable. Europe is not yet so "small" that it cannot affect the development of globalization. Its member states could easily realize that being a "lone knight" guarantees only transitory advantages, whether it is a question of the special relationship between Great Britain and the United States; the ambition to become the platform for Japanese investments in Europe; wars in Europe and elsewhere, decided outside any coordinated common effort by Great Britain and France; the refusal on the part of Great Britain, Sweden, and Denmark to join the Economic and Monetary Union; or the temptation to manage certain aspects of globalization through individual participation in the G8 (or perhaps the G9 once an invitation is extended to China).

The Economic and Monetary Union and the euro, but also the recent decisions concerning defense and the new planning of the enlargement process and its completion that have been announced with a new revision of the treaties in 2000, offer Europe real possibilities of growth, from the state of being a "political midget" to that of an indispensable partner, not only in the current geo-economy, but also in the new geopolitical scenario of regulated and politically organized globalization.

This new role for Europe cannot be defined and inscribed in the framework of the preceding period. It must seek allies and propose hegemonic solutions in the sense defined above, that is, not to resist or to defend itself against globalization, but to make a decisive contribution in mastering it. Europe more than others has the "winning cards" to be able to work effectively in this direction, since it is something other than a nation-state of the past, and it is accustomed to working while respecting a complicated consensus that involves states and their citizens. Thus, should we reinforce European unity, especially political unity, in order to better resist the trends and pressure of globalization? And what will be the consequences of further expansion for this hypothetical state, which confronts formidable dilemmas in such a perspective? Or for relations with the United States and the rest of the world? Or for the world economy as we know it today?

These are two strategies that must be discussed fully, directly, and in all their ramifications, not just by allusions. The first greatly resembles an abdication, the second an illusion. In any event, these are answers to the questions that Europe is asking about itself. And what if Europe asked these questions in relation to the problems that globalization is raising for the rest of the world in almost the same terms?

11. Toward a European Contribution to Global Political Management

What if, for example, we asked the question of the limits and serious risks of globalization left to itself, without a historical project or plan of action, without political, social, and ecological—indeed cultural and moral—regulation? In this case the need for a process of overall structuring of the world would be evident. Certainly it would have to be undertaken step by step and with political and institutional innovations on a historical scale, indeed, on the scale of the real challenges that are already present: those of globalization! Because of its history and political culture Europe would be better suited than any other political entity to make proposals that would safeguard this historical project and build on what already exists—separate peoples and states—with the original and hence legitimate methods of political and democratic management. The process of globalization could then be transformed from something inevitable to something desirable. Certainly Europe could do all this provided it rapidly attains the status of a political entity. But we must also admit that this will only create the possibility of having a voice and the means for making it heard. On the other hand, what Europe says and what it will be able to do, once it has these possibilities, depends on other factors and specifically on the debate and the struggle that are still lacking on the level of analyses, expectations, and political relations based on power.

CHAPTER 12

Globalization and Environmental Protection

ALEXANDRE KISS

If there exists a domain in which globalization is inherent, it is that of the environment. Economic globalization is a product of ideology and market strategies, that of communications is the result of technological advances, and that of civilization is the result of the combined globalization of economic activities and communications.

The environment is different. Human activities necessitate a global approach not because these activities stem from intentionally harmful policies and strategic planning, but because they inevitably and often unwittingly cause environmental degradation. To give one example, the threats to biological diversity are certainly anthropogenic, but the harmful activities are usually undertaken without awareness or understanding of the real effects they produce on the biosphere and the importance of their impact. Merely stating and understanding this problem makes evident its global character. Intensification of communications has certainly played a crucial role in raising and disseminating awareness of ecological problems, so much

Alexandre Kiss is director of research emeritus at the National Center for Scientific Research, France. He is president of the European Council for Environmental Law, and vice-president of the International Institute of Human Rights. He has published five books and approximately 350 articles in a dozen languages. He has taught throughout Europe, Africa, the Americas, and Asia. He is consultant to nearly all international organizations concerned with environmental protection.

so that environmental consciousness now extends throughout the global village in which we live.

Global awareness does not mean that deterioration of the environment at local, regional, national, and international levels was not subject to actions and reactions even before this form of globalization was understood. It is useful to briefly examine the motivations which have guided such responses, before attempting a synthesis of societal reactions. The conclusion draws out several broad tendencies which seem important in this field at the dawn of the twenty-first century.

I. Why Protect the Environment?

Even the term "environment" is new in many languages, including French (*environnement*), German (*Umwelt*), Dutch (*miljeu*), Spanish (*medio ambiente*), and Italian (*ambiente*). Based on their current understanding, scientists today point to increased levels of pollution over short and long distances, depletion of the stratospheric ozone layer, reduction in biological diversity, and anthropogenic climate change as wake-up calls which should incite action to avoid fatal degradation of the biosphere over the long term.

The problem of human relations with nature and its elements can be traced back through history. Over time, an evolving series of motivations has appeared to protect that which today is denominated the environment. In the beginning, the belief systems of numerous ancient civilizations of Africa, the Americas, and Asia viewed the earth as the mother goddess of humanity. She was seen as sacred and her animals and plants were entitled to respect.

Belief that the universe belongs to God, its creator, is a concept common to the three great monotheistic religions. In the book of Genesis, a text common to Judaism, Christianity, and Islam, God warns Noah, a good man, of the impending flood and orders him to construct an ark in which he will take not only humans but also males and females of every species "to keep seed alive upon the face of all the earth." And "they went in unto Noah into the ark, two and two of all flesh, wherein is the breath of life." After several months, "God remembered Noah, and every living thing, and all the cattle that was with him in the ark," and the waters were abated. At the end of the flood, although God had given humans power to reign over all the other species, he established his Covenant not only with humans, but also with "every living creature."[1] Islam emphasizes that man executes divine commandments; he is the manager and not the owner of the earth; he can enjoy its fruits but not dispose of it. From this derives the responsibility of humans to safeguard and conserve creation, albeit humans enjoy rights of utilization and development.[2]

Another conception with a long tradition is that man is part of nature and thus should respect the other elements to which he is linked. A Buddhist text, dating from the third century before the present era, reports a sermon on Buddhism in which the son of an emperor recalls that the birds of the air and the beasts have as equal a right to live and move about as the king himself; the earth belongs to the people and all living beings and humans are only its guardians.[3]

This same conception reappears in new forms: humanity is part of the biosphere, the only place in the universe where life is possible, and thus man cannot destroy the biosphere without destroying himself. The World Charter of Nature, adopted and solemnly proclaimed by the United Nations General Assembly on October 28, 1986, recalls that "Mankind is a part of nature and life depends on the uninterrupted functioning of natural systems which ensure the supply of energy and nutrients . . . every form of life is unique, warranting respect, regardless of its worth to man, and, to accord other organisms such recognition, man must be guided by a moral code of action."[4] In sum, humanity ought to be considered as one species among millions, comprising part of the global ecosystem.

A third concept is anthropocentric. Seemingly born in the eighteenth century, it proclaims that man should manage and improve nature for his own benefit. This conviction was integrated in certain ideologies prophesying a new society where man would be the sole master of the universe, subordinating all to the satisfaction of human needs. The materialism that permeated Western societies, progressively extending to the rest of the world, led to the unparalleled exploitation of the biosphere, considered and significantly described as the sum of the utilizable natural resources. Even the first manifestations of concern to protect aspects of the environment were explicitly anthropocentric: specific elements of the environment, such as fish stocks, birds, and fur seals, were managed because of their utility for mankind.

With the growing awareness of the dangers menacing the biosphere, a more global economic explanation emerged during the 1970s. It perceived elements of the environment as natural resources necessary to life and to the development of economic systems. Traditionally, the list of resources has been limited to arable land, forests, minerals, wild plants, and animals. Unpolluted oceans, fresh water, and clean air only now became elements of economic value to be taken into account, and the cost of their use internalized. This naturally led to the principle of rational utilization and optimal use of natural resources.

Less materialistic conceptions, based on ethical principles, also placed humans at the center of environmental concerns, but took into account moral considerations. Thus, the "right to environment" of each individual, which is increasingly recognized as a right, linked environmental protection to human needs. One of its formulations incorporates the temporal dimension in seeking to take into account not only the present needs of humanity, but also those of future generations of humanity. The most common expression of this today is the concept of "sustainable development," development which does not compromise the capacity of future generations to satisfy their own needs.[5] This conception could lead to long-term thinking, based on the fact that human existence on the earth is a relatively recent phenomenon, not necessarily a permanent given of life on the planet. It is thus indispensable to safeguard the biosphere.

A synthesis of these different concepts could be founded on the recently developed principle of "environmental justice" and its three aspects. In the first place, it signifies equity among humans living today: they should share environmental benefits and burdens in endeavoring to meet the basic needs of all. Secondly, it demands intergenerational equity between present and future generations. Finally, it introduces the concept of equity between species, between humans and other living things.

The ultimate consequence of these developments is globalization, posing the problem of environmental protection for the entire planet. Overall, it can be seen that the natural tendency of environmental problems is to impose themselves on the political and economic structures of the world. At the end of the 1960s, international legal instruments recalled that the environment knows no frontiers. In the 1980s it became recognized that the major threats to the biosphere have a global character: depletion of the stratospheric ozone, climate change, desertification, deforestation, rapid loss of biological diversity, and exhaustion or pollution of natural resources such as fish stocks or fresh waters. No country, no continent, however powerful, is capable of responding to these problems alone. Globalization is imposed by the necessity of solidarity in the face of these threats.

2. How Can the Environment Be Preserved?

How can a single indivisible environment be preserved? A dialectical method appears the best adapted to attempt a synthesis of reactions from the "global village" to the new challenges. On the one hand, all legal authorities at every governance level—local, national, regional, international—should take action to respond to environmental dangers. On the other hand, the role of individuals and groups becomes increasingly important.

In any structured society, human or even animal, there exists a concept of common good whose safeguarding is a condition of survival, or at least the good functioning of the society. Safeguarding the common good, whether tangible or intangible, is in the general interest. It is evident that this last should govern the particular interests of individuals and groups which compose the society. In this regard, societies have recognized the general interest as including actions to defend against external or internal aggression, protection of public health, education of the young, protection of fundamental rights of individuals, and, for the past thirty years, environmental protection.

The problem of environmental protection as a whole involves global dimensions and the interests of all humanity, who must be responsible for its safeguarding. Thus is born the awareness of a general global interest in this field, as part of the general interest of humanity which also includes human rights, maintenance of peace, and human development.

A principle formulated by the International Court of Justice in 1996 and reaffirmed in 1997 may be recalled in this regard. The environment is not an abstraction, but rather the space where human beings live and on which depends their quality of life and their health, including future generations.[6] Thus, the concept of the general interest of humanity must be translated into concrete realities. The question is who determines the public interest at the general level and in daily life.

Preservation of the Environment: The General Interest of Humanity

Within each state a fundamental act, the constitution, announces the principles which define the basic values that guide the action of authorities and other citizens. The state's legislature and executive must determine the general interest and act on it case by case, within legal limits

In the society of states, which is largely global society, there is scarcely a constitution or legislature, no executive, and no mandatory judicial branch. The concepts and principles expressing fundamental values which humanity should respect are proclaimed for the most part by all or a large majority of states. The procedure is to inscribe these values in treaties or sometimes in nonbinding instruments, such as the Universal Declaration of Human Rights of 1948, the Stockholm Declaration on the Human Environment of 1972, and the Rio Declaration on the Environment and Development of 1992. The principal characteristic of international instruments which define the elements of the general interest of humanity is that the states which have accepted them derive no immediate advantage. The instruments contain only obligations, which can weigh heavily on states and restrain their sovereignty by requiring them, e.g., to protect the fundamental rights of all those who are within their territory, assure the survival of living species, and disallow certain activities that harm the environment of other states, or even their own.

One of the first international instruments that reflect the concept of the general interest of humanity in the field of the environment is the Antarctica Treaty of December 1, 1959. This text declares in the preamble that in the interest of all humanity the sixth continent should be forever reserved for peaceful activities,[7] but it also foresees that the contracting parties should jointly formulate measures relative to the protection and conservation of flora and fauna in Antarctica (Art. 9.1.f).[8] Subsequently, this idea was developed in Canberra on May 20, 1980, with the adoption of the Convention on the Conservation of Antarctic Marine Living Resources, whose preamble recalls for its part that it is in the interest of all humanity to reserve the waters around Antarctica to exclusively peaceful purposes. Above all, the Madrid Protocol of October 4, 1991, expresses this concept. It recalls the designation of Antarctica as a special conservation zone (preamble) before renaming it a nature reserve consecrated to peace and science (Art. 2). One of the paragraphs in the preamble of the Madrid Protocol expresses the conviction of the contracting parties that the development of a global regime of environmental protection in Antarctica and its dependent and associated ecosystems is in the common interest of all humanity.[9]

A series of international conventions related to the conservation of living species as part of the general interest of humanity affirms the same principle. In 1946 the International Convention for the Regulation of Whaling recognized "the interest of the nations of the world in safeguarding for future generations the great natural resources represented by the whale stocks."[10] The preamble of the African Convention for the Conservation of Nature and Natural Resources of 1968 speaks, for its part, of action to ensure conservation, utilization, and development of soil, water, and the resources of flora and fauna that constitute a capital "for the present and future welfare of mankind."[11]

This idea is developed in the Convention of Washington of 1973 on International Trade in Endangered Species of Wild Fauna and Flora. Its preamble recognizes that "wild fauna and flora in their many beautiful and varied forms are an irreplaceable part of the natural systems of the earth which must be protected for this and the generations to come" and adds that peoples and states are, and should be, the best protectors of their own wild fauna and flora. Thus, it proclaims a general interest of present and future generations of humanity in safeguarding species threatened with extinction, on the one hand, and imposes obligations to undertake such protection, on the other.[12]

The Bonn Convention of 1979 on the Conservation of Migratory Species of Wild Animals takes up the same ideas and develops them:

> The Contracting Parties
>
> Recognizing that wild animals in their innumerable forms are an irreplaceable part of the earth's natural system which must be conserved for the good of mankind;
>
> Aware that each generation of man holds the resources of the earth for future generations and has an obligation to ensure that this legacy is conserved and, where utilized, is used wisely;
>
> Recognizing that the States are and must be the protectors of the migratory species of wild animals that live within or pass through their national jurisdictional boundaries. . . .[13]

Adopted several months later, the Bern Convention of September 19, 1979, on the Conservation of European Wildlife and Natural Habitats declares that "wild flora and fauna constitute a natural heritage of aesthetic, scientific, cultural, recreational, economic and intrinsic value that needs to be preserved and handed on to future generations."[14]

The Convention on Biological Diversity opened for signature by states during the June 1992 Conference of Rio de Janeiro on Environment and Development equally declares in its preamble that "the conservation of biological diversity is a common concern of humankind."[15] Similarly, the Framework Convention on Climate Change opened for signature during the same Conference proclaims that "change in the Earth's climate and its adverse effects are a common concern of humankind" and that the States are determined "to protect the climate system for present and future generations."[16]

An international instrument from another legal domain, the protection of human rights, shows that environmental protection has been recognized as being part of the general interest of humanity beyond the framework of environmental agreements. Article 11 of the Protocol Additional to the American Convention on Human Rights in the Area of Economic, Social, and Cultural Rights, adopted at San Salvador on November 17, 1988, provides that "the States Parties shall promote the protection, preservation and improvement of the environment."[17]

Parallel to the evolution taking place on the international level, a growing number of constitutions impose on states the obligation to protect the environment. In a progressive development, the European Community recognized first implicitly, then explicitly, that environmental protection constitutes an essential component of its action. It is thus universally recognized that the conservation of the biosphere is one of the essential aspects of the general interest which should be safeguarded and should guide public authorities at all levels.

Is the General Interest Respected by Cooperation between States?

Are the international proclamations translated into action? In general, the problem is to determine to what extent the behavior of the principal actors, the states, is really influenced by statements and instruments that express the general interest of humanity. The task is extremely difficult. How is it possible to evaluate the effectiveness, that is, the effective respect given to norms generally, be they religious, moral, social, or legal? In most cases, only violations of norms receive attention: no one notices the pedestrians who await a green light before traversing the road or the citizens who regularly pay their taxes. The application of law by courts is founded precisely on situations where a violation of law is alleged.

On the international level a distinction is made in the application of international instruments, whether treaties and instruments, that are formally nonbinding, such as Agenda 21 adopted by the Rio Conference in 1992. First, an international norm is legally applicable in states party to an instrument when that norm is incorporated into the laws of those states, which can be automatic upon agreement to the instrument or can require a formal domestic legal enactment. But it is not always certain that the norm now incorporated will actually be applied: the state may lack the political will or the means to do so. The example of the prohibition on international trade in specimens of endangered species illustrates the situation. The battle against poachers, smuggling, and the black market can require considerable funds and a strong will on the part of public authorities. Other factors are relevant, such as lack of training for customs officials and the police who should regulate imports and exports. These factors can also hamper the application of norms prohibiting such trade. Thus, the promulgation of international norms within states is not always enough: their effective application may require the adoption of other rules and policies, as well as the marshaling of considerable means.

Two responses are possible. The first is to utilize or create international mechanisms which induce states to go beyond the simple promulgation or legal incorporation of international norms. Initially, it is tempting to think of international responsibility in terms of rules that would oblige a state in violation of an international norm to repair the resulting damage. However, international responsibility does not play an effective role in this area because of a series of obstacles difficult to overcome. Notably, proving the causal link between the wrongful act and deterioration of the environment is extremely problematic, given the possible multiplicity of actors and acts and the possible intervention of natural causes, such as fog that aggravates air pollution or catastrophic rains. The example of the nuclear accident at Chernobyl demonstrates the limits of application of the rules of responsibility: How could it be proven that a case of cancer arising since April 26, 1986, in the region of the accident was caused by radioactivity released into the environment? Instead, unofficial claims focused on the cost of preventive measures, such as the prohibition on eating vegetables and fruits, but the Soviet Union rejected the idea that these measures, whose severity varied from one country to the next, were truly necessary.

It is essential, therefore, to pursue other methods which could assure a better application of global rules. These methods are also global, for they appeal to a certain will of states to appear virtuous in respecting the general interest represented by environmental protection. They consist of demanding from governments a report on the manner in which they apply international conventions, with the understanding that these reports will be discussed by the totality of states party to the convention, sometimes in the presence of associations for the protection of the environment. The most advanced methods in this area permit a state which cannot satisfy its obligations to call for aid from other states in order to bring its actions into conformity with its obligations.

A second type of approach that should encourage better application of norms of environmental protection is international cooperation. Global environmental conventions contain numerous clauses anticipating aid to developing countries, including financial assistance, transfer of technology, education, and training to develop technical and administrative capacities.

Thus globalization, in the sense of the solidarity of every state in the world in the face of threats to the environment, is an important factor in the preservation of the common heritage. But what position should be taken on globalization in the sense in which the term is most often used: the institution of global free trade?

It is useful to recall the problem that appeared during the 1970s in the European Common Market because of the emergence of the "ecological era." Free circulation of goods, services, and capital was the founding principle of the institution; the newer preoccupations were ignored by the constitutive texts because the texts were drafted in the 1950s. While certain member states of the European Community already had developed rules to protect the environment, others had much less in the way of legal regulation. There was thus a risk that the old phrase "good money chases after bad" would find a new application in this field, with good environmental regulations being weakened because of the supplementary costs of production they impose that distort competition. The choices were either to let this happen, at the risk of rendering impossible any environmental protection within the European Community, or to impose common rules. The latter was the path taken, and despite the absence of any direct allusion to the environment in the Treaties of Paris and Rome, a large amount of Community legislation has been created essentially on the basis of Article 100 of the Treaty of Rome, which provides for the harmonization of national laws having a direct effect on the establishment or functioning of the common market. The juridical basis of about 150 Community instruments adopted in this way was only made explicit in 1986 by the Single European Act, followed by the Treaties of Maastricht and Amsterdam.[18]

This example provides food for thought about economic globalization. Without the establishment of legal frameworks limiting the freedom of exchanges that environmental protection in the general interest of humanity requires, the existing protective measures could disappear.

However, it is necessary to pose the question whether the measures taken by the states are well-adapted to the problem; as a general rule, can the politics of the environment, which are inevitable, respond to the needs for environmental protection? One of the principal problems with environmental protection is the time lag between public or private action and the demands of environmental protection. Too often, governments, like the heads of corporations, are obliged to think and act in the short term: the date of the next elections or the annual meeting of shareholders. The environment, in contrast, consists of natural processes which can change over years, even decades: repopulation of wooded areas, rehabilitation of a river or lake. Besides, environmental deterioration may only manifest itself after many years, such as the drying of a wetland or pollution of underground aquifers.

Prevention requires the adoption of scientifically-based measures with a long-term objective. Since the beginning of the 1990s the principle of precaution has added supplementary considerations which should be taken into account to avoid irreversible or serious harm to the environment, even in the absence of scientific certainty quantifying the risk.

Of course this last principle theoretically concerns only those who must make the decisions, but in reality it is also addressed to the public, which has been made increasingly aware of the problems by ecological catastrophes. It is useful, therefore, to consider the role of individuals and groups in safeguarding the environment, in recognition of the public interest.

Role of Individuals and Groups

Given the inevitable globalization, the role of individuals has been affirmed since the beginning of what may be called the "ecological era." One of the founding documents of environmental protection, the Declaration of the Stockholm Conference of 1973, begins by proclaiming the fundamental right of man to live in an environment whose quality permits him to live in dignity and well-being and, at the same time, imposes a solemn obligation to protect and improve the environment for present and future generations. The first formulation of this right in an international treaty is found in the African Charter of Human and Peoples Rights of 1981. Its article 24 guarantees all peoples the right to a general satisfactory environment favorable to their development.[19] Similarly, Article 11 of the Protocol Additional to the American Convention on Human Rights in the Area of Economic, Social, and Cultural Rights affirms that each person has the right to life in a healthy environment.[20]

From the numerous debates over the content of the right thus proclaimed and whether its violation would be susceptible to sanctions by the tribunals, there is general agreement that it is above all a procedural right which can be formulated as "the right to the protection of the environment," comparable to the right to life or the right to personal security. Like these last, in order to guarantee rights, the state must prevent and sanction any attempted violations of them. As for the environment, it is a question of recognizing the right of the public to information on the environment and on its potential modifications, the right to participate in decisions that can affect the environment, and the right of access to remedies in case of violation of these rights.

The European Community has contributed largely to this evolution, notably by imposing the obligation to inform the public, among other things, about the quality of bathing waters, about requests for licensing permits for industries that cause air pollution, about the risk of major accidents, and in general about projects submitted to environmental impact assessment procedures. Directive 90/313 of June 7, 1990, on freedom of access to information about the environment made general the duty to inform the public about anything which can affect the environment.[21] The Rio Declaration on Environment and Development adopted in June 1992 took this procedural interpretation of the "right to environment" to the global level:

> Environmental issues are best handled with the participation of all concerned citizens, at the relevant level. At the national level, each individual shall have appropriate access to information concerning the environment that is held by public authorities, including information on hazardous materials and activities in their communities, and the opportunity to participate in decision-making processes. States shall facilitate and encourage public awareness and participation by making information widely available. Effective access to judicial and administrative proceedings, including redress and remedy, shall be provided. (Principle 10)

This text is not legally binding, but the principle has been developed in detail for Europe and North America by a treaty, the Aarhus Convention of June 25 1998, on information, public participation in decision making, and access to justice in environmental matters.[22]

These developments on the legal plane were in part preceded and in part accompanied by developments within civil society, which has organized itself, thanks to growing awareness of problems that concern all individuals, primarily in three areas: the protection of human rights, consumer protection, and environmental protection. In regard to the last, public opinion from the beginning (during the last half of the 1960s) was characterized by its international nature. The presence at the Stockholm Conference of 1972 and the Rio Conference twenty years later of thousands of representatives of environmental protection associations, not to mention the demonstrators at the World Trade Organization (WTO) Conference in Seattle in 1999, manifest the birth of an international civil society alongside states and intergovernmental organizations.

Civil society, both national and global, actually comprises three categories of actors. Individuals and groups that seek to protect the environment, often protesting against pollution and other attacks on the natural world, are increasingly frequent partners of public authorities in the elaboration of policy and concrete measures. They can even exercise their influence during international meetings examining the application of conventions or negotiating new international instruments. A second group, not necessarily an adversary to the first, represents economic interests trying to weigh in on decisions of concern to them. Their influence can contribute to the adoption of realistic solutions: witness the negotiating history of the conventional system for the protection of stratospheric ozone during the second half of the 1980s. Industrial groups may also elaborate their own environmental norms to be applied by their members, such as ISO 14000 of the International Standards Organization on systems of environmental management. Finally, a third element of civil society is less visible, but not necessarily less effective: this consists of the epistemic communities composed of experts who do not necessarily know each other, but who share the same knowledge and the same convictions about our relations with the biosphere. For all that they are often invisible, they can exercise a considerable influence on the other groups.

It follows from this discussion that the principle of responsibility is the foundation of the role of society in environmental protection. On the one hand, the "right to environment" under its triple aspect of information, participation, and access to justice only makes sense if citizens make use of it. Like any right, this new right carries with it responsibility. On the other hand, civil society—local, national, regional, or global—is founded on the sense of responsibility to define and protect that which is recognized as the general interest.

Should protection of the environment, thus proclaimed as part of the general interest, be confided to public authorities or to civil society? Can there not be a synthesis akin to that of the two conceptions discussed above—first the general interests of humanity, and second the responsibility of individuals and groups—taking into account the different motivations which may justify such an approach? Can this also surmount the difficulty posed by the existence of so many different levels of responsibility, decision, and action?

3. The Global Village: Can It Resolve the Problem of Protecting the Biosphere?

The preceding discussion has described two types of tension. The first exists between, on the one hand, the global dimensions of the problem of environmental deterioration and the necessity to protect the environment, and, on the other hand, the different levels of decision and action. The second seems to oppose the role of public authorities—national, supranational, or international—to the roles of civil society in the definition and safeguarding of the public interest represented by the environment.

The solution can perhaps be found in the idea of the "global village," which has so well expressed the phenomenon of globalization. One of the characteristics of a village is the existence and multiplicity of links between its inhabitants. These are increasingly found on the global level as well: they are the essence of globalization, which gives rise to a responsibility, also global, that must be assumed in part by the international community and in part by individuals. From this perspective the principal question that arises is how to distribute the responsibilities among the various actors.

A response to this question involves a legal technique which is increasingly recognized as a general principle: subsidiarity. Well known among specialists of European Community law, its application can be usefully extended across different issues to allocate competences in a given domain. In the domain of the environment, problems should be resolved by the different actors by rigorously following the principle which demands that resolution begins from the smallest unit. Thus, the first level of environmental protection should be individual behavior. It should consist of electing to reduce waste and to avoid destroying wild flora and fauna. A larger grouping is necessary to resolve those problems that cannot be addressed by the individual: social sanction of neighbors or legal measures at the municipal level. This fashion of proceeding is inspired in part by a concept of human rights that aims at assuring the maximum liberty of action for the individual, and in part by the norms of a democracy that favor local consensus and regional action over centralized decisions, as a way of affording maximum respect for local conditions. It is evident that global action is needed for the largest problems and will necessitate cooperation among all people and all states. The simple adage "think globally, act locally" expresses in reality the fundamental rule of the game in a globalized and diverse world.

NOTES

1. Genesis 7:3, 7:15, 8:1, 9:10.
2. World Conservation Union (I.U.C.N.), *Environmental Protection in Islam*, 2d ed., IUCN Environmental Policy and Law Paper no. 20 rev. 1994, pp. 2–3.
3. Mahavamsa, chapter 14.
4. Resolution 37/7.

5. See Christian Stoeffaës, "Le développement durable comme idéologie," in *Espérances et menaces de l'an 2000* (Paris: Descartes et Cie, 1999), p. 13f.

6. *Legality of the Threat or Use by a State of Nuclear Weapons in Armed Conflicts* (Advisory Opinion), 1996, International Court of Justice (I.C.J.) paragraph 29, and *Case Concerning the Gabcikovo-Nagymaros Project,* 1997, I.C.J. paragraph 53f.

7. EMT 980:39. In *International Environmental Law: Environmental Multilateral Treaties* (The Hague, Boston: Kluwer, 1991).

8. EMT 959: 91.

9. EMT 991:74.

10. EMT 947:76.

11. EMT 968:68.

12. EMT 973:18.

13. EMT 979:55.

14. EMT 979:70.

15. EMT 992:42.

16. Art. 3 al.1, EMT 992:35.

17. 28 International Legal Materials (I.L.M.) 156 (1989).

18. See in particular Articles 15–152 of the October 2, 1997, Amsterdam Treaty on European Union.

19. 21 I.L.M. 59 (1982).

20. 28 I.L.M. 156 (1989).

21. Official Journal of the European Community (OJEC), no. L 158, June 23, 1990.

22. EMT 998:48.

REFERENCES

Apostolides, C., G. Fritz, and J.-C. Fritz. *L'humanité face à la mondialisation: Droit des peuples et environnement.* Paris: L'Harmattan, 1997.

Barrère, M. *Terre, patrimoine commun: La science au service de l'environnement et du développement.* Paris: La Découverte, 1992.

Bosselmann, K., and B. J. Richardson. *Environmental Justice and Market Mechanisms: Key Challenges for Environmental Law and Policy.* London: Kluwer Law International, 1999.

Le Cercle des économistes. *Espérances et menaces de l'an 2000.* Paris: Descartes et Cie, 1999.

Collège de la prévention des risques technologiques. *Le risque technologique et la démocratie.* Paris: Documentation française, 1994.

Coste, R., and J. P. Ribaut. *Sauvegarde et gérance de la création.* Paris: Desclée, 1991.

Kiss, A., and D. Shelton. *International Environmental Law.* 2d ed. Ardsley, New York: Transnational Publishers, 2000.

Rens, I. *Le droit international face à l'éthique et à la politique de l'environnement.* Stratégies énergétiques, biosphère et société (SEBES). Geneva, 1996.

United Nations Environmental Program (UNEP). *Global Environment Outlook.* London: Earthscan Publications, 1999.

CHAPTER 13

Actors in a Globalized Society: "Médecins du Monde"

JACKY MAMOU

INTERVIEW CONDUCTED BY
MARINA RICCIARDELLI AND SABINE URBAN

I. "Médecins du Monde," A Nongovernmental Organization (NGO)
Operating on a Worldwide Scale

Sabine Urban: In this era of globalization, we are seeing an explosion in the number of NGOs, a sort of new player operating on a world scale in the crucial areas of human existence (humanitarian action, human rights, environmental protection, etc.). Despite the attention these organizations have received from the news media, seen from the outside the acronym NGO remains somewhat mysterious. Could you describe to us the major characteristics of an organization such as yours?

Jacky Mamou: "Médecins du Monde" is a nongovernmental organization, French in its origin, whose aim is to provide health care and testimony. Created in March 1980, Médecins du Monde arose out of the French

At the time of this interview and until 2001, Jacky Mamou, M.D., was president of *Médecins du Monde*, a nongovernmental organization (NGO).

Doctors movement which was conceived in 1971 on the initiative of Bernard Kouchner, Max Récamier, and several colleagues who first founded Médecins sans frontières (MSF, or Doctors without Borders). Upon returning from Biafra, where they served with the Red Cross, this group, whose members had had the experience of providing medical care in extreme conditions, created a flexible and promising way of breaking with the neutrality and silence of large health care organizations. Thus the first nongovernmental organization specialized in emergency medical care was created: Médecins sans frontières.

Beginning in 1978, tensions arose between the founders and young doctors who sought to professionalize and institutionalize the organization. The rupture was consummated in 1979; the breakup was over a basic issue, that of speaking out during the Vietnamese boat lift operation. The discussion involved the opportunity for a mission in the China Sea to help the Vietnamese boat people who were fleeing their country.

Bernard Kouchner supported the idea that a boat should be deployed with doctors and journalists aboard in order to provide care and to witness any human rights violations firsthand. A committee for the China Sea operation was created with the support of several French intellectuals, in particular Aron, Sartre, Glucksmann, Montand, Signoret, Foucault, etc. For those who were opposed, the most urgent need was elsewhere. This difference in conception of humanitarian medicine led to the departure of some fifteen individuals who then founded Médecins du Monde in March 1980.

Marina Ricciardelli: Because Médecins du Monde is the only NGO included in our book, we would like to understand more generally what, in the Western world, are the ancestors of the NGOs? Are these organizations based on an ideal of solidarity? Does an association become an NGO when it decides to become legally registered? Do NGOs, numerous around the world (several hundred thousand or more), belong to networks, with, for example, international or European meetings, platforms for discussion or debate?

J.M.: Yes. NGOs have existed for a long time, linked to the right of free association (law of 1901 in France). The 750,000 associations declared in France in 1999 have a wide variety of aims and social objectives. Associations with a humanitarian focus have existed since well before the creation of Doctors without Borders, or Médecins du Monde, and have been primarily aimed at development issues and long-term support; they have often had a religious base (Catholic or Protestant organizations, for example).

S.U.: Like the foundations in the Middle Ages?

J.M.: Yes, exactly, but a new element was introduced by the French Doctors movement: that is, international emergency action by the rapid deployment of doctors in the field.

S.U.: And how does an association become an NGO?

J.M.: Well, de facto. By creating an association, you are already creating an organization, or an association of citizens. Whatever the topic, the theme that is the social aim of the association, it is "nongovernmental" in that it is independent of government structures, either financially or administratively. In fact, the question of an NGO's legal status is not resolved. Right now, each country has its own laws governing associations and foundations. There is a European agreement on the recognition of the legal identity of NGOs, aiming to facilitate their activities on an international level. But the agreement has yet to be ratified by many member states.

It is an important question, because NGOs are vehicles of opinion and of the expression of citizen needs, linked to the globalization of the economy. With the new concept of the right of humanitarian interference, we have enabled an individual who is suffering to be given a place in the political decision-making process. It is henceforth much less possible to oppress with the protection of borders.

Since 1996, the international network of Médecins du Monde has been recognized as a nongovernmental organization with a general consultancy status with the Economic and Social Council of the United Nations. Médecins du Monde is an operational partner with numerous international organizations (United Nations Children's Fund [UNICEF], United Nations Development Program [UNDP], High Committee for Refugees (HCR), Red Cross Organization, World Bank, etc.), but it is a private organization, which is left to defend its own point of view, regardless of the points of view expressed by governments.

At the time of their creation, all associations or NGOs function exclusively with private funds, and then gradually the importance of the programs leads the NGOs and governments to collaborate. A government thus may see the advantage in having a nongovernmental organization work in a specific area on behalf of a particular population, because it is less expensive, sometimes more efficient, the abilities are more specialized, or because the mode of intervention is sometimes more flexible. An NGO might also see the advantage of such cooperation in that it enables the NGO to have greater funds than those available through private sources alone. But at the same time, this brings about other problems: funding from government creates a certain dependent relationship.

S.U.: Possibly conflictual?

J.M.: In reality, no. The development of NGOs has in fact been linked to the disengagement of the state in a whole series of areas, either inside the country (reduction of the traditional role of the welfare state, leading to difficulties in terms of housing, nourishment, etc., for some marginalized segments of the population) or on an international level. There, NGOs act because the governments do not act or do not act well, whereas the population is in danger, is vulnerable, or is enduring acts of violence.

S.U.: How then does an NGO like yours make the decision to intervene or not, where to intervene, and how?

J.M.: There are several scenarios. There could be a call for international solidarity launched by a given world region or by a government, as in the case of natural disasters. In such cases NGOs naturally respond to the extent that they have the resources or the means. There could also be a solicitation from groups of people from within a zone of conflict. We can mention, for example, the Kurds who need support to take care of women, children, and invalids. In these specific cases the populations call on NGOs because the governments, for political reasons, cannot help them, since they risk entering into immediate conflict with others, in this particular case, with Iran, Iraq, Syria, and Turkey. NGOs can intervene with a certain technical competence, in terms of medical care, nutrition, education, etc.

M.R.: Does this mean, on the one hand, that NGOs can intervene with the state's blessing at a rate that is much faster than the state could ever do because of bureaucratic processes (a sort of cooperation alliance between the governmental institution and the NGO based on flexibility), and that on the other hand, in other cases, you would intervene to try to resolve the problems created by the government, or at least the very negative results of their actions (for example, with the war in Kosovo or other areas of conflict); here, might you intervene even against the wishes of the government?

J.M.: Yes, there are the two sides. Sometimes it's an alliance with certain governments, and sometimes an alliance against them.

M.R.: Does this type of relationship, sometimes conflictual and sometimes collaborative, exist with other types of international institutions, such as, for example, the United Nations, which also has an organized assistance network?

J.M.: Yes, of course. We can benefit, for example, from subsidies in the case of a program of aid for refugees, which enables us to intervene in refugee camps in such and such country; and we can do so while not agreeing with the policies developed by the United Nations in other regions of the world.

M.R.: So, you can get the financing, then act in a way. . . .

J.M.: Yes, but if we are really in disagreement, we don't accept the financing.

M.R.: Even though one might consider this to be a sort of socialization of funds?

J.M.: Yes, that has happened.

M.R.: In fact, one can well imagine that in the case of natural disaster, say, an earthquake, the principle of a "paid" collaboration is simple, but in other cases the system of financing and the freedom to maneuver later on might pose a problem. . . .

J.M.: In truth, it all depends on the type of action developed by the NGO, the context of intervention, the conditions placed on the financing, and the extent to which the NGO wants to conserve its freedom to maneuver. In the case of missions initiated in areas of acute humanitarian crisis, Médecins du Monde has the ongoing concern of participating in the financing of its activities using funds from its own coffers. This fact is a sort of insurance that we retain a nongovernmental identity.

S.U.: As far as financing and dialogue are concerned, I imagine that in many cases you are not the only organization to be solicited: you'll find yourselves among other comparable organizations, American, German, Dutch, English, with whom you are forced to collaborate.

J.M.: We have no choice!

S.U.: So each site calls for a new form of collaboration, with a different sharing of tasks and resources?

J.M.: Yes, that's correct.

S.U.: So, you put into place a coordinated decision-making structure on the international level with a well-defined goal.

J.M.: Yes, that can happen, but it is not the most common scenario. Each case is different. It often happens that it is a rebel movement that asks for our help. This population occupies a zone in which there may be grave humanitarian problems and needs help (Médecins du Monde responds then to health problems, but they are not normally the only problems). Discussions then begin: is the intervention well founded? Will we be independent to act while we are in the field? Can we be witnesses to the situation?

S.U.: Could you elaborate on the concept of "witnessing"?

J.M.: Serving as witnesses to events is extremely important to us. It is the terrible memories of those doctors who went to Biafra and who saw how the famine and the acts of violence against the population were organized that inspires us.

The call for international awareness through testimony is an essential weapon for bringing these situations to a halt. For a long time, humanitarian aid workers solicited the media, saying to journalists: "Come see what we see." Then the means of communication enabled condemnation. Today, information is spread more rapidly; our relationship with journalists has evolved, but for a time there were only humanitarian aid workers to attract attention to this or that often forgotten conflict, or to this or that oppressed population. In Afghanistan, for example, after the Soviet invasion, only NGOs were allowed to enter the country; they were able to sneak journalists in on their teams so they could see what was going on: bombings, mistreated populations, etc.

S.U.: Is that to say that NGOs are used to infiltrate a situation, to offer a view, opinion, or pressure. . . .

J.M.: Yes, but with Médecins du Monde, it is an essential part of our mission. We believe that bearing witness to the atrocities that the population is experiencing is a fundamental element of our activities. Thus, during the war in Kosovo, we were positioned in Macedonia, Albania, and Montenegro where we welcomed thousands of Kosovan refugees; we systematically gathered accounts of the situation that we then took to the War Crimes Tribunal in the Hague.

There, it wasn't only emotion that guided our action, but a systematization of our work in the realm of bearing witness. There are numerous examples of this.

M.R.: In fact, in light of the complexity of the real world, there would be numerous requests for aid from an NGO like yours. You mentioned that there are three or four types of intervention. Could you list these before we move on to another point?

J.M.: Yes. The first scenario, we saw, is a request from a country in the grip of a natural disaster, calling for international solidarity. The second scenario is driven by a population in difficulty who, following a rebel movement, for example, is in a tragic situation. The third case corresponds to an initiative on our part because we are concerned by what we have read in the media or by information we have received using other means. The fourth case would occur when agencies or other NGOs call us to fill a specific void in their program (in our case, medical) within a framework of partnership. Other modes of intervention exist as well.

M.R.: Those that correspond to a disengagement of the welfare state?
J.M.: Yes, of course.

M.R.: But in any case, since you cannot be everywhere, you are obliged to select your field of intervention. Is there then an ideological component to the selection, or does it happen that you decide to intervene, for example, with rebel groups whose politics you oppose?

J.M.: That's an extreme case. For these specific cases, we use a range of criteria, including how much freedom to act we will have. Can we, for example, evaluate the needs of a population independently, without depending on the figures provided by other groups? Can we work in agreement with our own ethical principles, that is, without ethnic, political, or religious discrimination (for us, visiting a hospital or a dispensary cannot be reserved only to members of one tribe or other specific group).

M.R.: Does that mean that you make value judgements in selecting your operations?

J.M.: Yes, there are some behaviors, such as ethnic selection, that we cannot accept.

S.U.: Are your criteria linked to any kind of ethical charter?
J.M.: Yes, of course.

S.U.: Is this ethical guarantee emphasized at the time that funds are raised? This is a question we might ask as external observers because it is extraordinary to see NGOs that represent in some sense a parallel power around the world, beyond the institutions that are elected or controlled by the established powers, and that intervene (efficiently) with a large freedom to maneuver, without any control, it seems. This new worldwide community of citizens is intriguing.

J.M.: What you are saying is debatable. The idea that there is "no control" is not true. There are procedures we must respect. We cannot intervene whenever or wherever in the world. It is true that we have political independence, but it is relative in reality (we need advance authorization for our interventions). Military, political, and humanitarian relationships are more complex; the access to populations in need is rendered difficult in that the civil populations are taken hostage as human shields, and also in that the contexts for intervention are becoming more and more dangerous; violence tends to disregard the immunity of humanitarian aid workers.

Citizen involvement is for us a completely fundamental issue, but it does not necessarily simplify the operation of the organization. I am a doctor; I have an office in the Paris suburbs; and I donate time to Médecins du Monde. All of our system of organization and management is based on this idea of citizen involvement.

M.R.: That means volunteerism?

J.M.: Yes, exactly, volunteerism and voluntary service. The "volunteers" are people who, like me, donate time to the functioning of the association; those in "voluntary service" are the individuals who agree to go out in the field for six months, a year, two years. They have a status that is somewhat unusual: they are not employees but they receive a stipend that corresponds *grosso modo* to the cost of rent and some other expenses.

The "volunteers" are in the field for a short period of time, or they work in France where we develop numerous activities for those who do not normally receive medical care, or they contribute time to the administration of the organization. All of the leadership of Médecins du Monde is volunteer; the fifteen members of the administrative council are volunteer; they do not receive any payment whatsoever for their services. But there is also a permanent structure of paid employees, who are given the responsibility to make sure that the missions function smoothly (in terms of logistics, recruitment of volunteers, financial management, communication, development, and follow-up).

S.U.: How many professionals, volunteer physicians, make up your organization?

J.M.: It's difficult to say because the number is constantly changing. It fluctuates anywhere between two thousand and three thousand.

We also try to include local physicians in our teams. We think that is important because we need to consider the future: when the emergency is over, there are still needs to be met (AIDS prevention, drug addiction, opposing child labor, medical and social help to homeless children, construction and management of clinics, pre-natal care, health education programs, care of the elderly, etc.). It is easier to disengage when we have provided high quality care and training on site.

S.U.: One can imagine that for a physician it is difficult to abandon a practice for a relatively long period to become an emergency volunteer in the field, or to participate in training missions in developing nations.

J.M.: Yes, we have real problems in recruiting. It is usually the young doctors who are available, just out of medical school, or those at the end of their career.

S.U.: Do you find significant support in Europe with doctors from other countries who join your organization?

J.M.: There are two phenomena, linked to the internationalization of Médecins du Monde. First, we have African or Latin American doctors who originally worked with us on programs in their countries and who agree to be sent to other destinations. Then, we have created a network of twelve international delegations (in Belgium, Spain, Portugal, Greece, Cyprus, Italy, Sweden, Switzerland, the United States, Canada, and Argentina) and representation offices (in Japan, China, Great Britain, Germany, and the Netherlands) with whom we collaborate.

M.R.: And you create shared programs, or a coordination of intervention, with these organizations?

J.M.: Yes, we try, but we have to struggle, because NGOs have a strong sense of independence, even when it concerns others in the same network. In certain cases, the partnership is difficult. We have, for example, seen serious conflict with Médecins du Monde in Poland on questions related to AIDS (the Polish defended a traditional Catholic position of abstinence). Médecins du Monde France retains ownership of the "brand" and logo Médecins du Monde: it is our only means of ensuring that there is no ethical drifting.

M.R.: You mean that the ethical value that you defend is a secular value at bottom?

J.M.: Yes, completely.

M.R.: But that could also pose problems in Arab countries, for example in Afghanistan?
J.M.: Yes, it does.

2. Europe Supports Social Partnership

M.R.: The Treaty of Amsterdam brought forward the concept of social partnership, giving NGOs the role as direct interlocutors of the European Commission. Has this disposition had a concrete effect on your organization? Has it given you more room to maneuver? Up to now, in order to obtain cofinancing, NGOs had to be part of a team. From now on, as a "direct interlocutor," an NGO can apply alone, with its own plan in relation to a grant request. Does this disposition create a new relationship between money and freedom? Does this source of financing put NGOs in competition with one another, to a splitting up of resources, or, on the contrary, does it lead to a coordination of initiatives relative to the needs expressed?

J.M.: We haven't yet seen the impact of the new arrangements. What is clear is that for the last several years the European Union has been a very important partner. On the whole, Médecins du Monde receives 60 percent of its funding from private sources (a million donors, private grants, sponsorship, bequests). Most of the 40 percent of public funds (four-fifths) comes from the European Union. In particular we solicit the DG I (Department of Foreign Affairs) and the DG VIII (Department of Economic Development) of the European Commission. Moreover, sector-based budget lines correspond to NGOs' realms of intervention (for example, the line "human rights"). More than competition, there is a de facto breaking apart of the initiatives brought forward individually by NGOs. Since 1996, the European Union encourages associations to regroup in consortial relationships (with an NGO leader, taking ownership for the project and its budget).

There is also the issue of respecting a certain balance between the tendency in the European Union to fund the larger NGOs, on the one hand, and the respect for the rich diversity of European associations, recognized as such by the EU itself, on the other. Overall, we are not thrilled with these complicated and redundant bureaucratic procedures, even if we understand the need for coordination in this area. The problem is that the management of projects replaces the bureaucratization of European authorities in the nongovernmental arena. This is an extremely perverse logic because it will tend to institutionalize NGOs, to create a humanitarian bureaucracy, with a multiplication of controls (auditors at the national and European level).

We are increasingly obliged to devote more human and financial resources to respond to all kinds of controls.

M.R.: Formally, it is the efficiency of certain bureaucrats, of certain leaders of constituencies, that will lead the competition between social partners to have access to funds: is this democratic?

J.M.: No. I'll give you another example: that of financial backing. The European Commission now requires, when it funds a project, a guarantee from an NGO's bank, in an amount that equals that of the total financing for the project. That, in effect, breaks all the small NGOs in favor of a few very large NGOs that will become bureaucratized "institutional partners." On the one hand, we can understand that the European Commission, out of concern for its own internal management, wants to limit the number of interlocutors, but this disposition discourages and reduces new initiatives from the start. There is something paradoxical here, in that the words of the European Commission concerning NGOs are quite the opposite: "You are full-fledged actors, associations of citizens that make up Europe's social fabric." These words evoke the unique nature and richness of Europe's associative milieu, but at the same time . . . !

M.R.: You hit the nail right on the head.

J.M.: In the end, institutional funds have a way of shrinking. In exchange, we can hope for more funding from private sources, foundations like Kellogg, Ford, and Succhi in Taiwan. Things aren't extremely clear, however. Every country has a different point of view in terms of humanitarian action. On the European level, the new General Conditions (regulation of the European Commission on the cofinancing of European NGOs in matters of development), which have been applicable since 2000, plan for an increase in funding from the EC for NGO projects from 50 to 75 percent.

The availability of private funds is not a condition imposed by the EU for cofinancing of NGO projects (complementary funding can be drawn from national sponsors). However, the availability of private funding guarantees to some extent the nongovernmental independence and identity of the projects carried out by NGOs.

3. The Ambiguous Effects of Globalization

S.U.: Do you think that one of the good effects of globalization is that, thanks to new information and communication technologies, your humanitarian work of care and testimony is better known in the world and that this recognition makes it more likely for you to obtain financing in Taiwan, the United States, and elsewhere?

J.M.: Yes. The benefit of this is also that we are able to diversify our funding sources, reinforcing the organization's independence vis-à-vis sponsors. But it also happens that private foundations are not interested in funding an NGO as such, but rather a particular mission, concerning the Kurds, the Kosovans, or the Rwandans, for example. In other words, they will limit their funding to a specific program.

M.R.: Could that also be an experimental medication program, for example, with the support of the pharmaceutical industry?

J.M.: For us, that has never happened. On the contrary, we are fighting against a certain lack of interest on the part of pharmaceutical labs. Let's take the example of AIDS: 90 percent of the afflicted are in the Southern Hemisphere, and 90 percent of the money is in the Northern Hemisphere. It is extremely difficult to get new types of AIDS treatment in the South.

M.R.: Why is that?

J.M.: Because the prices charged for the medications are beyond the reach of countries in the South. Initiatives have been taken so that laboratories will lower their prices a little, but these measures are not common; these are only a few pilot cases that do not reach the great majority of those suffering with AIDS.

M.R.: The process of globalization that we see growing before our very eyes, leading to a new worldwide, supranational architecture, also leads to the globalization of disease. In the framework of negotiations led by the World Trade Organization in Seattle (December 1999), it seems that NGOs are rather opposed to a liberalism they deem excessive. How did the Seattle meeting affect your organization?

J.M.: The Seattle event affected us in two ways. First of all, on the question of pharmaceuticals, that is, medication. To our mind, the price of medications should not be tied solely to free market conditions but also to pathological reality. Medicine should be manufactured at prices that are affordable for everyone in the human community, not only for those in the Northern Hemisphere.

M.R.: And do you think that globalization is stimulating an increase, rather than a decrease, in the prices? Franco Modigliani has expressed the opinion that the globalization of the economy would protect consumers against powerful monopolies. Are you more skeptical?

J.M.: Yes, we are concerned. We see that there are medications that are not being manufactured because "there is no solvent market," whereas parasitical illnesses, such as malaria, are rampant. Under the pretext that the Southern Hemisphere markets are not solvent, medications that target them directly are produced in small quantities or not at all.

Seattle affected us in a second way, relating to systems of social protection. In this regard, the idea of liberalization means free competition for private insurers on the social security market. Henceforth, it is necessarily the concept of profitablility that will dominate, and therefore, as concerns those who are sick, a risk factor will be applied. In the long run, we risk keeping a part of the world's population from having access to social protection or to health care, including in economically developed countries.

M.R.: Who are the afflicted that are most vulnerable, those who are marginalized by poverty? There is a renewed outbreak of tuberculosis, for example. . . .

J.M.: Yes, there are also illnesses that are easily avoidable, such as measles, for example, that kill millions of children around the world, because they are not vaccinated, although we have the scientific and technical means to vaccinate all these millions of children; but the vaccination programs in the Southern Hemisphere are largely insufficient. These children also die regularly of acute diarrhea and respiratory infections. Simple treatments could prevent death in these millions of children, if there were a minimum of sanitary infrastructures in these countries, that is, a certain number of clinics capable of delivering first aid, providing antibiotics, applying certain rules of hygiene or isolation to keep infections from spreading, etc.

S.U.: Do you think that globalization accentuates the disparity of health care, or that more simply it doesn't enable us to fill the existing gap, given that these sanitary disasters have always existed in the world? From this perspective, couldn't you say that in the long run the pharmaceutical industry can't ignore these immense markets and that it is, at the same time, strong enough to stimulate a program of health funding, for example, through the World Bank?

J.M.: Many of these health problems are linked to poverty. The resurgence of tuberculosis in the East is linked to the widening of poverty and to the disintegration of the traditional protective sanitation system that previously contained the spread of diseases like tuberculosis. The political measures taken by the International Monetary Fund (IMF) have considerably reduced national budgets in the least developed countries in Africa, Asia, and Latin America. The statewide health systems have been adversely affected in consequence, and most sick people do not have the means to call upon private medicine. The vulnerability of a segment of the third world population is aggravated in terms of health, nutrition, and education.

M.R.: Beyond the state of poverty, does this evolution seem to you to be linked to the reduction of national governments' power to intervene?

J.M.: No doubt. Take the example of Mali, which I visited not long ago. Until recently, Mali had a national health system that functioned pretty well; then a decision to regionalize health care was made: regions now must contribute to finance their hospitals, clinics, their doctors. But, in Mali, only one or two regions are "rich"; outlying regions (particularly in the north where Médecins du Monde operates and the Tuaregs live) have very limited resources. The disengagement of the state has really disorganized the system, led to a shortfall of medication. . . . For the time being, we don't see an alternative.

S.U.: New structures need to be put into place, to be invented. Do you think that NGOs can represent the initiation of a potentially stable civil structure that is not simply linked to temporary emergency care or testimony?

J.M.: I see the role of NGOs in two areas. The first is that of public opinion, of awareness. Here we must attract attention to the perverse effects of globalization as it concerns social protection systems. Privatization is faced with limitations in a certain number of countries. The survival of millions of people depends upon the distribution of state funds.

The second sphere of influence concerns the modes of organization within communities, to enable them to face up to things. Again, in the example of Mali, we are helping communities to organize themselves so that there is a pharmacy in each village, operating through a small contribution of funds or in kind, where it is possible to buy more antibiotics or antidiarrheics when people run out. We are trying to transfer some know-how, to stimulate exemplarity, to develop pedagogical virtues.

But it is clear that NGOs such as ours can only exercise a small counterinfluence without working within the logic of the market, with the power of the interests that are mobilized within the framework of globalization.

M.R.: Yet, to emphasize a positive side to globalization. . . .

J.M.: Wait—we don't approach the problem in terms of "positive" or "negative." We are, first of all, practitioners, confronted by a reality more than an ideology. Globalization is real. What we can do is sound the alarm regarding this or that aspect of things, but the world will remain globalized. The AIDS epidemic, like the radioactive cloud of Chernobyl or global warming, has crossed borders effortlessly. We live in this global world; we can't say that we are "against" it.

M.R.: Of course you are right. I would, however, like your opinion on one aspect of globalization in particular, that is, the spread of information. Can the new means of communication stimulate more human solidarity?

J.M.: Yes, of course. You know, doctors and medical NGOs understood the importance of AIDS before the questions of international solidarity had strongly marked the spirit of the medical NGOs. Very quickly, we understood that the AIDS epidemic wasn't going to respect borders and that policies of protection within a fortress were destined to fail. That means that it will not do any good either to lock up those who have AIDS (there have been such experiments in Cuba and in other countries), or to close borders, or to require an AIDS test for travel across borders. The real issue is that of prevention, public education. It would be useless to close our eyes and say, "AIDS is not in our country." But prevention measures are obstructed by prejudice, conservative reactions. Nonetheless, health problems have become global; people travel, communicate on the Internet; if a measure of prevention succeeds in such and such country, it is immediately known in others; ethical rules are also diffused far and wide, and fast.

M.R.: A local doctor, all alone, can he be helped?

J.M.: Yes, he can, but for epidemics such as AIDS, the problem isn't only having access to information, but also to medication.

CHAPTER 14

Globalization and Its Statistical Challenges

PHOTIS NANOPOULOS

I. Introduction

Mankind has a long history of debates about the significance of terms that can take on different meanings depending on who uses them. The famous dialogues between Socrates and powerful men and the sophists clearly illustrate the power of semantics. At the beginning of the twentieth century, the big word was "imperialism," while at the end, the magic word "globalization" was the center of attention among the majority of our intellectuals, philosophers, economists, and sociologists.

These debates stem from the fact that, since the Second World War, the whole world has been moving toward a new liberal order that has no borders and is standardized according to the American model of society, which is more concerned with the freedom of economic operators than the commonweal.

Photis Nanopoulos, formerly a professor in the Department of Mathematics at the Université Louis Pasteur in Strasbourg and at Athens Polytechnic University, is currently director of the Statistical Office of the European Commission (Eurostat), in charge of the systems of statistical information, of the analysis of conjuncture, of the statistics of the new economy, and of technical cooperation with the Phare and Tacis countries.

The word "globalization" has a basic geographical meaning of "covering the whole planet." It therefore has connotations of abolishing or transcending all sorts of national borders, be they physical, cultural, linguistic, legal, or commercial. It also suggests lifting natural or artificial constraints by letting people interact at the world level.

As mankind moves toward its destiny (whatever that may be), changes occasionally occur in thinking and knowledge, and this in turn changes the way our societies are constructed and run, or even the goals we are trying to achieve. Whenever this happens, human psychology being what it is, groups of "enlightened ones" always emerge, determined to make everyone think and act in the same way as they do. This determination, together with an urge to dominate and conquer, leads to one civilization imposing, for good or ill, some of its features on the others.

In this way the great conquests and the building of great empires have spread certain languages and philosophies over vast areas of the globe. Western civilization—which emerged from the melting pot of Europe, with its many different cultures and peoples, and is based on Judaeo-Christian moral principles, Greek philosophy and democratic principles, and "Anglo-Latin" languages—has spread and established itself over a large part of the world over the centuries.

The split resulting from the rise of liberal capitalism and its great successes in the New World, compared with the failure of the totalitarian models (be they fascist or communist), has created favorable conditions for genuine globalization in some areas. The fact that economic considerations take precedence over social questions and that greater value is attached to performance in terms of economic rather than social indicators is merely an expression of the view of the pragmatists who like to think that social success must be achieved through economic means.

According to Enrique Baròn Crespo, "The main factor of globalization is undoubtedly the universalization of Democracy, as a political system desired by most of humanity, with the affirmation that Human Rights are essential values vis-à-vis the supremacy of Reasons of State."[1] However, stabilizing the democratic systems, on the basis of human rights, would not be enough to establish favorable conditions for globalization. There are also the virtues of a free market and a privatized liberal economy, as exemplified by the highly successful model of the United States. The adoption of this model by a large number of countries paved the way for the multilateral agreements aimed at favoring the development of world trade. This idea, which dates from 1947, led to the signing of the General Agreement on Tariffs and Trade (GATT) and the General Agreement on Trade in Services (GATS) (1986–1993), which in turn led to the establishment of the World Trade Organization (WTO) in 1995.

The instruments that have permitted the development from internationalization of trade to globalization of the production apparatus and the proliferation of multinational companies are the policies of "deregulation" and "privatization" and the new role in the economy played by the "information and communication technologies" (ICT).[2]

The fall of the Berlin Wall was symbolic of the failure of planned economies compared with liberal capitalism and led to the opening of the borders of virtually every country in the world, including China—which is one of the last bastions of communism, but is nevertheless now open to the liberalization of trade.

The history of the world since the Second World War has seen a number of developments in various fields that have a common feature: they affect the world as a whole. The most significant of these is, I think, the nuclear threat, be it from military or peaceful applications, which still hangs heavy over the whole of humanity. Environmental problems have also taken on a planetary dimension because of the threats to the climate from the buildup of CO_2 and the destruction of the protective ozone layer, not to mention the local imbalances that are nevertheless a threat to the planet as a whole. The problems of overpopulation, poverty, and migration on a massive scale for reasons of famine or war also have global implications.

There is no escaping the fact that throughout the second half of the twentieth century, despite the constant "world summits," the world leaders did not manage to reach a single significant agreement to protect the planet from these threats of catastrophes of biblical proportions. Ironically, spectacular progress was made in another area, where there were no real threats to mankind—the worldwide liberalization of trade and business in general.

2. Globalization and the Information Society

A New Pythagorean Society

Our societies are in a state of flux. Technological progress is turning our industrial society into an information society. Transitions of this kind are nothing new: they are constantly repeated over long cycles, but these cycles are getting shorter and shorter. I think there is a strange parallel between the philosophies of ancient Greece and the cycles in the development of mankind. These philosophies are summed up in the following passage from a book by Catherine Collobert:

> Whether philosophy addresses Nature with the Milesians, Criticism with Xenophanes, Number with the Pythagoreans, Opposition with Heraclitus, Being with Parmenides, the Intellect with Anaxagoras, Forces with Empedocles, or the Atom with Democritus, it always reveals, in true sense of the word, a different perspective—not a partial, fragmented or exploded view, but a perspective. It is in this freedom of perspective—a token of thought itself—that philosophy has developed since its genesis.[3]

There is a good correlation between these philosophical concepts and the phases of varying importance and length that our civilizations have gone through, at least in the West. Our Milesian phase, the agricultural era, was followed by a phase typified by the Forces of Empedocles—the industrial revolution. Nowadays we are in a Pythagorean phase, in which Number is the prime concern. According to the Pythagoreans,

> everything has a number . . . without the number, it is impossible to think or to know. The figure is the form. It is through its figure that one entity distinguishes and differentiates itself from others. It is through its form that it becomes specific—individualized. The figure is determined by a given relationship between its sides or parts. . . . An entity therefore possesses a structure that is knowable through number. It is by virtue of this that it is said to have a number. Is number not merely a principle of knowledge rather than a principle of being?[4]

Here we are at the dawn of the twenty-first century and the information society, which we can dub a "Pythagorean society" because its progress depends on its capacity to *associate a number with everything*. In other words, everything visible, audible, or tangible becomes a numerical vector, a string of digits that represents it. Thanks to this digitizing of concepts we can establish a *digital economy,* a *virtual world,* and a *knowledge-based society*.

Infrastructures and Telecommunications Networks

Everyone agrees that globalization would not be possible without the progress made in the information and communications technologies in the second half of the twentieth century. Computers, with processing and storage capacities increasing exponentially, and communications satellites and networks linking the entire world are the backbone and nervous system of globalization. Data capture and digitization techniques enable easy and inexpensive storage, processing, and transmission.

These technologies enable the instantaneous, automatic, worldwide management of the big systems of banking and financial information, thus speeding up the flow of worldwide transactions. Thanks to ICT, businesses can use new types of decentralized management and hence new, less localized ways of organizing production.

The shift from analog to digital signals enables the large networks to be exploited efficiently and ensures a return on the investment needed for setting them up. The big telecommunications companies are all eager to have a hand in setting up these privatized "information highways," as Al Gore, then vice-president of the United States, called them in 1996, and which are coming to be organized at planetary level through mergers or takeovers. We are witnessing the development of high-capacity networks; towns are wired with millions of kilometers of optical fibers; all circuitry is becoming digital, the market in mobile phones is booming, and prices are falling.

Borne on the wind of liberalization and privatization in the telecommunications sector, many related businesses are reorganizing on a world scale in order to get a foothold on the markets, and are investing in development of new services.

Internet and Cyberspace

The Internet, which integrates and promotes the technological arsenal, is the innovation par excellence that enables the general public to "join the globalization party." The Internet is not a technology in itself, but an intelligent exploitation of the possibilities afforded by the information technologies for sharing the information produced by anyone anywhere in the world. By integrating a whole range of technological tools (computers, modems, networks, satellites, video cameras, mobile phones, programming languages, html, etc.), a common communication protocol and a set of digital applications and services in worldwide networks, the Internet enables transparent continuous access to virtually all the computers in the world. The Internet creates new jobs (access providers, site managers, content managers, etc.), exploits multimedia resources on a world scale, and creates new sectors of economic activity. More than that, it changes man's relationship with his environment, affects his cultural identity, and transforms the very foundations of the ways in which our societies and nation-states are run.

The Internet has given birth to electronic commerce and is nurturing its development. The new way of doing business has a catalytic effect. It is synonymous with greater market transparency and immediate world competition. It is a vital factor in encouraging change and a competitive attitude—not only in the new sectors but also in traditional ones such as the labor-intensive industries. It favors the distribution of a wide range of goods and services, thus making good use of the diversity of the productive fabric and know-how. At the same time, electronic commerce generates completely new activities, including in particular intermediation services such as logistics firms, certification and authentication services, and credit-rating agencies. In 1996, the Internet created 1.1 million new jobs throughout the world. Of these, 760,000 were in the United States.

The Internet is spawning a whole new world—Cyberspace. It has no material existence, it knows nothing of borders or administrative rules, it lets everyone voice their ideas, it is liberal and has no ethics or morals. One of the features of Cyberspace is the dizzying growth in interaction between individuals, involving both commercial transactions and exchange of information. The access to information places individuals in a new interactive relationship with a virtual environment. A question or information search may yield hundreds of thousands of replies, but there is no guarantee of their accuracy and validity. The human brain will never be able to absorb all the knowledge available, but it can stretch its limits.

Cyberspace is challenging all the rules of the economy with the emergence of three factors: speed, intelligence, and adaptability. The countries and businesses that corner certain sectors of Cyberspace have the advantage of getting in first. As we see in biology, it is very difficult for a species to dislodge another from its ecological niche. This is known as the "lock-in" effect and is very familiar to the new generation of economists.

Equipment and Infrastructures

If we are to understand the progress various countries have made in the process of globalization and the tactical positions they have adopted, we must look at the development of their technological infrastructures, since this is one of the factors that determines a country's capacity to keep pace. By infrastructures, I mean telecommunications networks, networks for the processing and exchange of information, and the tools available to households and businesses for making use of these infrastructures.

An important factor is the digitization of these networks. Digital networks are important because they can transmit speech, sounds, data, and images simultaneously after these things have been digitized—in other words, translated into numbers. The capacity of these networks, measured in terms of throughput, is another factor. Integrated Services Digital Networks (ISDN) are the most widespread at present because they can offer all high-throughput services.

The European source par excellence for information on technological developments in Europe and the world as a whole is undoubtedly the European Information Technology Observatory (EITO), which publishes each year, under the same title, a factual report with a statistical appendix. The only negative aspect is that the methodology used and the information given on the sources do not permit an assessment of the quality and validity of the figures. The table below is significant, however, showing the development of the technological infrastructures in the various countries and regions of the world up until 2000.

TABLE 1. ICT Market

Billion Euros	1996	1997	1998	1999	2000
Europe (including Eastern)	372	405	436	470	509
USA	437	477	517	558	603
Japan	162	170	164	172	182
Rest of World	258	291	326	361	401
TOTAL	1,230	1,343	1,444	1,562	1,696

Source: EITO

Clearly Europe is hard on the heels of the United States when it comes to investment in ICT. This investment (by the state, businesses, and households alike) is reflected in the development of communication via the Internet.

Equipment—Businesses and Households

In order to give an idea of how the households and citizens in the European Union (EU) are dealing with globalization and the information society, we refer to a recent European Commission survey on the tools used for connecting to the various networks.[5] These figures show the differences that might exist, even between European countries.

Of the people consulted in all the member states, 30.8% said that they used a personal computer at home. This figure exceeded 50% in three member states: Sweden (59.8%), the Netherlands (58.8%), and Denmark (56.7%).

The next group was made up of Luxembourg (42.5%), Finland (38.6%), the United Kingdom (35.2%), Belgium (33%), Austria (30.8%), and Germany (30.5%). A third group was below the European average, but nevertheless had an overall market penetration of more than 20% (Spain with 28.4%, Italy 26.6%, Ireland with 26.3%, and France with 22.8%).

Among the EU population, 9.3% said that they used a fax-modem at home. The figures were highest in Sweden, the Netherlands, and Denmark, with 34.3%, 24.7%, and 24.5% respectively. These were followed by a group of seven countries for which the figure was average or slightly above: Finland (17.7%), Luxembourg (15%), Germany (10.2%), Belgium (10.1%), Austria (9.6%), the United Kingdom (9.3%), and Ireland (9%). The lowest figures were found in Italy (7%), France (5.5%), Spain (4.6%), Portugal (4.2%), and Greece (2.4%).

An average of 8.3% people in Europe have Internet access, but here, too, the figure varies widely from one country to another—from 39.6% to 2.9%. In 1999, Internet access was most widespread in Sweden, where 39.6% of the people interviewed had a connection, followed by Denmark (24.6%), the Netherlands (19.6%), Finland (17.2%), Luxembourg (14%), and the United Kingdom (10.7%).

In some member states, fewer than 10% of the people interviewed said they used the Internet at home. These countries were Ireland (8.4%), Belgium (8.2%), Germany (7.1%), Austria (6.8%), Spain (5%), France (3.9%), Portugal (3.4%), and Greece (2.9%).

Mobile phones are also on the up and up in a good number of member states. On average, 30.2% of people in Europe have their own mobile phone, the biggest users and owners being the Finns with 64.4% and the Swedes with 60.3%, followed by the Italians with 44.2%, the Danes with 43.1%, the Luxembourgers with 36.9%, and the Austrians with 35.7%. Lower than average figures are found in the United Kingdom (32.2%), Portugal (29.9%), Greece (29.3%), Ireland (28.3%), Spain (26.3%), Belgium (25.8%), France (25.5%), and the Netherlands (24.2%). Germany has the lowest percentage of mobile-phone users in Europe (19.4%).

These figures show how rapidly globalization is spreading in Europe. We would need more systematic, coordinated surveys of all the countries in the world in order to conduct a new development-aid policy to help the least developed countries enter the information society.

Research and Technological Development

Virtually the sole factor that determines technological progress is investment in research and development, which is being conducted on an increasingly global scale (American firms, for example, invest more than 10 billion dollars per year on research and development conducted outside the United States). R&D has always been the preserve of the rich countries, which have the necessary resources and can take the corresponding financial risks. As in biotechnology, where sometimes unforeseen products can result directly from basic research, the combination of public and private investment, together with the ways in which basic and competitive research complement each other, is very fruitful for ICT.

One way of assessing "research output," both public and private, is to observe the filing of patents and the acquisition of intellectual property rights to protect trademarks and licenses. The imbalance between the United States and Europe, both in terms of the number of patents and royalties earned, is on the increase—particularly in the research-intensive sectors such as information technologies, pharmaceuticals, and biotechnology. Between 1985 and 1995, Europe's share of patents filed in the United States fell from 21% to 16%, while the number of U.S. patents filed by American inventors remained stable at around 55%. Over the same period, American patents filed with the European Patent Office rose from 27% to 34%, while Europe's share fell from 50% to 44%. The United States is a net exporter of intellectual property: royalties and fees it received from foreign businesses were on average three times what American businesses paid for access to technologies owned by businesses in other countries.

3. Effects and Challenges of Globalization

Emergence of a New Economy

The impact of the information society on the economy has been acknowledged.[6] The changes that technology made to the world economy in the second half of the twentieth century were much more radical and complex than simple developments in trade patterns. The new technologies shifted the core of the economies from sectors representative of the first and second industrial revolutions (machinery and textiles, electricity and chemicals) to electronics (the information revolution).[7] Alongside an industrial economy based on the constant improvement and optimum exploitation of the "material value-added chains," a new economy is rapidly developing with "nonmaterial value-added chains" as its basis. The burgeoning of the services sector—particularly financial and communication services—and worldwide electronic commerce is slowly but surely eroding the traditional economy's contribution to the world's total value added.

This new economy, which owes its existence to ICT and the liberalization of trade, is producing spectacular results—at least for the American economy. In the United States, average annual growth in Gross Domestic Product (GDP) since 1994 has been around 4%, unemployment has fallen from 6% to 4%, and inflation has been kept below 2%. It is just too bad that the trade balance showed a deficit of more than $235 billion in 1998!

According to Michael J. Mandel,[8] these achievements of the new economy are thanks to seven virtues or basic principles of action:

- giving new life to investments in ICT;
- restructuring businesses to reduce costs, improving flexibility and use of the new technologies;
- opening up the financial markets to direct capital to the best uses;
- developing venture capital to help innovative small and medium-sized businesses;
- encouraging the business culture and facilitating the establishment of new businesses;
- speeding up deregulation, particularly in telecommunications and the labor market;
- adjusting monetary policies to the realities of the economy by non-anticipatory adaptation of interest to inflation.

The benefits of the new economy are not sufficiently distributed throughout the world. A "gazelle" economy based on information and knowledge is not accessible to everyone and does not put all the countries of the world in the same producer/consumer relationship. There is a real danger of a social rift between those who are in and out of this international race.

The dangers are real but should not be seen as catastrophic. Globalization and the information society are also a source of opportunities, and the first to take them are the political leaders. In a Communication of 1998, the European Commission called for optimism and action:

> The joining of new technologies and the globalization of markets increase the comparative advantages of industrialized economies that specialize in products involving a high degree of knowledge and organizational competency. This implies a great increase in investments in research, education, and of expenses in company-related services, activities characterized by a very high rate of wage expenditures. Contrary to what is believed, if an adaptation to these new conditions of competitiveness is actively pursued, this should then be translated by

a decrease in the unemployment rate. This has been the case in the United States in the last few years. Highly technological businesses represent 40% of industrial growth in America in the last two years. Employment Directions for 1999 and the recent report of the Commission concerning employment opportunities in the information society have brought to light the potential that exists in these sectors for growth and employment in the European Union; they have emphasized the need for concerted action in order to optimize that potential.[9]

The Information Society and the Protection of Privacy

The protection of privacy for individuals, families, and businesses is a commonly accepted principle in our Western societies, even if it is often insufficiently or poorly regulated. This protection has several aspects and objectives. For example, there is the secrecy observed by doctors, lawyers, notaries, and priests with respect to information about an individual that they can obtain through the exercise of their profession. Then there is postal secrecy or the confidentiality of communications guaranteed by the state which has the monopoly on communications; industrial secrecy on procedures and techniques developed by industry; military secrecy; and finally, statistical secrecy, which is less known but as old as the hills. Computerized transactions and credit cards are already giving rise to problems of protecting individuals in their electronic transactions.

The emergence of the information society and of globalization, together with the possibilities afforded by computers and communication networks, brings a new dimension to this problem of the circulation of information that individuals wish to keep secret and of the fraudulent or simply unwanted use of such information by others.

A classic example is that of a user ordering consumer goods over the Internet. Not only do the data transmitted from the server to the user need to be protected against forgery, but it must be impossible to intercept the user's credit-card data in transit. The data must also be protected against simple repetition or "playback." The dangers are real, and it is impossible to put a figure on the costs they entail. Piracy and industrial espionage, etc., complicate the matter still further.

Obviously these techniques may be used by Mafia-type groups to encrypt messages or by groups of "crackers" to exchange pirated software. We think, however, that they should be allowed to proliferate for the following reasons:

- banning them could prove to be futile since the algorithms are widely known;
- there is no equivalent on commercial networks of an envelope that has to be unsealed;
- searching for key words (such as credit cards) can easily be automated, even on a large scale;
- guaranteeing confidentiality of communications by other methods would mean reducing the number of suppliers and hence increasing prices;
- banning these methods would mean that only people acting outside the law had access to them.

No satisfactory solution has yet been found to this problem of security that would guarantee the confidentiality of systems for digital transactions and the protection of data stored on computers linked to the World Wide Web, while helping combat crime. Efforts at present are concentrating more on protecting the operation of the information society and globalization than on repressing criminal use of these systems.

The Cultural Challenge

The interpenetration via the media of foreign cultures and life-styles has been both stimulating and unsettling. There is a general fear that the dominance of the transnational media will lead to a convergence of cultures at the expense of diversity. There may also be a danger that media images will increase the levels of consumerism in our societies. There are distortions and imbalances, in that world news tends to pass through American filters before it reaches us. The concern about a concentration of influence in the hands of the media is linked with fears that the power of the sector to affect the political agenda is not counterbalanced by a sense of social responsibility.

Globalization and culture do not seem to mix, therefore. On the one hand, globalization gives greater access to culture, but the means that must be put in place and the language barriers favor the "big" and economically powerful cultures over the "small" and weak. Some people think, therefore, that the biggest challenge to the cultural sector is to give the producers of culture access to capital in order to support their position vis-à-vis international competition or give them a national presence in a sector that is greatly dominated by foreign products. A related challenge is to identify the most appropriate ways of ensuring that adequate account is taken of cultural identities in international commercial agreements.

From a different angle, broader access to information has been a healthy factor for the development of democracy, which benefits from having its citizens better informed. It is also beneficial for economic development, scientific and professional collaboration, and many other activities. The vast network of linked information can also help to bring people throughout the world closer together. Media images of human suffering have led people to express their concern for and solidarity with others far away, by contributing to humanitarian aid efforts and calling for explanations and action by their governments.

4. Measuring Globalization: Major Challenges for Statistics

The Burgeoning of Trade

In a recent Eurostat publication on foreign trade,[10] we see that the postwar period was marked by an acceleration in trade, which grew by 6.7% between 1948 and 1953, by 7.4% between 1958 and 1963, and by 8.6% between 1963 and 1968. Despite the oil crises, this trend continued during the 1980s and 1990s, reaching 10% in 1997 compared with the previous year. However, according to the report by the World Trade Organization, growth in world trade in 1998 was only 4%, not as steep as it had been in the past. Despite variations over time and space, these figures show that trade has increased everywhere and that the share accounted for by the three biggest partners (USA, EU, and Japan) is diminishing, which suggests that a redistribution between rich and poor countries is taking place in the world. In fact, if we analyze the studies on intra-company trade, we see that this shift is largely explained by trade between parts of companies that have relocated some of their production.

The Burgeoning of Transnational Companies

Recent literature on the foundations of foreign trade has revealed the limitations of the traditional explanatory variables such as the relative availability of resources and factors of production, the geographic and cultural proximity of the partners, or the comparative advantage resulting from productivity. A new variable needs to be taken into account: the type of company. We will henceforth distinguish between companies that principally operate at the national level, and transnational companies that have transferred production units to countries where the labor costs and taxes are lower.[11]

These companies "externalize" some of their activities by shifting their production to different sites and countries, and by promoting the distribution of their products on several markets in order to benefit from economies of scale. Links between companies at the international level reflect the same ideas.

Statistical Observation of Transnational Companies

The existing statistical system does not enable us to measure the structure and activities of the population of transnational companies. However, on the basis of the various sources, mainly professional, the European Commission states in its 1998 Communication to the European Council and Parliament:

> In 1998 the number of transnational companies rose to more than 45,000; these control more than 280,000 branches throughout the world. In 1994, these companies represented more than one-third of world production, and their internal exchanges about one-third of world trade.
>
> In 1997 the total quantity of goods and services produced by multinational companies on local markets rose to $6,000 billion, or more than the entire volume of world international trade.[12]

In the same Communication, the Commission describes the current trends, gives a diagnosis of European companies, and proposes the direction a new industrial policy should take. It stresses, among other things, the need for new definitions:

> The acceleration of globalization and the rapid emergence of new forms of competition, the challenging of traditional barriers between industrial sectors, demand a reassessment of the concept of competitiveness. As companies are segmenting "the chain of value" of their products and services through distinct markets, traditional criteria of separation following various industrial sectors lose their relevance: the true measure of competitiveness should not be that of sectors, but that of activities and markets.
>
> National or regional competitiveness is also becoming difficult to measure: with the increase in transborder investments, the relocation of operations, the rapid changes in ownership, and the advent of "telework," geographical identity is becoming increasingly diffuse. Finally, it should be noted that competitive positions established on the mastery

of advanced technology, or great intellectual know-how, if they prove to be capable of rapidly creating increased value, are also much more volatile.

Statistical observation of transnational companies is therefore vital. A first series of questions is quite straightforward. How many are there? What is their annual turnover? What are they investing in and where does their capital come from? Who are their suppliers and how much do their orders total? Where are their production units and jobs? Where are their markets and how big are they? How do they distribute their profits? Where are profits ploughed back?

Unfortunately, no reliable statistics can currently be obtained on these points. The definition of an "enterprise" given in the European Union's regulations on statistical units cannot be applied to national entities that form part of transnational groups. We would have to be able to retrace the links between large companies on the international level and produce statistics on the basis of transnational groups of companies in order to obtain a clear picture of those aspects of globalization that are at present most obscure. This would not run counter to the interests of the transnational companies—indeed, it would enable more light to be shed on a highly controversial field in which the debate is largely based on speculation, since none of the parties has data which are both precise and equally accepted by the other.

Observation of Investments

The new economy is based on knowledge and the intangible, and predictions cannot be made using traditional methods and indicators. One of the major statistical challenges, therefore, is to measure non-material investment—and not only in national training and research, but also in training in large multinational companies and commercial networks. Given that it is difficult to obtain data on the operations of transnational companies, *Foreign Direct Investments (FDI)* may be used as a means of approximating these data. Eurostat provides detailed figures on stocks and flows of financial capital between partners in its annual publication *EU Direct Investment Yearbook.* It provides important information on alliances between companies in another publication entitled *European Report on Science & Technology Indicators* (the second in the series appeared in 1997). The publications *External and Intra–European Union Trade, Statistical Yearbook,* and *International Trade in Services—EU* also give detailed information on imports and exports of goods and services.

On the basis of recent statistics, therefore, we were able to observe an exceptional increase at the world level in direct foreign investment over the period 1992–1998, marked by flows of capital to the emergent markets that have contributed to the rapid development in domestic demand and trade by these economies.

Monitoring the New Labor Markets

Two elements affect the globalization of the labor markets: the first has to do with the liberalization of these markets and the second with the development of teleworking.

An international division of labor is gradually taking a new direction because of the costs of labor and the need for a qualified work force. The same phenomenon can also be seen in certain sectors that lend themselves to teleworking, such as the production of software.

These new phenomena are not statistically observed because we have no method and there is no world-level coordination system. The debate—which is full of assertions and speculative questions, but at present has no statistical basis—reminds us of the new need for employment statistics and social statistics in general.

5. The Need for a World-Level Statistical System

The Role of Official Statistics

The essential role of official statistics in society today is to provide our society with a consistent conceptual and methodological framework for impartial, independent, and scientific observation of socioeconomic phenomena of common interest. In an increasingly globalized society, this role becomes primordial and calls for a universal language.

The Need for Statistical Observation of Globalization

This need has been voiced by all decision-makers—political, economic, and social—in all countries. We need to observe this planetary reality by measuring all the variables in an objective, independent, and scientific fashion. In other words, we must imagine a new and appropriate statistical system, particularly since events at the World Trade Conference in Seattle in December 1999 and the abundance of literature on the subject show that the atmosphere in which the world-level debate is being conducted has become increasingly heated and confused in the absence of reliable information. This debate should not be conducted in a state of confusion arising from contradictory and biased information produced by partisan sources, but should draw on a reliable and complete statistical system for the observation of globalization that is accepted by all concerned.

The crucial questions are simple. What must we observe? Who is going to do it? How is it to be done? Who will provide the means?

The development of a statistical system is very similar to a business project. One needs people with vision, investors, customers, a manager, a business plan, a work program, an objective, a quality audit, workers, and an organization that meets the needs of all the parties involved, including society as a whole.

The existing systems are not satisfactory for a number of reasons:

1) They are not specifically geared to observing globalization, as they were designed with a different purpose in mind and on the basis of a different view of the world. This is a problem of vision.
2) Each of the existing systems has its own investors, who guide their investments according to different views, priorities, and objectives.
3) Each has its own customers to satisfy, which means that the design of the service is very different depending on the producer body.
4) Insufficient resources are allocated to developing methodologies and producing information, with the result that quality suffers.
5) The total absence of a plan or quality auditing by the producer bodies means that there are always some doubts about the validity of the figures. This creates a pernicious atmosphere of distrust.

If there is a positive aspect, it is that there are managers all over the world: thousands of statisticians, specializing in all possible areas and working with various civil institutions—particularly the International Statistical Institute—in accordance with precise and ethical codes of practice. They will be able to carry out a project of this kind as soon as they are given the necessary resources and freedom to act.

The Various Global Statistical Systems

At present, a whole range of sources are quoted as references in the study of globalization. These include in particular:

- the World Trade Organization (WTO), which periodically publishes figures on world trade in goods (not in services) by region of the world and by sector of economic activity;
- the United Nations and its associated regional or specialized bodies, such as the United Nations Statistical Department (UNSD), the United Nations Economic Commission for Europe (UNECE), the United Nations Industrial Development Organization (UNIDO), and the Food and Agriculture Organization (FAO). Generally, the production of statistics by all these bodies depends on the good will of the member states, and there has unfortunately been very little harmonization of methodologies in many areas. The data are therefore neither very up-to-date nor precise, particularly with a view to comparability;
- the World Bank (WB) and the International Monetary Fund (IMF)—mainly monetary and financial statistics.

The real sources of statistics, however, are national. The National Statistical Institutes (they are not all called this, but no matter) and other ministerial departments are responsible for producing statistics. Whatever happens, these bodies will apply the international methodological agreements after they have been translated into national contexts; these bodies will apply the standardized definitions of statistical units and populations in their countries, in order to produce national statistics which will then have to be converted into international statistics by means of post-harmonization and aggregation.

These, then, are the people and bodies that produce today's world-level statistics. But the question is also "how?" They are produced by a myriad of experts, divided into working groups of national representatives, who meet at various intervals in the four corners of the globe and produce tons of paper containing conventions and definitions from scraps of information, which are often the result of a relatively insignificant compromise. Funding, which is spread very thinly over the many organizations and national government departments, often depends on local decisions made in the light of the interests and resources of those concerned.

Expertise and production capacity also vary widely from one country to another, and this fact, together with the differences in approach, explain why the international bodies receive products that are not sufficiently similar to be aggregated. Of what value, then, are international statistics? For want of anything better, they are still a precious source of information for many purposes—particularly when we have to use them for evaluating national situations. They become more problematic when we have to aggregate them in order to eliminate the national elements, which is precisely the case when studying many aspects of globalization. There is clearly a need, therefore, for better international cooperation.

The New Role of the Public Information Systems

A New Approach for Public Administrations

We are only at the beginning of the revolution resulting from the information society and globalization, which is very rapidly changing many things, including the way in which public administrations, companies, and households function. Public administrations at all levels—city, region, country, Europe—are called on to enter the era of *new governance* through total quality and transparency. This requirement is based on the information that the public administrations have to produce or collect, process, transform, and disseminate. The ability to manage large volumes of information, to extract relevant and reliable knowledge, and to offer high-quality service is the key to success in fulfilling their role as public administrations. This accumulated information will be spread over various administrations and stored in a multitude of public information systems without harmonization. For this information to be re-used and undergo trans-system processing, concepts used must be standardized to a high degree and their consistency and semantics must be checked over time and space.

Because of globalization, public administrations will have to (and have to be able to) provide other parties with more information and receive more from them in return. Obviously, it will be very important to harmonize the contents of the information systems as far as possible, unless we want to end up with a Tower of Babel. Language will once again be a major stumbling block for those outside the English-speaking world, since at the end of a protracted struggle, all we will be left with is a translation into the national languages of concepts produced by the American culture.

Diversity as a Handicap in Europe

With this technological challenge facing its national and European Community administrations, Europe is at two major disadvantages that compromise its chances of success and threaten to lead it to a subordinate position vis-à-vis the United States, not only regarding the hardware and software to be used for public information systems, but also the conceptual framework underlying their content.

The first disadvantage is the disparity of the linguistic and semantic vehicles for conveying information concepts. This problem is very clear to anyone needing to compare the information disseminated by the various EU member states. Concepts as basic as "household" and "business" or "professional activity" or "accident" are semantically close but nevertheless not identical in different countries.

The second disadvantage is that the levels of technological development and capacity are not the same in all the countries or at all the different administrative levels within a given country. This problem becomes even more acute if we think about enlarging the European Union.

In the 1990s, the development of information highways overthrew the traditional means of communication. E-mail and the Internet are part and parcel of the new communication tools that the people of Europe use every day both at work and in their private life, for purposes of consumption, instruction, or discussion. These same people, as citizens, also call for electronic services to enable them to deal with administrative matters at both the national and the European level. The existing public information systems should therefore offer new services, accessible to the general public at any time via their PCs, for filling in tax returns, for requesting documents and keeping track of their requests, or for electronic voting, for example.

If they are to be able to perform this new role, the public information systems are obliged to go onto the public information networks, such as the Internet. The real danger here is that they will become a potential target for electronic attacks aimed at lowering the quality of the service, disrupting operation, or copying, changing, or even destroying the data manipulated by these systems. In order to take up this challenge, the administration of the United States takes the view that since the Internet is used as a common platform for communication by American public information systems, it should have the same level of security as other critical infrastructures in the country (nuclear power plants, the oil infrastructure, etc.).[13]

In general, this calls for new constraints in terms of software and hardware architectures, data protection, and the confidentiality of public information systems. All tasks involving transfer, processing, and storage of information by these systems will be affected.

If Europe is not to succumb to the consequences of American hegemony in this field, it is vital that all parties concerned, both at the level of member states and at the level of the European Union, realize what is at stake and become aware of the impact and importance of the new information technologies in the construction or transformation of public information systems. This will involve in particular:

- the establishment of think tanks to examine the role of the information technologies in administrative processes;
- training and informing the decision-makers in public administrations and making them aware of the need to harmonize the content of information systems;
- launching pilot projects involving several administrations of EU member states.

The Need for a European Initiative

We therefore need European-level initiatives to deal with the problems described above—for example, by promoting the establishment in the member states of centers or institutes responsible for keeping track of standardization of the content of public information systems and offering assistance and training for national, regional, and infra-regional administration in the development and integration of their information systems.

European support must be provided for the establishment of structures of this kind, and to promote cooperation between them and coordination of their activities at the European level. This could be done by launching a new program providing both the financial support and the legal and technological framework for the establishment of a network of such centers or institutes. This new program would complement the Interchange of Data between Administrations program (IDA), which aims at developing infrastructures for telecommunications between administrations. It provides the networks and the tools, without concerning itself with content.

6. Conclusion

The move from a society of forces to a society of numbers must be based on an ontological philosophy so that the change can be guided by universal principles. Globalization must not take place blindly and simply in order to serve the economic interests of a few powerful entities, but should occur in the general interests of all the peoples of the world in such a way as to ensure a better distribution of wealth and a leveling of the right to prosperity, while guaranteeing that the environment is protected. We must not, however, fall into the neoconservative trap of trying to seek refuge in the old values of "fortress nations" with ethnic and religious identities, and rejecting any idea of opening up to the world. Globalization is a fact of life; it is a process of opening up to the interpenetration of all cultures; it is a change in our worldview.

To be in control of this process, we must understand it. We must, therefore, be able to observe it. We must be able to systematically measure all the aspects of globalization, the way they develop and are adopted by all the various peoples, and their interactions with social and environmental aspects.

It is the task of the United Nations and its Statistical Commission, with the help of other international organizations and all the national statistical services, to conduct a vast program for the collection and dissemination of the statistics needed to achieve this goal of transparency in globalization.

Only in this way will governments and peoples, armed with the same knowledge, be able to efficiently play their respective roles so that globalization will be the globalization of democracy, freedom, human rights, and solidarity between peoples the world over.

Finally, I think that globalization as we see it today is one of the first manifestations of a greater and more profound phenomenon—the emergence of a new world order, a global society based on freedom and the right of human beings to live together on this earth enjoying an equal share in the right to happiness. The first stage in this process is the information society that we have just entered.

NOTES

1. E. Baròn Crespo, *La globalisation de la démocratie* <http://www.global-progress.org/frances/aportaciones/baron.html>.

2. International Monetary Fund, *Globalisation, Opportunities and Challenges,* World Economic Outlook (Washington, D.C., May 1997).

3. C. Collobert, *Aux origines de la philosophie* (Paris: Editions Le Pommier-Fayard, 1999).

4. Ibid.

5. See *Eurobarometre,* Opinion polls taken by the European Commission (Luxembourg: OPOCE, 1999).

6. See J. De Rosnay, "Stratégie pour le cybermonde," *Le Monde Diplomatique,* "Révolution dans la communication," *Manière de voir* no. 46 (July–August 1999).

7. M. Kwanashie, "The Concept and Process of Globalization," *CBN Economic and Financial Review* 36, no. 4 (December 1998).

8. M. J. Mandel, "The New Economy. It Works in America. Will It Go Global?" *Business Week,* European edition (January 2000): pp. 36–39.

9. European Commission, "Communication au Conseil et au Parlement européen, au Comité des régions et au Comité économique et social," *La compétitivité des entreprises européennes face à la mondialisation-Comment l'encourager?* COM (1998) 718 Final.

10. Eurostat, *External and Intra-European Union Trade, Statistical Yearbook, 1958–1998* (Luxembourg: OPOCE, 1999).

11. P. Dicken, *Global Shift: Transforming the World Economy,* 3rd ed. (New York: Guilford Press, 1998), pp. 24–25.

12. See note 9.

13. See the Report of the President's Commission on Critical Infrastructure Protection, the United States <http://www.info-sec.com/pccip/web/report_index.html>.

CHAPTER 15

The Globalization of Justice

DINAH SHELTON

Globalization is generally regarded today as an economic and technological phenomenon that has blurred, if not erased, state boundaries and made it harder for states to regulate their own affairs. With the exchange of more than $1.5 trillion in the world's currency markets each day, and with the trade of nearly twenty percent of the world's goods and services each year, there can be no doubt that we are experiencing unprecedented technological change and a deepening of global economic interdependence. Yet globalization goes beyond a simple expansion of transnational markets and information. The interdependence of the world's people is not only economic, but social and cultural as well. Globalization may be defined as "the contemporary tendency for persons, corporations, and institutions to expand out of the confines of a nation or civilization, towards participation in and identification with a world community. This expansion takes the form of trade, investment, communications, culture, sport, citizen affinities, law,

Dinah Shelton is a professor of international law, human rights, and international environmental law at the Law School, University of Notre Dame. She is director of the doctoral program in human rights at the Center for Civil and Human Rights at Notre Dame, and a fellow of the University's Joan B. Kroc Institute for International Peace Studies and Helen Kellogg Institute for International Studies. She has been a visiting professor and lecturer at universities throughout the world and is the author of numerous books and articles on international law topics. She also serves on the executive councils of various human rights and environmental organizations and institutions.

223

and other contacts."[1] Thus, globalization is a holistic transformation of the international system, incorporating new actors and values that limit and even redefine state sovereignty. As such, globalization is reinforcing but also changing the paradigm of human rights, presenting unprecedented challenges and opportunities.

I. Human Rights as an Example of Globalization

The international protection of human rights is itself an aspect of globalization, perhaps its first great manifestation. Human rights express universal values that limit the power of the state and breach the concept of absolute state sovereignty by making the treatment of individuals and groups within each state a matter of international concern. During the past fifty years, international law concerning human rights has aimed at restraining powerful governments from infringing the fundamental rights and freedoms of those within the state's territory and jurisdiction. The 1993 Vienna World Conference on Human Rights, held forty-five years after the adoption of the Universal Declaration of Human Rights, produced a unanimous reaffirmation by the participating states that "human rights are universal, indivisible, and interdependent and interrelated. . . . While the significance of national and regional particularities and various historical, cultural and religious backgrounds must be borne in mind, it is the duty of States, regardless of their political, economic and cultural systems, to promote and protect all human rights and fundamental freedoms" (Sec. I, para. 5).

This revolution in favor of human rights has led to the adoption of global norms and the creation of regional systems to enforce those norms through judicial and quasi-judicial bodies. Beginning with the adoption in 1950 of the European Convention on Human Rights, regional systems have spread to the Americas and Africa, with a similar system nascent among the Arab states. Today only Asia lacks a regional system, and efforts are underway to create one, if not regionally, then subregionally. While there are clear differences among the protections afforded, all legal instruments creating regional systems refer to the Universal Declaration of Human Rights and to the Charter of the United Nations, providing a measure of uniformity in the fundamental guarantees and a reinforcement of the universal character of the Declaration.

The various regional instruments not only mention the global instruments, they also contain similar guarantees and in many instances use language identical to that contained in other instruments. The economic, social, and cultural rights proclaimed in the Universal Declaration of Human Rights are found in the American Declaration, the European Social Charter, and in the African and Arab charters. The Arab Charter and the African Charter include the principle of self-determination from Article 1 of the two United Nations (UN) covenants on human rights; indeed, the Arab Charter iterates virtually all of the rights contained in the International Covenant on Civil and Political Rights (ICCPR). The result is a global normative basis for human rights.

The global norms are applied by states within the context of UN and regional human rights systems. The term "system" encompasses the inter-dependence, complexity, and punctuated equilibrium that characterize the norms, institutions, and procedures particular to this field. Each human rights system has developed (1) a list or lists of internationally guaranteed human rights; (2) permanent institutions; and (3) compliance or enforce-ment procedures. The subsequent functioning of the systems has led to a growing democratization and spread of the rule of law to regions previously governed by repression and terror. The European system has had an unde-niable impact in these developments. The Council of Europe was the first organization to require that every member state accept the principles of the rule of law and of the enjoyment by all persons of human rights and funda-mental freedoms. It also was the first to create an international court for the protection of human rights and a procedure for individual denunciations of human rights violations. These crucial aspects of human rights protec-tion have spread to other regional systems, as have subsequent innovations in the European system, because each successive regional system has looked to the normative instruments and jurisprudence of the systems that were founded earlier, as its models.

In Europe, there has been a proliferation of regional institutions con-cerned with human rights and a broadening of human rights activities. In 1990 the Council of Europe created a program to strengthen genuine de-mocracy. It subsequently launched an initiative entitled "Globalization with-out Poverty." The project aims to promote the idea of social inclusiveness and concepts of global citizenship that focus on the rights and responsi-bilities of individuals. It affirms that extreme poverty and social exclusion are a denial of human rights. The 1993 Vienna Summit Declaration adopted by the Council of Europe Heads of State and Government included a com-mitment to combat racism, xenophobia, anti-Semitism, and intolerance. The Council then established a new mechanism, the European Commission against Racism and Intolerance (ECRI), to review Member States' legisla-tion, policies and other measures to combat racism and intolerance and to propose further action at local, national, and European levels. In May 1999 the Council of Europe acted again, to create the post of Commissioner for Human Rights. The function of the independent commissioner, who is elected for a nonrenewable six-year term, is to serve as "a non-judicial institution to promote education in, awareness of and respect for human rights, as embodied in the human rights instruments of the Council of Europe."

The Organization on Security and Cooperation in Europe and the European Community (EC) also are engaged in human rights activities. The Organization on Security and Cooperation in Europe (OSCE) has tended to focus on conflict prevention and mediation and the development of regional democracy. The European Community, in its transformation into the European Union (EU), has established that respect for basic rights is an integral part of EC law. In December 2000, the European Union approved a Charter of Fundamental Rights and Freedoms, which has adopted a Declaration of Fundamental Rights which has broader guarantees than the European Convention. The Parliament's Human Rights Sub-Committee has emphasized the global nature of its concern by producing an annual report on human rights in countries throughout the world.

The human rights revolution has been global not only in its norms and institutions, but in its impact. Democratic transitions in Africa, Central and Eastern Europe, and Latin America have emerged from the breakdown of authoritarian, repressive regimes, with a resulting dramatic decrease in the worst governmental abuses: disappearances, summary executions, torture, and other brutal violations of personal security. Yet, democratic transitions—especially when coupled with economic reforms—also pose enormous challenges when the countries involved attempt to build institutions that go beyond free elections, such as independent judicial systems, professional police and military, a free press, and accountable administrations. The response of human rights institutions suggests a broadening of human rights concerns. The global and regional bodies are occupied increasingly with issues of democracy, internal armed conflict, transnational crime, environmental protection, economic development, science and technology, and, indeed, the full range of activities that relate to equity, justice, and human dignity.

2. The Impact of Economic and Technological Globalization on Human Rights

Deregulation, privatization, and the opening of global markets have both contributed to and undermined the movement for human rights by loosening and even weakening state control over information, economic actors, and the movement of people, goods, and services. The opening of markets and incentives for exports are standard prescriptions for economic development, to help growth and raise per capita income. For many countries the results have been positive, but the link is not automatic. Increases in trade and investment can be accompanied by increased deprivation and human rights abuses.

On the positive side, global technology and the information revolution have made it virtually impossible for governments to control knowledge and restrict the right of individuals to seek, receive, and disseminate information. Ideas and information now flow freely, as do people. These developments can be seen as an implementation of Article 19 of the Universal Declaration of Human Rights, which states that everyone has a right to "receive and impart information and ideas through any media and regardless of frontiers." Other human rights benefit in turn, as the idea of human rights spreads and its values are strengthened.[2] Entities such as the Cable News Network (CNN), the fax, and the Internet mean governments are no longer able to hide human rights violations or prevent their citizens from having access to the outside world. With the number of television sets per thousand people doubling between 1980 and 1995, and the number of Internet users surpassing 700 million, monitoring human rights compliance and "mobilizing shame" have become far easier. Ease of travel and communications also have enabled networks of transnational nongovernmental organizations to develop in strength and influence. Nongovernmental organizations (NGOs) have become effective advocates for human rights not only vis-à-vis governments, but with respect to corporations and international agencies such as the World Bank. NGO efforts, motivated by concern for human rights, were largely responsible for defeating in 1998 a proposed Multilateral Agreement on Investment.

Globalization arguably also promotes at least some human rights by weakening or eliminating governmental interference with individual economic decision making. Like the law of civil and political rights, trade law is largely aimed at limiting state power. Economic, social, and cultural rights, in contrast, more frequently call for state regulation, and it is here that globalization may pose the most problems.

While weakening the state, globalization is enhancing the capability of non-state actors to violate human rights. Powerful multinational companies and individuals seeking competitive advantage can leverage weaker governments to allow trade and investments to proceed without respect for the fundamental rights of their citizens and foreign workers. From environmental disasters such as Bhopal to the use of forced labor in Myanmar, human rights guarantees are undermined by economic interests seemingly beyond the control of the state. Violations of human rights that are often observed in export processing zones and in the factories of multinational corporations generally go without redress because human rights treaties were written to govern the conduct of state agents, not private actors.

Unregulated markets also produce inequities that concentrate power and wealth in a small group of people, companies, and states, thereby marginalizing large groups and depriving many of basic needs and economic, social, and cultural rights. According to the United Nations Development Program's 1999 Human Development Report, in 1998 the assets of the three wealthiest individuals in the world exceeded the combined gross domestic product (GDP) of *all* the least developed countries and their 600 million people. With mergers and acquisitions, by 1998 ten companies controlled 85 percent of the $31 billion pesticide market, and ten networks controlled 86 percent of the $262 billion telecommunications market. Given these concentrations, and despite transnational investment and trade, more than eighty countries had per capita incomes lower at the end of the 1990s than they were at the beginning of the decade. During the financial crisis in Asia more than 13 million people lost their jobs. Even in less troubled areas, restructuring, mergers, and acquisitions have led to massive layoffs, with the result that economic growth has done little or nothing to reduce unemployment even in wealthy, industrialized countries. In such conditions, governments may lack the capacity to ensure respect for human rights in the workplace and society at large. In short, human rights problems increasingly stem not from governments that are too strong, but from those that are too weak.

Various human rights violations linked to globalization can be cited. International crimes involving gross human rights violations are burgeoning. Illicit trade in drugs, weapons, laundered money, and even people is on the increase. The traffic in women and girls for sexual exploitation is estimated to be a $7 billion-a-year business. Organized crime syndicates are estimated to rival multinational corporations in economic power, thereby undermining personal security and an array of human rights. Free movement of capital, a precondition of increased foreign investment, allows for money laundering if currency controls are removed before a proper regulatory environment has been established. Free transit of goods can include stolen cars as well as new products. New technologies allow for the theft of intellectual property.

The weakening of state authority can also be seen in the number of ethnic conflicts that have arisen in recent decades. These are supported by an unregulated trade in conventional arms and the growth of mercenary armies. Of the sixty-one major conflicts fought between 1989 and 1998, all but three were internal armed conflicts. In failed states, armed tribes, families, or political groups hold sway over territories where there is little or no rule of law or government authority. Human rights, like other legal restraints, give way to anarchy and unrestrained exercise of power.

Specific human rights are threatened by globalization. Privacy, for example, is under threat from lack of computer personal data protection. The business community is concerned to maintain access to and transfer of electronic information across borders, but in many cases the protection of personal privacy is inadequate. Europe has responded with several regional initiatives as well as national data protection laws.[3] Other states and regions have been slower to respond to the problem, but several are in the process of adopting privacy laws similar to those of Europe. More important would be the adoption of a global agreement authorizing the blocking of data transfers in order to protect personal privacy, something now lacking.

Cultural and linguistic rights also face an onslaught from open markets, but the trends are seemingly contradictory. There is no doubt that globalization stimulates the transfer of cultural goods. A study by the United Nations Organization for Education, Science, and Culture (UNESCO) indicated that trade in cultural goods tripled between 1980 and 1991, stimulated by new technologies such as satellite communications, the Internet, and videocassettes. In this field, like others, mergers and acquisitions have produced a concentration of ownership and driven out local industries. Hollywood films controlled 70 percent of the European film market in 1996—more than double the percentage of the previous decade—and 83 percent of the Latin American film market. At the same time, in contrast, cultural traditions from throughout the world are penetrating increasingly multiethnic states, and there has been a resurgence of interest in local cultures and in the preservation of languages.

Human rights also come into conflict with intellectual property rights in the pharmaceuticals industry. Property rights undermine the right to health in poorer countries that lack the resources to purchase necessary medications. In addition, the development of many medicines is based on knowledge acquired without compensation from indigenous groups and on the appropriation of their biological resources.

3. Integrating the Two Faces of Globalization

The responses of the international community to the problems posed by globalization are nascent and multifaceted. Some are more promising than others. Part of the difficulty lies in the conflicting predictions about the impact of economic globalization. On the one hand are those who are convinced that market mechanisms and global economic integration will lead to better conditions for all. On the other hand are those who believe that economic growth will not suffice by itself in guaranteeing social progress and that therefore some set of basic rules and institutions is necessary to protect workers and other vulnerable parts of society from disadvantage and abuse of power. A further complication arises from a North-South division over whether guarantees of minimum worker rights and other trade conditions related to human rights are legitimate or whether they instead constitute a disguised form of protection for domestic industries and producers in industrialized countries.

United Nations human rights bodies have begun a general effort to study the impact of globalization on the full enjoyment of human rights.[4] Based on a recognition that globalization is not merely an economic process but one that has social, political, environmental, cultural, and legal dimensions affecting human rights, the UN Human Rights Commission and Sub-Commission have authorized studies on issues related to globalization. The Sub-Commission also unanimously adopted a resolution on trade liberalization and its impact on human rights[5] in which it requests all governments and economic policy forums to take international human rights obligations and principles fully into account in international economic policy formulation, while opposing sanctions and "negative conditionalities" on trade as a means for integrating human rights into international economic policy and practice. The resolution also requests the UN High Commissioner for Human Rights to collaborate with the World Trade Organization (WTO) and its member states to emphasize the human rights dimensions of trade and investment liberalizations and to take steps to ensure that human rights principles and obligations are fully integrated in future negotiations at the WTO. Finally, it calls on civil society to promote within states the incorporation of human rights obligations into economic policy processes and to monitor and publicize the effects of economic policy that fail to take such obligations into account.

The issue of minimum labor standards has arisen in several fora.[6] First, the International Labor Organization (ILO), with its unique tripartite structure, has affirmed a code of fundamental workers' rights applicable in all states without regard to the ratification of particular ILO treaties. ILO conventions and recommendations ensure, inter alia, freedom of association and the right to form trade unions and to negotiate terms and conditions of employment; they protect vulnerable groups against abuse and prohibit forced labor. The new legally binding code sets forth the minimum standards applicable around the globe in the face of deregulation and privatization, stemming the "race to the bottom" in the name of competitiveness. It is based on the ILO Constitution, whose preamble begins by affirming that "universal and lasting peace can be established only if it is based upon social justice" and that "the failure of any nation to adopt humane conditions of labor is an obstacle in the way of other nations which desire to improve the conditions in their own countries." The ILO's 1998 adoption of a treaty on child labor is another reflection of this response to labor abuses worldwide.

In contrast to the ILO, the WTO has rejected adopting a "social clause" or other standards relating to minimum labor standards because of objections from developing countries. Prior to and during the Seattle meeting of WTO member states in 2001, developing countries unanimously opposed any discussion or negotiation on labor standards in the WTO. Industrialized countries generally recommended increased collaboration between the WTO and the ILO Secretariats, while the United States called for a work program to address issues relating to labor standards. It is also clear that there is considerable opposition to recognition by the WTO of the legitimacy of trade sanctions for egregious human rights violations, either unilaterally or pursuant to the decision of an international human rights body.

Third, the issue of social conditionality arose in the context of negotiations for a further Lomé agreement between Europe and the Africa, Caribbean, and Pacific states. The previous agreement expired in February 2000. The European Union (EU) sought to make good governance, democracy, respect for human rights, and protection of the rule of law essential elements of the next agreement. Failure to respect any of these would allow the suspension of assistance. The developing countries expressed reservations about this approach, and this hesitancy is reflected in the Cotonou Agreement that replaced Lomé IV.

Those concerned with ensuring respect for human rights not only by states but by non-state actors are taking other actions, as they perceive the ineffectiveness of the traditional regulatory approach. Victims of violations are increasingly seeking legal redress against abuse by individuals and multinational companies through litigation brought either in the country of incorporation or wherever the violator is found. Such actions provide compensation for victims and may help deter future violations. The prospect of expensive litigation or awards of damages in turn has stimulated companies to draft codes of conduct for their enterprises.[7] Consumer boycotts, selective investments, and labeling programs (e.g., "Rugmark") provide further impetus for corporate action. Today the best codes of conduct are detailed and monitored by outside auditors. A study by the ILO in November 1998[8] compiled documentation on more than two hundred private initiatives, including codes and labeling programs.

Perhaps the most significant development in the area of human rights in response to the challenges of globalization is the increasing willingness of the international community to impose direct human rights obligations on non-state actors. The actions are considerable, and several can be cited: efforts within Europe to prosecute Pinochet and other human rights violators; work by the International Law Commission to draft a code of offenses against the peace and security of mankind; adoption by the General Assembly of a declaration of human duties; and creation of a growing number of international criminal tribunals. The establishment of a permanent international criminal court and the concomitant identification of conduct that constitutes an "international crime" represent the furthest development to date of the notion of international justice in response to globalization.

Taken together, these developments signal a recognition that as a matter of international law and policy, all actors—individuals, companies, and states—ought to be accountable for violations of fundamental norms of international justice. The restriction on immunity for heads of state reflected by the Pinochet case is perhaps the most dramatic example to date of this development. Yet, it merely reflects the reality articulated a half century ago by the chief judgment at Nuremberg: "crimes against international law are committed by men, not by abstract entities, and only by punishing individuals who commit such crimes can the provision of international law be enforced." The ad hoc International Criminal Tribunals for Yugoslavia and Rwanda and the establishment of a permanent International Criminal Court expresses the world community's interest in imposing sanctions on violations of fundamental international norms of justice, while avoiding the problems inherent in domestic prosecution of international crimes.

If direct imposition of responsibility on non-state actors for human rights violations or consumer actions fails to sway multinational enterprises, economic studies can provide a basis for these enterprises to be concerned with human rights. A recent study of ninety-three countries by a trade economist showed that repressive countries pay less in wages per worker output than do democratic developing countries; the indications are that the repressive countries' wages are not being set by the free market.[9] Failing to require autocracies to adhere to fundamental labor standards allows them to maintain an unfair trade advantage. The study also demonstrated that economic returns and economic growth are greatest in countries that are demo-cratic and generally respect human rights. It thus may be that the goals of human rights and of the market reinforce each other, and that the two faces of globalization are both molded on the model of human dignity and justice.

4. Effectiveness of Human Rights Regulations

It is important to assess the real impact of human rights norms and insti-tutions, i.e., human rights governance, on state behavior, in order to reflect on whether imposing similar human rights obligations on non-state actors would be effective and what strategies could be developed to improve com-pliance. While abuses and assaults on individuals undoubtedly continue to be perpetrated around the world, it is also clear that human rights gover-nance has led to an overall improvement in the treatment of persons by states during the past half century. Despite continuing controversy about its aims, normative content, and the powers of the institutions it has created, human rights governance can be said to have restrained many dictatorial powers and established the criteria for the transition to democracy and rule of law. It has also succeeded in challenging many totalitarian and authori-tarian governments, although it cannot claim sole credit for the surge of democratization over the past two decades.[10]

Success in human rights governance can be attributed to several factors. First, unlike many global issues, human rights governance is aided by its moral and ethical dimensions and the innate desire of every human being for fulfillment of the norms. No one wants to be the subject of human rights violations, and there are far more persons identifying with victims than with violators. The very *idea* of human rights as a legitimate claim of every individual, founded in theology, morality, and philosophy, is thus a power-ful governance tool.[11]

Second, and linked to the first factor, civil society has insisted upon and achieved the right to participate from the beginning in the development of international human rights governance structures. Nongovernmental human rights organizations have played an essential role at every stage, from nego-tiating norms and standards to enforcing them, creating a global human rights movement. Nongovernmental organizations represent the assembly of individuals who are actual or potential victims of human rights violations and who are concerned to prevent and remedy governmental actions con-trary to human rights guarantees.

Third, the human rights movement of civil society and like-minded states produced relatively early consensus about the general normative content of human rights, reinforced by repetition in subsequent global and regional treaties and declarations.[12] This development of human rights as international law produced a normative pull toward compliance.

Fourth, states are held accountable through a still growing, interlocking set of institutions with a mandate to address human rights issues through a variety of techniques. Global and regional intergovernmental institutions provide the forum for NGOs to place issues on the human rights agenda. In turn, states and intergovernmental institutions rely on the information brought to them by human rights groups to expose violations and pressure states to conform to their obligations. Regional courts are proving particularly effective in securing redress for individual victims and consequent changes in the laws and practices of member states, in part because of the prestige attached to courts, but also because of the quality of the judges and their carefully crafted judicial opinions. This has led to a virtually unblemished record of compliance with judgments of human rights courts.

Fifth, some of the major human rights successes stem from linking the topic to other issues, such as peace and security, economic development, and environment. Such linkage can provide incentives for states less motivated to respect human rights, increasing the compliance pull and the effectiveness of human rights guarantees. Developments in Central and Eastern Europe initiated by the Helsinki Conference on Security and Cooperation in Europe and its transformation into one of the largest regional organizations concerned with human rights are instructive in the value of linking human rights to other topics of international concern. The United Nations represents the largest example of issue linkage. A state wishing to join the United Nations and participate in programs it finds useful must accept human rights obligations in return.

While there have been successes, human rights governance has also failed in some highly visible instances to prevent or halt massive abuses, including genocide. The reasons are many. First, there are legal restraints. Human rights has been hampered by traditional concepts of state sovereignty and domestic jurisdiction, as well as by the consent-based nature of international obligation that prevents enforcement of norms against nonconsenting states. This legal barrier is reinforced by the conflict of interest inherent in a system where states violating human rights also participate in standard-setting, compliance monitoring, and enforcement. At an extreme, this leads to challenges to the normative basis of human rights governance from ruling elites, who seek to retain power by invoking cultural relativism. They challenge the universality of human rights despite their participation in drafting normative instruments guaranteeing such rights and their subsequent voluntary consent through ratification.

In a more subtle challenge, the lack of political will to take human rights seriously is reflected in the underfunding of monitoring bodies and in efforts to undermine the independence of commissions and committees. Underfunding and understaffing are problems in nearly every human rights body. At the United Nations, human rights activities account for less than 2 percent of the budget of the organization. The regional African Commission on Human Rights has repeatedly complained of shortage of staff and equipment. An Organization for African Unity (OAU) budgetary crisis has meant several projects of the Commission had to be suspended and one session was cut from two weeks to eight days. As of June 2, 1998, Organization of American States (OAS) members owed more than $48 million in contributions, an amount that represented one and one half times the annual budget of the organization.[13] Only twenty of the fifty-three members are up to date in their assessments. Two states have not paid for twelve years and two others for ten years.[14]

Second, and more generally, most states exhibit a reluctance to criticize others for human rights violations, unless there are independent political reasons to do so, such as ideological conflicts or unfriendly relations. In many cases, the reluctance stems from concern about reciprocal complaints, but it also derives from the multifaceted nature of international relations. States usually must balance, and often subordinate, consideration of human rights issues in relation to other international concerns, including trade, military and strategic policy, and foreign investment. When human rights does become a cornerstone of bilateral and multilateral relations, particularly on the part of a powerful state or a group of states, it can have a significant positive impact on compliance with human rights norms.

Third, human rights governance is limited by its own design, whose objective is to restrain powerful government agents. It has not succeeded in addressing the massive violations that occur in weak or failed states where anarchy and civil conflict prevail, because violations by non-state actors that cannot be controlled by a state generally fall outside the scope of most human rights law.[15] International human rights institutions and systems thus lack the power to step into failed states, and so far they have been unable to develop new institutions and procedures to prevent or remedy violations in such states. Even where the state is a functioning entity, increasing deregulation and globalization are creating powerful non-state actors outside the governance structure. These will call for new governance mechanisms in the future as states voluntarily renounce some of their power in favor of the private sector.

Despite these problems, overall there is considerable evidence that states have responded to recommendations of the UN Human Rights Committee, the Committee on the Elimination of All Forms of Racial Discrimination, and other UN bodies, such as the thematic rapporteurs appointed to study specific problems. Over time respect for human rights has become a test of legitimacy for governments, making it important for them to do something about violations. Judgments of the regional tribunals have led to changes in laws and practices as well. In Europe it is relatively easy to demonstrate the effect of the European Convention on Human Rights and European Court judgments: Austria, for example, has modified its Code of Criminal Procedure;[16] Belgium has amended its Penal Code, its laws on vagrancy, and its Civil Code;[17] France has strengthened the protection for privacy of telephone communications;[18] Germany has modified its Code of Criminal Procedure regarding pre-trial detention, given legal recognition to transsexuals, and taken action to expedite criminal and civil proceedings;[19] The Netherlands has modified its Code of Military Justice and the law on detention of mental patients;[20] Ireland has created a system of legal aid;[21] Sweden has introduced rules on expropriation and legislation on building permits;[22] Switzerland has amended its Military Penal Code and completely reviewed its judicial organization and criminal procedure applicable to the army.[23] According to Buergenthal, "the decisions of the European Court are routinely complied with by European governments. As a matter of fact, the system has been so effective in the last decade that the Court has for all practical purposes become Western Europe's constitutional court. Its case law and practice resemble that of the United States Supreme Court."[24]

The impact of the system in Europe is relatively easy to demonstrate because of the follow-up procedure, which requires states to report to the Committee of Ministers on their compliance with decisions of the European Court. In a similar fashion, the Inter-American Court maintains open files on cases until the defendant state carries out the judgment. It has closed a number of cases following compliance.[25]

The very success of human rights governance is creating new problems. Beginning in the early 1980s, the caseload of the European system, for example, began to double approximately every five years.[26] During its first eighteen years, the European Court decided 26 judgments while the next eighteen years brought 472 decisions. During 2001 the Court issued more than one-third of the total number of judgments delivered since it was created.[27] It now receives close to 800 letters every day. From 1988 to 1999 the number of provisional applications grew from 4,044 to 20,538. Then in one year, the number jumped to 26,398. In 2001, the number again jumped, to 31,393. The number of cases registered after preliminary examination shows a similar increase. During 2001, 13,858 cases were registered, some 2200 more than during the entire first 30 years of the Convention. Not only do the statistics reveal a huge surge in complaints, they show the origin of the complaints in every member state. This means the Court must work in thirty-seven national official languages in order to ensure that the right of petition is real and not illusory. The Inter-American Commission's caseload is also expanding; on January 20, 1998, the Commission had 976 cases under consideration and a staff of twelve lawyers to handle them. The question is whether even a full-time court can cope with the increase.

Finally, there is always the risk of "backsliding." On May 26 1998, the government of Trinidad and Tobago denounced the Inter-American Convention on Human Rights, the only state ever to do so. It also denounced the Optional Protocol to the ICCPR. In January 1998, Jamaica withdrew from the ICCPR Optional Protocol on the death penalty, and the government of Barbados announced that it was considering denouncing the American Convention. While these events challenge both regional and global standards, so long as the states remain members of the Organization of American Studies (OAS), they are bound by regional norms and subject to the jurisdiction of the Inter-American Commission.

5. Conclusion

Global governance, that is, a framework of rules, institutions, and established practices, can set limits and provide incentives for individuals, organizations, and states. In this respect, further mechanisms must be devised for making human rights norms binding for corporations and individuals, not just governments. A common core of values and a widely felt sense of responsibility must guide globalization. Concepts and principles of economic efficiency and competitive markets must become the means to the end of human well-being and not ends in themselves. Otherwise, the promotion of increased international trade, investment, and finance will come at the expense of the observance and protection of fundamental human rights. In this case, it may be expected that the numbers of economic and environmental refugees will swell, conflicts will erupt, and economic benefits will be transitory at best.

Thus, the most important issue for global governance in the next century will be reconciling free markets with support for human rights.

NOTES

1. Pendleton M. D., *A New Human Right—The Right to Globalization,* 22 Fordham Int'l L. J. 2052, 2054 (1999).

2. But rights do not always benefit from technological innovations. In Rwanda, the Radio-Television Libre des Mille Collines was a significant instrument in inciting the genocide.

3. See Organization for Economic Cooperation and Development, *Recommendation of the Council Concerning Guidelines on the Protection of Privacy and Transborder Flows of Personal Data,* Sept. 23, 1980, O.E.C.D. Doc. C(80)58 Final, reprinted in 20 I.L.M. 422 (1981); Council of Europe, *Convention for the Protection of Individuals with Regard to Automatic Processing of Personal Data,* Europ. T.S. No. 108, reprinted in 20 I.L.M. 317; Council Directive No. 97/66/EC of 15 Dec. 1997 concerning the *Processing of Personal Information and the Protection of Privacy in the Telecommunications Sector,* O.J. L24/1 (1998).

4. See Commission on Human Rights, Resolution 1999/59 of 27 April 1999 and Sub-Commission Resolution 1999/8 of 25 August 1999 on *Globalization and Its Impact on the Full Enjoyment of All Human Rights.*

5. Sub-Commission resolution 1999/30 of 26 August 1999.

6. See OECD, Trade, Employment and Labor Standards: A Study of Core Workers' Rights and International Trade (1996).

7. E.g., the Sullivan Principles; the McBride Principles; the Minnesota Principles; The Valdez Principles; the Caux Principles; the Kyosei Principles. See Compa L. and Hinchliffe-Darricarrère T., *Enforcing International Labor Rights through Corporate Codes of Conduct,* 33 Colum J. Trans. L. 663 (1995); Perez-Lopez J., *Promoting International Respect for Worker Rights through Business Codes of Conduct,* 17 Fordham Int'l L. J. 1 (1993); OECD, *Trade Employment and Labour Standards: A Study of Core Workers' Rights and International Trade* (1996).

8. GB 273.WP.SDL/1; see also Hilowitz J., *Labelling Child Labour Products: A Preliminary Study* (ILO, 1997); Sajhau J., *Business Ethics in the Textile, Clothing and Footwear Industries: Codes of Conduct* (ILO, 1997).

9. Rodrik D., *Democracies Pay Higher Wages,* NBER Working Paper No. 6364 (1998). See Bernstein A., Labor Standards: Try a Little Democracy, *Business Week* (Dec. 13, 1999), 42.

10. Demonstrating causality in the field of human rights is a perennial problem. Governments generally deny that human rights abuses are taking place and are not inclined to admit that any positive changes are due to international pressure. Much of the evidence for the impact of human rights norms and institutions is therefore anecdotal or circumstantial, apart from those instances where evidence of compliance must be transmitted by a state, as is the case with judgments of the European and Inter-American Courts of Human Rights.

11. See Lauren P. G., *The Evolution of International Human Rights: Visions Seen,* University of Pennsylvania Press, 1998.

12. Subsequent debates about the details of the rights have emerged, of course, as well as questions about priorities and resolution of problems when rights conflict. These developments, as well as recent efforts to add to the catalogue of human rights show the importance of normative consensus. Claims that development, environment, drinking water, and other issues are matters of human rights have provoked political debate and division that have prevented normative or institutional evolution to deal with them as human rights matters.

13. Gaye S., *OAU Owed 48 million by Member States,* Pan African News Agency, June 2, 1998.

14. Id.

15. Non-state actors are covered by humanitarian law and international criminal standards concerning crimes against humanity and war crimes, but these topics are usually, if mistakenly, treated separately from human rights in international law.

16. See Neumeister, 8 Eur.Ct.H.R. (Ser.A) (1968); Stogmuller, 9 Eur.Ct.H.R. (Ser.A) (1969); Matznetter, 10 Eur.Ct. H.R. (Ser.A) (1969); Ringeisen, 13 Eur.Ct.H.R. (Ser.A) (1971); and Bonisch, 92 Eur.Ct.H.R. (Ser.A) (1985).

17. De Wilde, Ooms and Versyp (Vagrancy Cases), 12 Eur.Ct.H.R. (Ser. A) (1970) and Marckx, 31 Eur.Ct.H.R. (Ser. A) (1979) (discrimination between legitimate and illegitimate children).

18. Kruslin and Huvig, 176B Eur.Ct.H.R. (Ser.A) (1990) (wiretapping).

19. See e.g. Luedicke, Belkacem and Koc, 29 Eur.Ct.H.R. (Ser. A) (1978) (interpreters fees).

20. Engel, 22 Eur.Ct. H.R. (1976) (military penal code) and Winterwerp, 33 Eur.Ct.H.R. (Ser.A) (1979) (mentally ill).

21. Airey, 32 Eur.Ct.H.R. (Ser. A) (1979).

22. Sporrong and Lonnroth, 88 Eur.Ct.H.R. (Ser. A) (1985).

23. Eggs v. Switerland, Committee of Ministers, 1980.

24. Buergenthal T. & Shelton D., *Protecting Human Rights in The Americas: Cases and Materials,* N.P., Engel Pub., 3rd ed., 1996.

25. See, e.g., Velasquez Rodriquez v. Honduras, Inter-Am.Ct.H.R. Order of 19 September 1996, reprinted in Annual Report of the Inter-American Court of Human Rights 1996, OAS/Ser.L/V/III.35, Dec. 4 (1997) at 209; Godinez Cruz Case, ibid. at 213.

26. In 1982, the Registry inscribed more than 500 applications for the first time; in 1988 more than 1000 applications were registered. By 1992, the number of registered applications reached 2,037. See European Commission of Human Rights, Survey of Activities and Statistics (1993). The number of court judgments has similarly risen. During its first fifteen years, it issued 17 judgments in regard to 11 cases. During the next ten years, 59 judgments were adopted. From 1984 to 1993, the number jumped to 372.

27. The Court delivered 888 judgments in 2001 out of the total number of 2,597 judgments delivered by the Court since 1959. Statistics taken from the European Court of Human Rights, Survey of Activities 2001 (Council of Europe 2002).

CHAPTER 16

Globalization: A New Framework for Women's Rights

ELISABETH G. SLEDZIEWSKI

Having arisen out of the great abstractions of Western modernity, globalization has also surpassed them. Wherever globalization builds links among humans, it also imposes a new link between what is universal and what is unique. This relationship is not only richer and more concrete, but also more fragile than that brought about by the liberal movement and two centuries of socialist offshoots.

We underestimate this evolving movement to a large extent by limiting its impact to production, trade, and administration. On the contrary, globalization is affecting little by little all spheres of human activity and all levels of the representation and creation of social ties. This evolution risks becoming all the more evident in a sphere where profound upheavals have been occurring for some fifty years, the sphere of relations between the sexes. Confirming and easing the revolutions of the second half of the twentieth century, the "global moment" moves the issue of women's rights to a planetary scale. It renews the status and the content of social claims, as well as the decisions that are made in this sphere.

Elisabeth G. Sledziewski, who holds an aggregation in philosophy and a state doctorate in literature, is a lecturer and director of research in political science at the University of Rennes 1. Her work concerns the birth of modern political society (the French Revolution), the role of women in democracy from the eighteenth to twentieth centuries, and changes in women's identity. She is an expert consultant to the Council of Europe on gender equality.

These tendencies, today unequally explicit, call for analysis. Touching on the most minute stitches of the human fabric—the male-female relationship—the movement brought about by globalization takes on an anthropological importance which it is clearly still difficult to grasp but which it is appropriate to emphasize.

Along with the global moment there seems to be, in effect, a reuniting of the conditions for a deep reform of the schemas which up to now have ordered the feminist logic of winning rights and equalizing conditions, both in terms of intellectual categories and in terms of political objectives. It is necessary to understand the ingredients of such a reform, both as a doctrinal critique and as a possible exit from the impasses of Eurocentrism and abstract universalism. It is also appropriate to evaluate this historical opportunity from the original context of globalization. This opportunity obviously does not come from a simple chronological coincidence, but rather from a structural affinity between the paradigms of the global society and the values called for by the new dynamic of male-female relations.

I. The Equality of Men and Women under the Regime of Abstract Universalism

To evaluate the extent of the transformation that has occurred, we must return to the historical construction of the women's rights issue, from the revolutions of the second half of the eighteenth century to the present.

Democratic modernity has in fact taken two centuries to develop, very laboriously and very imperfectly, its thinking about the equal role of men and women in the democratic society. In the process, it has displayed tremendous inconsistency, alternating between progress and regression, voluntary advances and deliberate delays, without ever coming to terms with the ontological contradiction between the universal abstract and its pluralist personification, between the creation of human rights and their realization by sexual human subjects. It is on this a priori principle of egalitarian universalism that we are forced to place the accent.

If women's issues seem to be of lesser importance in today's global context, against criticisms offered in the name of parity and group identity, it is perhaps because they are repressed by the emancipatory logic which surrounds them. This discourse can itself be an instrument for excluding women from the public sphere, providing arguments for its perpetuation.

Western democracy, differing in this respect from Christian thought, has discovered rather tardily the social relations between the sexes: while recognizing that democratic society is composed of men and women, it did not know what role to assign to the latter group. If it has taken decades to integrate, often through violent conflict, social rights within a doctrinal framework, it has been even more difficult to integrate women's rights. In this culture fashioned by Christianity, multiple egalitarian references were available to rethink the relationship between the rich and the poor according to modern, rational norms. But for the relationships between men and women, conceived for centuries under the sign of schism or even submission, modern society has had to improvise.

On the one hand, modern society has chosen to bring forward, even accentuate, the inequalities inherited from a compartmentalized society. The infantilized and morbid woman of the nineteenth century, and the woman as submissive adornment for a large part of the twentieth century, have each fulfilled their reassuring function as an antidote to the dizziness of the acceleration of history. On the other hand, modern democratic society has developed a resolutely egalitarian doctrine, which finally accords men and women—at least in principle—the same prerogatives, freedoms, and place in society—on the condition that women do not recognize their sexuality or any difference between them in this regard. The denial of any heterogeneity between these two concrete modes of human existence, masculinity and femininity, and the ensuing repression of the sexual dimension by political leaders have formed the framework of modern democratic universalism, with its resolutely abstract orientation. Sexless citizenship has been defined as the only possibility in the eyes of the law.

The development of women's rights, the modernization of the social relations between the sexes, and the entrance of women into democracy's mainstream were conceived in the spirit of the Enlightenment, that is, in a style which is both progressive and Newtonian. According to these criteria, based on those from deterministic physics that see the universe as an intelligible continuum, every moral and cultural recognition of an ontological discontinuity between the sexes appears to validate the oppression of women, notably, by giving a rational foundation to their exclusion from public life. From this point of view, admitting that "les femmes ne sont pas des hommes comme les autres,"[1] that is, taking into account the most elementary reality, purely and simply forbids asking the question about their rights. Conversely, insisting on putting women's rights on the political agenda suggests the exclusion from this same agenda of the male-female discontinuity, by pretending that there are not two sexes, or that the difference of sex doesn't exist. In other words, ignoring women's rights cannot be fought except by ignoring femininity. The equality between the subjects of masculine or feminine rights cannot be produced except by the reduction of differences to singularity, that is, at the price of denying sexual duality, a source of unmanageable antagonisms, thanks to the rational fiction of an indivisible and asexual human whole. This explains the position that certain convinced feminists have long held—and hold still—against the feminization of functions and professional titles. In its feminized version, the title for a position heretofore reserved for men is devalued, and women have the impression of having fought for nothing. Even affirmative action measures are formulated in terms of the dualist doctrine of parity, as is every positive active measure favoring the promotion of women in public life. The women who benefit from these measures are ashamed to be there as women, denouncing these "biological alms," with the recognition of their gender unjustifiably substituting for their human rights.

Let us recall that this universal, asexual definition of women's rights in the beginning, and for a long time, had as its effect the removal of women from the public sphere. This was the point where the culture of civic abstraction was historically the most pronounced, and where the semantic slippage in French of human rights to men's rights ("droits de l'homme") went most unperceived. In France in the First, Second, and Third Republics, the most effective barriers were erected against women's suffrage (until 1944), and this by political leaders who called for universal suffrage.

The inclusion of women's rights in this continuist and deterministic rationality has long been perceived as necessary, particularly for those who, in good or bad faith, act as the bugbear of the community as soon as the question of cultural identity or parity arises. Beyond the system that serves to desexualize the feminine subject in order to recognize her as a bearer of human rights, femininity is simply not thinkable. The feminine subject has the status of biological accident, cultural contingency, and political parasite, whose very evocation endangers the foundations of democracy, threatening to shake political society into clan regression and a chaos of values. From a classic liberal approach, in fact, only a homogenous world can produce and receive laws. This demand for monolithic univocity has been historically constituted through the centuries of the expansion of market capitalism, then industrial capitalism, based on the intellectual model of classical, physical, and mathematical science. The universe is a system that is integrally decipherable and that reacts to a uniform law. This model is not completely incompatible with pluralism, but on the contrary, it allows and even favors it, in the sense that it sees itself as capable of reining in centrifugal force, preventing a destabilizing effect. It is the same paradigm—of a universal law reflecting order and integrating the diversity of a world presumed to be homogenous—that structures the political concept of a common will, unique and indivisible, so central in French Republican doctrine. The result is a continuist and deterministic conception of history, where the individual is always marked by a distinctive identity and where all difference conceals possible discrimination. With so many threats present in the multiple realities of life and history, facing them requires all the unifying power of the law, all the simplistic strength of abstraction, and, in short, a strategy that dissolves the individual being to save the universal.

2. Global Paradigms

There are signs that the global moment is one of rupture with the challenge of the ontological effacement developed by liberal and socialist modernity. In a world characterized by connectivity and the coexistence of differences, globalization inaugurates a new configuration of the universal, where one can consider the reconciliation of individual and group dynamics, and where the substantial complementarity between humanity's masculine and feminine modes is affirmed. This change in the perception and treatment of the social relations between the sexes is manifested across two great emerging issues: male-female parity, and subsidiarity in national decision making in favor of equality.

The parity problem and the subsidiary approach, both at the center of the debates of the United Nations (UN) Fourth World Conference on Women (September 1995), mark a turning point in history. These illustrate, in fact, each in their way, a departure from abstract universalism. Although each has its own logic, the first ethical and the second political, they are, however, animated by the same general dynamic, that of the development of interdependencies within a network of concomitant and complementary expressions: the dynamic of globalization.

Let us return to this double rupture, which attests to the fact that in terms of women's rights, as in other areas of social practice and intellectual debate, the global moment imposes a renewal of the paradigms of modern humanity. It is that which accomplishes a revolution for parity, in denying one gender the faculty of expressing the entirety of humanity. It is that which also accomplishes the subsidiary revolution, by denying to the centralized authorities the monopoly on producing norms for the realization of universal goals of equality.

For ten years, with the initial impetus of the Council of Europe, which added the doctrine of the rights of the individual person to the agenda,[2] the problem of parity has enabled a philosophical, legal, and political critique of the universalist abstraction. Humanity is dual. If, in the context of a homogenous, centralized, and one-dimensional universe, the human being cannot be thought of as two species at the same time, it must then be brought into one simple view: that is, the masculine, which is seen to express the total human essence. But it is completely different in a universe that is multipolar and woven with interconnections, a universe no longer horrified by the non-uniqueness of the human being. Humanism, thus liberated from the need to reduce the duality to make it fit the masculine mold, can be emboldened to conceive of the human *being,* in its proper sense, in all of its ontological depth, and to recognize the authentic richness of its dual sexuality. This is precisely what modern democratic humanism and a part of the feminist movement have refused to do, by seeing in this dual sexuality merely a mutilating dispersion of the subject of human rights. From the new perspective of a global universal enriched by different modes of being, the making taboo of humanity's dual sexuality will be seen rather as a danger that leads to the misunderstanding of social realities and a more or less complacent impotence in the face of the persistent hegemony of schemas associating virility and civic capacity. If we pretend not to distinguish between men and women, how can we fight against the confiscation of public power by one group, how can we promote the rise of the other group to the responsibilities of public life?

It is this line of thought which prevailed in Peking, where the platform adopted by the states following the Fourth World Conference on Women consecrated the principle of balanced participation of both sexes in decision making and detailed the strategies and means for its accomplishment. This involves a dimension that is completely new in the doctrinal and strategic approach of women's rights. These rights are no longer considered to be the prerogative of a specific category, of a feminine minority requiring the protection of the collectivity, but rather as essential attributes of a humanity made up of two genders. The recognition of these attributes constitutes a vital challenge for all of society, even more so now that it must be assured jointly by men and women, with women now serving as partner political subjects, rather than as objects of concern for male decision makers. This integration of women's rights as fundamental, rather than a specialized application of an abstract model, in a balanced universal of human rights is given equal footing among the tendencies that characterize the global age as a new age of the "universal." In dynamic harmony with globalization, the idea of parity between men and women aims to move universalism toward the concrete. It is universalism because it connects the rights of women not to specificity (as was the case with the feminist agenda of specific rights from the 1960s through the 1980s, which limited the demands of the female subject to a sexual and procreative habeas corpus), but to the ontological duality of humanity as a whole. It is concrete because a political doctrine pretending to ignore the sexual duality that is fundamental in human relationships is no longer credible: this doctrine might have been able to bring about change in a context of sexual apartheid, which legitimized the masculine confiscation of decision and understanding, but it can no longer do so in the context of the growing diversity of civil society, with its multiplication of initiatives and circulation of knowledge.

Finally, the dynamic of globalization is directly working to bring out the principle of subsidiarity in the policies for promoting women's rights. In the modern world, first centered on Europe and then Americanized, and governed until very recently by a pyramidal conception of hegemony, the norms of humanism have been dictated in conformity with Western ideals and from there declared universal. Because of this, they have drawn considerable criticism, notably in the developing world, from a critical anthropological perspective in the name of the irreducible singularity of cultures and in reaction to an imperialism of values. This difference between countries dictating universal norms and countries anxious to maintain their own ethical sovereignty has marked all of the international conferences of the last half century. We have seen the two sides face off irreconcilably with equally strong arguments. On the one hand, the relativists demanded their right to uphold differences and showed suspicion toward models imposed from the outside. On the other hand, the universalists suspected that this demand hid a questioning of human rights, conveniently qualified as Western. This standoff has naturally affected the question of women's rights, whether it deals with their very definition or the means to promote them.

The Peking Conference seems to have marked an important turning point here as well. It saw, in fact, the affirmation of a new balance between a doctrinal core, made up of intangible principles—such as the equality of sexes or the full civic and social capacity of women—and diversified points of view from heterogeneous cultures with dissimilar priorities, followed by dissimilar effects in their actions toward equality. From within a global framework where each of the multiple actors is called upon to express principles from a unique vantage point, the question of women's rights henceforth can be looked at in a way that combines universality and subsidiarity without contradiction. In short, there is a universality of canons, but not a universality in the pretension to legislate on the diverse ways of codifying them. There exists an absolute limit to the cultural autonomy of each society, namely, the respect of the inalienable rights of the human person and therefore of each woman to moral and physical integrity and full participation in the political life of the society. This means that no state may invoke any local tradition to escape protecting and promoting these rights. However, it falls to each member of the global community to translate the universal standards and to apply them according to the individual norms of their culture. In the system of interconnected initiatives—concurrent and weakly hierarchical—that underlie the global society, national institutions, internal laws, grass-root movements, local associations, and in some cases individuals themselves are best placed to ensure an efficient, realistic, mobilization and proposal in favor of women's rights. Who, for example, would formulate in the same terms the objectives of democracy for the women who head large families in the developing world and for their less fecund counterparts in Europe? And who would claim that this healthy adjustment of local strategies might question the universal nature and need for egalitarian democracy?

At the same time, we must recognize that voices have been raised to warn against the risks of democratic universalism bowing too quickly to the concrete. Some women feel that the masculine-feminine declination of rights for the human person, by relativizing these rights, will weaken them: we can see the parallel with the objection made in its time to the theology of the Trinity, reputed to be "divisive" of the divine universal. Others, notably in Southern Europe where there is a strong patriarchal tradition, suggest that parity risks introducing a breach in universalism and involuntarily reopens the path to a culture of separate development of the sexes, which the democrats, breaking with religious conservatism, had had such difficulty in overcoming.

This reticence, in turn, supports certain objections. They must all be taken seriously in that they suggest a decisive doctrinal evolution for twenty-first-century democracy. It is through transcending these impasses of abstract universalism, and by assigning a concrete anthropological content to what is universal, that democracy will be able to ward off regressions in society . . . and therefore to resist its enemies of today and of the future.

Globalization provides the historical occasion and the intellectual tools for a renewal of doctrine and strategy regarding women's rights. More generally, it makes available new paradigms enabling us to surpass the theoretical and practical quandaries of abstract universalism. The global moment is one in which it becomes possible to think of the universal concretely: to render the human being the plenary dimension of two sexual modes and to integrate positively, through a feminist humanism limited by Western norms, all the factors of diversity in a networked world.

NOTES

1. To borrow the fortuitous formula that is the title of the survey book by Janine Mossuz-Lavau and Anne de Kervasdoué (Paris: Odile Jacob, 1997).

2. The memory of these European beginnings of parity having been curiously erased, it is fair to recall that the Council of Europe took the initiative of holding a seminar in Strasbourg in November 1989, which was significantly entitled *The Democratic Principle of Equal Representation: Forty Years of Council of Europe Activity. Proceedings of the Seminar, Strasbourg, 6 and 7 November 1989* (Strasbourg: Council of Europe Press, 1992). On the notion of parity, introduced by Claudette Apprill, then secretary of the European Committee for Equality between Women and Men, see my report "Democratic Ideals and Women's Rights," pp. 17–27.

PART 3

Views and Testimonies

CHAPTER 17

The World of Music

PIERRE BOULEZ

INTERVIEW CONDUCTED BY JEAN-DOMINIQUE MARCO, MARINA RICCIARDELLI, AND SABINE URBAN

Sabine Urban: Pierre Boulez, you are a major figure in international cultural life, a renowned orchestral conductor, and a world class composer in the realm of contemporary music. You are also a Frenchman who, after World War II, at a very young age, developed successful relationships across borders, notably with Germany. In other words, you are a witness to European construction, you have lived through the gradual opening up of the world space, and you have observed and lived this from a multidisciplinary viewpoint. Moreover, you are an innovator, a creator, and a "modern" man involved in the technological revolution. Your thoughts about art, and especially music, in the context of a rapidly changing society—with the fear expressed by some at seeing a primacy of the development of economic issues—appears to us to be of primordial interest.

Pierre Boulez is a composer, conductor, founder in 1955 of the concert series "Domaine Musical," and founder and first director of the Institut de Recherche et Coordination Acoustique/Musique (IRCAM) and of the Ensemble Intercontemporain. Involved in musical creation, research, and education, he has been one of the most influential individuals of the second half of the twentieth century.

Jean-Dominique Marco is the director of Musica, Festival des Musiques d'aujourd'hui, Strasbourg.

Pierre Boulez: I think that we musicians live somewhat outside of the economy, because music, unlike the other arts, with the exception perhaps of poetry, is not subject to speculation. For film this subjugation is evident, because of the big budgets involved, the distribution network, and the numerous other factors that lead to a total invasion of certain films, against which it is difficult to fight. I know the United States well, and I go there often, but I realize it is very unusual to see a French film in its original version, even in New York or Los Angeles. For novels, the question of language also comes into play, and translations are very costly. Language is a barrier. This is particularly true in the field of general literature, less so in specialized scientific or literary works. As far as painting is concerned, it is clear that the phenomenon of the market plays an enormous role. Americans have an inventiveness for organizing the market that is infinitely superior to that of Europeans. There, the problem of taxes is also very different. If the major field of speculation is in the United States, it is because transactions are still tax free. And the behavior of the people counts as well, their idea of a kind of social status: people who have earned a lot of money are not embarrassed to show it; so they buy a collection, and their social status, remaining linked to their money (money that is somehow ennobled by the intermediary of their collection of paintings), becomes enhanced. In California, for example, I met recently wealthy collectors who showed their new acquisitions with great pride.

As for music, it is not at all the same thing. Speculation doesn't exist. Private sponsorship is not imaginable except for music that is already accepted, with a recognized master or a great orchestra. This is why in the United States the major orchestras are funded solely by private contributions, with only a few exceptions. I remember that in New York the concerts in Central Park were subsidized by the city, but the concerts during the season were funded entirely by private contributions. We see, in the United States as in Europe, that funding is given to visible organizations that are in sync with society. Private economic support goes to the large groups; the small ensembles have a difficult time. A group of chamber musicians will have trouble finding sponsorship while at the same time attendance at their performances shows that there is a demand. But the time that it takes for this demand to appear—I won't say "necessary" or "profitable," but visible—raises problems.

Difficulties of this type are also true of poetry: poetry is published only by university publishing houses, at least in the United States; otherwise not at all. The large publishing companies are not interested in poetry. So poets have a problem in the United States as well. On the other hand, we find in this country an efficiency and professionalism, and a clear decision-making power, that I like very much. While I was in New York for a season, I had planned a series of programs with six choral works. I was told that I could only do four. Okay. That was fine, but I knew that the budget was there. In Europe it is often more difficult for an organizer to know what to expect.

I. "Au fil du temps" (With the Passing of Time)

P.B.: Take the case of Germany and France. In the two countries—which in this area function on roughly the same model—many cultural organizations are subsidized by the state and are part of the cultural background. After the fall of the Berlin Wall, the famous Schillertheater was closed, or more precisely, rededicated to hosting musicals. A cultural space was practically and abruptly "cleaned out," if I may say so.

But there is more than the economic situation that affects budgetary decisions; there is also political involvement. I have been traveling and living in Germany for more than forty years. In the 1950s, the radio stations were extremely rich, with considerable budgets and managers devoted to the artistic world. These were people who were not compromised by the Nazi regime or who had fled Berlin with the rise of Hitler, and who stayed completely out of sight from 1933 to 1945. After the war, you could tell there was determination to catch up for lost time and to encourage not only contemporary art, but also a general knowledge of what had happened during all that lost time. The radio stations had huge budgets then (especially since television hardly existed) and were a strong innovative force. Today, these people who worked to manage the budgets for artistic promotion are gone. The new generation doesn't have the same creative ideology (there are, of course, exceptions), and the budgets for new creative works have been reduced drastically because they are encroached upon by television, and the audiovisual media in general.

At the same time we are led to believe that television is not costly to the creative arts, at least it costs less than the live arts, such as theater or music, which we accuse of . . .

P.B.: "Eating up budgets!" Yes, it is a false presumption, especially for contemporary music. I see, for example, with the Ensemble Intercontemporain, with IRCAM [Institut de Recherche et Coordination Acoustique/

Musique], we are always viewed as "eating up the budget," but if we compare our case with the National Orchestra of Radio France we place ourselves in a much higher quality-price relationship, both in the quality and number of concerts we offer.

Notwithstanding the influence of the Ensemble Intercontemporain, the IRCAM is also a formidable laboratory of multidisciplinary research characterized by the strong links that you personally have with science, literature, poetry, technology, creative arts; it is a kind of beacon, even on a world-wide level. . . .

P.B.: I am more of an exception. This is no doubt explained by the time in which I was born; I was twenty years old in 1945, when everything was at its lowest point and we started from nothing. The time was bizarre, and I'll make you laugh: in France there were people who wanted to bring back "pre-war quality. . . ." So when we found a good steak, it was a steak "like before the war," and if we found a good pair of shoes, "Ah! Just like before the war," etc. There was an establishment in French music in the period 1945–50 who also wanted to bring back pre-war quality, even a pre-war lack of quality. We did not. That is why I told myself that it was pointless to discuss endlessly lost works that no one listened to. There was the German model that gnawed at me. I found that the Germans did lots of things, on the radio . . . (and if we compare the French radio of the time with the German radio, it was really a difference of night and day), and then "Darmstadt" [the summer academy where composers of the day would gather], a concept born in Germany. I thought we might try as much in France. But there was no way of getting any help from the government. We then had to turn to the private sector. The Domaine Musical was funded solely through private contributions. There were, of course, only four to six concerts each year, but we earned a certain reputation. I worked a lot with the German radio stations (the Südwestfunk in Baden-Baden, Cologne): they were very rich and we were able to count on their support, both musical and financial. The groups of the German radio stations offered their services free of charge and paid for their travel costs; we at the Domaine Musical hosted them, and they were happy to have this opening in Paris. Both sides benefited. But I never worked with French radio; it didn't broadcast our concerts. In the framework of the European Broadcasting Union (EBU), French radio did no more than lend us some of their technicians. In sum, our concerts were broadcast in Germany, but not in France.

I think—it's a question of character—that there are moments when you have to try and force the outcome. So, even in very precarious economic times, one must find a way to get by. Especially in this particular case, there were musicians who were there: young people of my age, twenty-five, twenty-six; they were very dedicated. At the time, I was responsible for the music for the theatrical troupe of Jean-Louis Barrault and Madeleine Renaud; that enabled me occasionally to find part-time jobs for the young musicians. This is how the small group of musicians of Domaine Musical was formed, with dedicated young artists, who came to do concerts even though they were poorly paid, but paid nonetheless, because I didn't want to depend on volunteers; there was always a salary.

You toured the world with the theatrical troupe of Jean-Louis Barrault and Madeleine Renaud; that was perhaps your first immersion in the globalization trend?
P.B.: Yes, it was then that I went on my first long voyages; well, I was part of the luggage at the time! That began in 1950.

But it is ultimately in Germany that the very close interdependent links between music, science, and technology impressed you?
P.B.: Yes, and they are still strong.

2. Birth of the IRCAM

P.B.: You know, the IRCAM is a project that was conceived in Germany (for Germany), as curious as that may seem. The idea came from the Max Planck Foundation. There are a number of Max Planck Institutes, specializing in a given scientific area, and in this framework the idea was born: why not an institute for music? We then imagined a department for pedagogical development, another for the manufacture of musical instruments, and so on. I was in charge of contemporary music and technology because I had contacts with Siemens, which had founded a "studio" in Munich. I regularly went to this studio each time I gave a concert in Munich. I was then aware of what was happening. I made a plan for "contemporary music and technology," which was submitted at several meetings to individuals connected with Paul Sacher [Swiss patron of the arts and conductor]. I remember the meetings also involved two or three Nobel laureates, including the brother of President Richard von Weizsäcker, who was himself a scientist.

So it was between 1966 and 1968. Then there was an economic recession in Germany, so the Max Planck Foundation had less funding, and curiously, if I was correctly informed, two people opposed the creation of this new music institute: a scientist and a musician. The first was the physicist Heisenberg, then president of the Max Planck Foundation, who said, "music doesn't need a research institute." The second, a musician, was the singer Fischer-Dieskau, and God only knows why he was against this project! So the German project sank, but the idea remained in my mind. So, in 1969, when President Pompidou contacted me expressing a desire to create the Center for Contemporary Art [Pompidou Center], I told him, "In terms of music, I already have a plan." But this plan was modified from the original plan for a Max Planck Institute (which was intended for Munich or Zurich).

Concerning the IRCAM, do you think Georges Pompidou realized that, thanks to your ideas, something might change dramatically in the French mind-set, making the public understand that the importance of contemporary music wasn't only cultural (artistic) but also social and political, that the modern-day challenges were transdisciplinary? Or was this presidential involvement linked more to the coincidence of interpersonal relations?

P.B.: There is a little of the latter, but the Center was *his* project; he really wanted to impose modern culture in France. In an article in *Le Monde,* he justified contemporary architecture, saying that the French were very far behind in this area. Pompidou was very conscious of the gap that existed between the general public—even the most cultivated—and contemporary art.

This was likely also true for music. Contemporary music still needed to be learned. In this context, we can understand why the IRCAM has focused on training and didactics: it was necessary to initiate. . . .

P.B.: Yes. There has always been pedagogical development, that was weak at first, but it has since grown, blossomed. When I drew up the proposal for the IRCAM in 1970, there were five departments: electronics, computers (I knew through contacts in New York that this was important, even though at the time computers were marginal . . . that has certainly changed!), instruments, "diagonal cooperation" (to bring all the areas together), and a fifth department of pedagogy. Later I completely modified this organizational structure along three axes: pedagogy remained, and then production and research.

Was this structure open to the international community as a place for meeting and dialogue?

P.B.: Yes, of course. You know, at that time I already traveled abroad often. I told Georges Pompidou that a condition of my creating the Institute was that it would be international, or else an institute of this kind would have no value. Pompidou agreed.

The IRCAM is clearly an international center for training; I think this is especially true in the training of composers, professional musicians, but is its role also the diffusion of "modern thought" in the schools . . . who is responsible for this?

P.B.: That is a big problem! It is the responsibility of the Ministry of Education, but it is not very active in this area. There are things that can be done, though. At the Cité de la Musique we work with certain high schools in the preparation of the baccalaureate exam (in music), and we willingly put on demonstrations. I recall presenting an hour-long analysis to a group of students between the age of sixteen and eighteen, a long one: they followed along with impressive attentiveness, really impressive. And David Robertson [conductor and musical director of the Ensemble Intercontemporain] does this as well. But we cannot do everything! There are I don't know how many music schools in France!

3. Music in the World

Ultimately, musical creation, contemporary music, is well established in Europe, with the Second Vienna School first, then Germany, France. . . . Do we find an equivalent creativity in other regions, for example in North America or Japan?

P.B.: In North America, yes, but that depends very much on the universities. Their budgets fluctuate; when there are spending restrictions, universities fund this or that department, depending on their specific orientation. It is often departments like music that suffer the most. Even wealthy institutions, like MIT, prefer to direct funding to scientific research that will a priori have industrial applications, or to the visual arts. Music finds itself with limited resources compared to the visual arts. It is always the same thing, the visual arts may offer a return on investment; it's that simple.

They sell better! But to return to the idea of globalization, this interdependence of just about everything, with all sorts of barriers—cultural, historical, linguistic, etc.—is finally more limited than it would seem. When we are observers, from outside the world of music, we have a tendency to think that music will encounter fewer barriers than other artistic forms; that music is a sort of universal language. Is this true, or is music also rooted in place, with barriers, for example, between tonal and atonal music, or the West and the East, etc.?

P.B.: It is clear that there are enormous cultural differences. Take the example of Europe/North America, or "Western" music. There is not a lot of interaction with "Eastern" music. What French musician, unless he is for example a specialized musicologist, will be interested in the music of India? If so, he will listen to recordings, know the material, but he won't know how to play; first because training takes place at a very young age, in families or groups, or in villages (in Bali, for example, you have small groups that meet like choirs do here). And then Eastern music is very different, it is a cultural, social, and religious phenomenon above all else. So there are very large differences: this is what poses the problem, for example to Japanese musicians who train in Western music.

We see Japanese musicians in western orchestras; but we may not see the opposite....

P.B.: No. We must really distinguish between traditional music, which is exclusively Japanese (like you have with the traditional theater of Nô or Kabuki), and western music. There is an astonishing parallel way of life in Japanese civilization. This is seen in their clothing: during the day, people are dressed like you or me, or like on Wall Street, but when they get home, they put on a kimono. That is, at home, tradition is important. For music, it's the same thing: they relate to Western music in a certain context (in Japan, there are six to eight Western-style orchestras), but they also play the koto, write a concerto for the koto, etc., although that never gets too popular because it very quickly turns into descriptive, "Hollywood" music, if I may say so.

Do you have the impression that, throughout the world, there is a feeling of Eurocentrism in contemporary music?

P.B.: Rather a Western influence; America is also very influential because of certain individuals, certain musical styles, like repetitive music, that corresponds to minimalist art. Painting has had a profound influence on music; I realized this during my first visit to New York when I went to see Cage. I was exposed to the people around Cage. It was 1952; I saw Pollock, de Kooning, all these painters. The New York movement was very much alive, more so than the French scene at that time.

... a question of a different paradigm ...

P.B.: Yes, there was also a kind of reaction to the European influence. Many painters took refuge in the United States during the war; I think of André Masson in particular who influenced the work of Pollock, of Max Ernst, of all the surrealists, etc. And that was the shock that started this kind of aggressiveness in American art as compared to European art, because they said "yes, now this is ours." And there is always, even among musicians (a little less so), this "us" and "them," that is, "we-the-Americans" and "they-the-Europeans." That is not recent; even in the 1920s when there was the first big wave of the "avant-garde" in the United States, we heard "we want to make *American* music."

But American composers like Edgar Varèse were very isolated in the 1920s.

P.B.: Not in the 1920s, but afterwards. He was, on the contrary, very well known—among a small group of people of course—in the 1920s, especially in the avant-garde movement in New York. His two principal orchestral compositions, "Amériques" and "Arcana," were performed by Stokowski and the Philadelphia Orchestra. I had the opportunity to study the New York avant-garde movement when I organized a mini-festival in honor of Charles Ives in 1974 at the 100th anniversary of his birth; for that, I worked at the musical library at Lincoln Center and studied everything about the New York avant-garde at that time, which was very interesting. And then there was a change, especially when Aaron Copland returned from Paris. A kind of neo-classicism developed, very much influenced by Nadia Boulanger. What surprised me is that we find a comparable evolution in Russia (even though the political regimes were completely different): there is an important period of avant-garde art in Russia until 1924–25 and a little later, that was the reign of popular art, "it must appeal to the masses," etc. In short, two different ideologies curiously had the same effect. In the United States, during the Great Depression of 1929–33, we also saw the concept of "popular art" and the idea that "art should correspond to the public's expectations," etc., . . . and so we get the folkloric ballets of Aaron Copland!

Today, in our media-driven democracies, isn't there a risk of returning to this invasion of the "popular?" It's a discussion we hear about.

P.B.: Yes, certainly. But at the same time, musicians who have precise intentions are less dependent than at that time.

You have the impression that cultural diversity, the will to create, is ultimately expressed more easily today than at the beginning of the last century?

P.B.: Yes, because there are more small organizations, which don't have many resources but which are at least doing something. We don't always rely on large official groups.

And these small organizations react against the sort of phenomenon of invasion or homogenization, or uniformity of lifestyles, behavior . . . driven by globalization. In your opinion, does art seem like a kind of reactionary response to this tendency of globalization?

P.B.: Yes, like a center of resistance: art is also a form of individual expression.

And you think that music is in a unique situation, that musical creation is more dynamic, stronger, than other forms of artistic expression?

P.B.: I don't know if it is more dynamic, but in any case it doesn't risk being "demonetized" rapidly, like painting or the studio arts do: there an artist can begin very successfully, with the support of a gallery or museum, be worth a lot, and then in several years lose value, because he goes in for mass production. This temptation exists in music too, for example with composers who want to write an orchestral score (but it is an exception): they know that in the United States, there can only be four practice sessions for a whole program; so they write something simple that can be rehearsed in three or four hours.

The ability to innovate has often been, in some periods, inscribed in social discourse with the political will to develop a project. Today (the avant-garde no longer exists for the time being) we have the impression that there is no longer this political will, or willingness, on the side of the creative artist.

P.B.: But the circumstances are not at all the same. You know, when you are dealing with a society that constantly demurs, you are forced to be aggressive, because you want to show who you are, that you exist. But today, I see the situation of the young composers who are hosted at the IRCAM: we receive them with open arms . . . if I had had that advantage, at twenty or twenty-two years old! These young artists are in a much better position than we were, at the time the doors were closed to us. I will tell you: in my entire career as a composer, I only had one commission in France in fifty-five years. From this point of view, it is not I who put a strain on the national budget!

At twenty-five years old, you hoped to change society, but now young composers aspire to social recognition. Isn't this dangerous for creation?

P.B.: That depends. In certain cases, yes, the ease of it is a danger.

What is surprising today is that in the context of a consumer society that is becoming more global, there is the emergence of standards: everything is being standardized, banalized, everything is available everywhere.

We are more interested in ethnic music now, but through modern American music: it's "world music." That seems to pillage musical richness.

P.B.: You know, it's today's form of colonialism: it's like when we went out in search of spices. Now we look for music that is somewhat different, but this kind of thing irritates me because—I repeat—it is really a new kind of colonialism. We take cultural merchandise and appropriate it, changing it so that it fits our tastes. There has been a reversal of the colonial hierarchy: the North Africans are numerous in France, the Indians and Pakistani in England. It's the opposite of colonization, that is, the backlash of colonialism in our countries. It is then very easy for their music to be "absorbed," because it is now part of our everyday lives.

This diversity is interesting, in that it is integrated at least in certain centers like Paris and London.

P.B. Yes, but it really isn't integrated. We can't say that Indian music, for example, is integrated in the mainstream of western music, in London . . . nor that it is *real,* traditional, Indian music; it is rather a kind of mixed music. The same is true of African music, that which is recorded in Central Africa and that which you hear in the "Goutte d'Or" [neighborhood in Paris]. Music has a tendency to remain confined geographically; I think, for example, of the big hero of pop music in France, Johnny Halliday. You go to the United States, and nobody has heard of him. He's unknown, I mean completely unknown. And that surprises me. We talk a lot about a kind of global culture, but it doesn't exist, except perhaps "American culture." Because there they have enormous resources for production and distribution. But the fact remains that there are some borders that are truly impassable.

But the Beatles, would they be an exception?

P.B.: Yes, they were an exception. There are exceptions, but the rule is that there are cultural borders.

4. Music and New Technologies

P.B.: Recording companies are really going through a difficult period; they will need to adapt quickly. Maybe in ten or fifteen years, music won't be sold in stores at all. Music will be distributed on the Internet. The recording will be put on the Internet and copied, you'll copy it yourself, and won't need the intermediary of the compact disc (CD) manufacturer. The recording

industry is now wondering how it will position itself in the future. For classical recordings, when you have an orchestra, these costs are such that the
investment is difficult to recoup; it's rare that such recordings are profitable.
For pop music, it's different: the cachet of the individual is very costly, but
the production of the CD is less expensive. Pop recordings feed the market
of creation; but there are limits to the transfer of resources. Given my age,
and what I represent, Deutsche Grammophon is willing to record my works;
but with the young composers of the IRCAM, it is more difficult.

*The name Boulez has such notoriety that when you have a new record-
ing, a work of contemporary music, it sells. Your name ensures not only
artistic value but also a certain market value. . . .*
P.B.: A very small market value.

*But as a general rule, what will this "Internet-ization," or demateriali-
zation, of the musical foundation change for the artist and particularly the
creator?*
P.B.: That's the big problem! There are copyright and sales issues. Just
like with the wireless telephone, the evolution is incredibly fast.

*We say you can't put a price tag on culture, but there is a cost. How will
we pay for (at a fair price) the music of the future? There needs to be a new
source of funding, resources that will enable creative freedom. The traditional purveyors, the government or public organizations, might have difficulty increasing their contributions.*
P.B.: It will be important to develop co-production. For example, we now
have co-productions of recordings with the IRCAM and the Ensemble Intercontemporain. The two organizations are subsidized by the government, so
it is the government that pays for the production in the end. If a recording
with an orchestra is very expensive, we ask the orchestra to coproduce it.

*So you recognize that it is absolutely necessary that the public authori-
ties (at a national or local level) support artistic creation, without any
immediate economic or social "return."*
P.B. Absolutely, but we're not just talking about supporting the creator.
I remember a meeting with the president of a large bank; he was ready to
do some sponsorship. But he didn't understand the problem of musical creation. I explained to him that to pay the commission of a composer wasn't
much, only the tip of the iceberg. What is expensive is to create the orches-

tral score, the various parts of the whole, to edit the printed material, to run the rehearsals, it's the concert, the recording, all of that is a lot more expensive than the composer's commission. I then told him, "If you want to commission some works, order the entire package from start to finish. If you pay the composer thirty or forty thousand francs, for example, you'll need to figure the entire cost at 200,000 or 250,000 francs at the end." And that he understood.

It appears, then, that with musical creation there is a problem of the finished product. For a painter or writer, the product is immediately visible: a painting or a book. For a composer who writes a score, the work only exists in an incomplete form: it will only really exist once it has been performed and recorded. Is this production chain more cumbersome than it was fifty years ago, for example?

P.B.: I don't know how it worked fifty years ago, but there have been significant changes in the past ten to fifteen years in this regard. On the other hand, in terms of sales, we see a discouraging change (if we want to be discouraged). Recording companies are rarely involved in marketing at sales outlets. A recording can be difficult to sell (because of its artistic nature), and it will be displayed in alphabetical order on a shelf with all the other recordings. The potential buyer has to make an effort to find it, rather than it being presented to him or having his attention drawn to this interesting record. There should be different approaches to selling this creative work than there are with popular recordings. Distribution has really declined. In the past, you had small music shops with their regular customers who were helped in making choices . . . just like the independent booksellers. Now these small music shops cannot survive with just sales of recordings, and they have practically disappeared. Now we have the large retailers; they put the recordings on a shelf, and that's it . . . just like carrots or cans of peas. Quality suffers in favor of quantity, shelves and shelves of recordings. . . . The large retailers aren't passionate about recordings, but about the rotation of stock, so, in the United States for example, when you have a book that doesn't sell or isn't successful, you don't keep it in stock; you get rid of it, destroy it, because it's less expensive than to store it!

And does this also happen with recordings?

P.B.: With classical music . . . no. It doesn't involve mass production. What I mean is that in certain ways, technological advances have done good things for music publishing. Now we don't keep printed scores in warehouses but on servers. This makes it easier to utilize certain resources: if you are missing four parts for violin, for example, there is no need to do a big print run, you can target production for a particular need. The distribution of the document is more flexible, faster, and less costly.

Finally, there are some aspects that are very ambiguous, both positive and negative, in this modern evolution. For example, it is more difficult to ensure coherence in a particular chain of decisions. But here, music should play an important educational role: in music, you compose, recompose, restructure sound elements: you learn in a certain way to live with and manage complexity. Do you have the impression that a process of this kind develops in the brain of the people you train?

P.B.: That depends. Ultimately, in daily life, what do you hear? Always the same thing, pop music, background music, in supermarkets, elevators. That's what forms people more than anything. This is why I wanted the Cité de la Musique [in Paris] to develop. We need to change the way people think about music, just as has been done for books. The library at the Pompidou Center in Paris has been a great success from the start. Why? Entrance was free and didn't require any membership or formal request. People could come in just like in a department store; they took whatever book was at hand. If they didn't want it, they put it back. They didn't have to ask a staff member at the entrance for anything. The contact with the book was direct, free, personal, and posed no difficulties (nor did individuals have to worry about looking like idiots because they didn't know how to formulate a formal technical request). It's the same thing with music: people don't want to attend a concert if they don't know how to behave at one. Today, technology allows an interactive apprenticeship; it's really crucial. People who are forty or fifty years old, for example, and who haven't had the time to read or learn about culture, may want to do so once they have more leisure time . . . but they don't want to take a class, they don't want to look uncultivated. Technology can help them learn. This is true as well in language learning: at the Pompidou Center, in the library, language learning is very successful: it's private, you go into a booth, you listen to yourself, and you aren't required to recite aloud like a kid.

Interactive learning can, and will, become very commonplace, no doubt.

P.B.: In my opinion, yes, it will, but it has to be available to those who are interested. I am constantly repeating this, and I really have to. In the realm of music, take someone who is cultivated and interested in the symphonies of Brahms, for example. He can say, "You know, I haven't heard that in a long time, I'll go to the Media Center and listen to a different interpretation of it." He reacquaints himself with the music that he is going to hear that same night, or compares different interpretations. He'll go through the archives and listen to a work the night before or the day after a concert. That's what is interesting. And then we can give him a biography of the composer; or other people will be interested in the social and political environment at the time of the composition. This all may take three or four days, if the documentation isn't available at the time, but it will be delivered. This is real democratization.

At the same time, for that to work, we need to build and connect networks. For now, we are still in embryonic form; between the IRCAM and the Cité de la Musique, there is a constant exchange of information, and the IRCAM's Internet network can be accessed from the Cité de la Musique. It's a start.

This is something that in a very short time may take on considerable importance.

P.B.: But we must construct a place for this and be equipped. Household use of computers is still lagging behind in France, compared to the United States or other European countries; individuals can't all be linked into our electronic networks. For the moment, we need a physical place that will attract them and inspire them to buy their own personal computers.

Is the IRCAM well-known in the world, in the United States or Japan, for example?

P.B.: Yes, in all of the specialized milieux it is very well known. You know, once a year, we organize a large meeting called a "forum," where among members of our network, we talk, discuss technological progress, the latest research, we sell our programs. . . .

So there is a kind of global network involving research, experimentation, sharing of know-how, interactive learning, creation. . . .

P.B.: At the IRCAM, we started very early on this path; we have called on specialists from Stanford University, MIT, Berkeley, and we have ongoing, very active links with the United States. In France, from the outset we have tried to build a network with small organizations, but they refused for fear of being "absorbed" (even though we really wanted to help them).

Do you have the impression that this kind of proliferation of initiatives, of networking, that is taking place, like it or not, around the world, and very rapidly in many areas, is something that can also stimulate the prolifera-tion of ideas and really be something that's very positive?

P.B.: Yes, absolutely. You know, my generation lived during the war, everything was closed to us. Then everything opened up, but only gradually, because during the postwar period until 1951–52 everything was still diffi-cult: we had to obtain visas, there were foreign exchange controls. It's curi-ous, but probably as a reaction we were very internationally-minded. This is why Darmstadt had such an effect, because there were Italians, Germans, French, English, etc. Everyone came together, and windows were opened in all directions. Now, on the contrary, I see a kind of fear linked to global-ization, a fear of losing one's identity and character. This is so much the case that people of a certain age, thirty to thirty-five, for example, are less aware of what's going on in the world than we were at their age. It seems to me that we are less curious now, we stay in our own countries. It's strange, now that we can travel at will, and very inexpensively, even with scholarships. In short there are ways to go to other countries, yet there are people who are com-pletely turned inward; they don't want to know what's going on elsewhere.

Yet cultural life can be sufficiently rich, and artistic creation (not just musical) sufficiently broad to counteract this fear of losing one's identity. I think that if one wants to, one can resist.

P.B. Yes, absolutely. Fear and withdrawal are not at all justified.

Faced with this movement of opening up around the world, you are ultimately quite optimistic. Do you see this as an opportunity?

P.B.: Yes, I do. You know, globalization is like wine; there are some wines—"local" wines—that are best consumed on the spot; but great wines can travel. In other words, good quality travels, poor quality does not!

CHAPTER 18

Theater and Creativity: "From the World of Approximations to the Universe of Precision"

SERGIO ESCOBAR

I will start with a provocative statement: the market and globalization suggest a great deal of optimism for me. I am absolutely certain that globalization will bring about a new humanism. I have said that this is provocative, and I believe that there are many who will shake their heads disapprovingly and many who will think that I am "pro-market" or even "pro-supermarket"—as the Left, which is part of my own life and history, often asserts: "If there is a market, give us supermarkets." It is not at all like this (it is exactly the opposite). I believe that the Left has enormous responsibilities, and each time anyone talks about the market, the Left invokes the negative image of the "supermarket." It is a connection that strikes all the neophytes, those who are discovering things for the first time. But, I don't want to waste time on this topic. Everyone is free to think the way they want, even the Left, and not only them.

In 1998 Sergio Escobar was appointed, along with Luca Ronconi, to direct the Piccolo Teatro di Milano–Teatro d'Europa, which was founded by Paolo Grassi and Giorgio Strehler. He has edited publications on the philosophy of science and analyses of the entertainment industry. This paper was presented in October 1999 within the framework of the 8th Festival de l'Union des Théâtres de l'Europe, organized by the Théâtre National de Strasbourg (TNS).

I will start with a hypothesis. By definition the theater is a positive marginality, a positive marginal element of society; this is part of its history. I believe that no one will be offended if I say that anyone who is in the theater bears an enormous resemblance to those who rummage through trash cans for rubbish, for things society has discarded, things that are no longer worth anything. The theater lives, and must live, by going against the grain of society. So, we must ask ourselves, what will be the destiny of this positive marginality in globalization, in the globalized market? This is the real question. Will it merely be a loss of identity? Will it be a loss of legitimacy? We are not useful, we do not produce merchandise. And I will stop at this point.

I do think one thing. Yesterday evening I went out with two friends who are here with me today. We went for dinner in a small village about one hundred kilometers from Strasbourg. There was a little boy celebrating Halloween while we Italians were drinking the must, fresh grape juice that is still fermenting in the bottle. It's the "new wine" that I believe is only available during one specific period of the year. What's its name in Alsatian? *Nejer Suesser!* We—*noi*—Italians! It sounds like a joke. But in reality, we have to ask a question: sitting across from this boy who is celebrating Halloween at the same table at which the must is flowing, where there is tradition, are we supposed to abandon him to two possibilities? The first possibility is that he will only cling to memories. And the second is that he will let himself be carried away with conformity, the conformity of Halloween. In other words, for us older persons, the only attitude we can adopt in the face of globalization is either subordinated love or rage (in Italian there is a stronger expression; we say, the rage of one who refuses). But in either case, and without being rhetorical, I wonder, what will become of this boy? What is our responsibility as people of the theater in this situation? Is it as a positive countercurrent, is it as an element of countercurrent optimism?

A highly renowned scientific philosopher, Alexander Koyré, who while not French, belongs to the French school of thought, wrote a memorable book entitled *Du monde de l' "à-peu-près" à l'univers de la precision.*[1] In essence, his thesis, with which I fully agree, is that expansion, the universe in which we are living, globalization, all imply, inexorably and positively, the exaltation of particularity, of specificity: from the world of the approximate we are moving toward the universe of precision. In technological terms, and applied to events today, to what we are experiencing, this thesis means that the development of the market contains a contradiction, a condition that is positive for us, which is that, in fact, the single market generates markets and submarkets. In essence, the market's history contains a denial of the market. To put it differently, the satellite also generates cable TV. But it is not technology that interests me. What does interest me is to understand what is happening in our world. The universal audience that some hope will develop actually exists already in the form of an audience of audiences, or rather, of fragmented audiences. The hypothesis is that if we can globalize the market, we can globalize public tastes, but—as Koyré said in his book—this, in turn, is countered by the fact that the more important expansion becomes, the more the value of the individual is reinforced, or the more the value of particularity or specificity is strengthened. Obviously, this is not fully evident in the market rhetoric that we see and hear. We must understand it, feel it, and use it.

I will put it another way. Mr. Morita, the president of Sony, passed away recently. Some years ago, Sony launched a very advanced technology item on the market, but Mr. Morita made a serious error. He forgot the creative element, the value of the creativity, the particularity, and the specificity of the theater, cinema, and poetry. Others, who were much less powerful in the market than he, understood this and allied themselves with the creative people, with the artists, and his system (the Betamax VCR) was pushed out of the market in favor of another, less important, less technologically-advanced system that was linked to the public and creativity.

There is no doubt at all that for many faced with the fragmentation of audiences, fragmentation is frightening. For those who create, for the artists, this is a great opportunity and an enormous responsibility. This is an extremely secular vision. To say it in other words, "hard times for ideologies, good times for ideas." The idea I support, and it is a paradox, is that the future of Europe, the future of the single market, will absolutely not be—for reasons inherent to the market—the future of standardization, since it will be impossible to reach a standardized audience. The "merchandise" of the future will increasingly be creativity and originality. It is a sort of self-destructive pact inherent in the market, but it is very positive. The danger we face is different: it is the fear that grips us as people who have a sense of society, of value, of public value, namely, a fear that fragmentation will become a total dispersion that cannot be put back together into a whole. It is easier to communicate through ideologies than to talk with people and audiences, or to convey passions on an individual basis. The first ideology that is reborn after the destruction of the others is that of the market. Faced with the market, we can adopt a behavior of mimicry: the theater must apologize for existing, for its marginality, and must seek to imitate the market, the visible market of globalization. And frankly, I believe that none of us have time to lose on this new ideology because the market in itself generates audiences, markets, passions, and curiosities; the universal dimension is the sum of these particularities and specificities. There is no artist, no theater director who can avoid this challenge. There is no excuse for not doing it, not even the market, because the market is, as I hope and believe, something else: able to surpass its own capabilities. This is an extremely uncomfortable position. It means thinking in secular humanistic terms, and that, obviously, presupposes a great utopia. No one can hide so awkwardly, and against all facts, behind the perverse market, because the market analysts would prove that he or she is wrong. The market is heading in another direction.

The other day a Nobel laureate, Arno Penzias, was in Milan. He is a great enthusiast of, and an expert on, the future. To the question, "How can we defend ourselves against a society that is becoming standardized?"—a standardization that would have pleased Marx but that comes from the market and not Marxism—he answered: "What we make must not become just any type of merchandise, but must become, must be, in some way unique and irreplaceable."

Let me go back to a specific theater, the Piccolo Teatro, so that we can understand what we are dealing with. Strehler and Grassi founded the Piccolo in 1947 when society was divided, broken, split in two. It faced challenges of the Right, the Left, post-fascism, and the recovery of social classes that had been cut off from beauty. In 1998, when Luca Ronconi and I were appointed its directors, we were also facing a fragmented society. We have the same needs, the same dream, the same utopia. For us it is a more difficult theater. But we cannot abandon it.

NOTES

1. See A. Koyré, "Du monde de l' 'à-peu-près' à l'univers de la precision," in *Etudes d'histoire de la pensée philosophique* (Paris: Gallimard, 1971), pp. 341–362.

CHAPTER 19

Inventing the Future of Surgery

JACQUES MARESCAUX

INTERVIEW CONDUCTED BY SABINE URBAN

Sabine Urban: Jacques Marescaux, you are a professor of digestive surgery and preside over two unique, world-renowned institutions that you have founded, the Institute for Research on Digestive System Cancers (IRCAD) and the European Institute of Telesurgery (EITS). Why are these institutions unique and what are their purposes?

Jacques Marescaux: The medical field is going through an inevitable and rapid period passing from industrial age medicine to information age medicine. So the idea came to me to create a unique structure, dedicated to focusing attention on fundamental research against cancer (IRCAD) and to developing new information technologies in the medical world (EITS).

I. IRCAD/EITS: An Original Structure for Research and Training in the Information Age

J.M.: The idea was to build a center where surgeons, oncologists, researchers, engineers, and computer technicians could bring together their

Jacques Marescaux is a professor of surgery at the medical school of the Université Louis Pasteur, Strasbourg. In 1994 he founded the Institute for Research on Digestive System Cancers (IRCAD) and the European Institute of Telesurgery (EITS).

energy in a single site. Such a structure didn't exist in Europe because it implied a strong industry-university partnership, of which the universities were suspicious. The various centers for training that existed in Europe (and in the United States) are either centers under university control, but poorly equipped, or centers that are well equipped, but controlled by industry. There was no system that closely associated researchers and engineers. So the Institute for Research on Digestive System Cancers (IRCAD) is not just another research institute; it is different. Rejecting the piecemeal approach to medical research that limits its effectiveness, the IRCAD sees itself as a federation of the efforts put forth in a range of disciplines and the interface between research and industrial worlds. This interface between industry/research/training is fundamental in surgery. In fact, the innovations have developed at such a pace that it seems impossible for a hospital or clinical surgeon to keep up with the technology that will guarantee his patients the use of the best materials for their treatment.

It is in this context that the idea for this training school was born. The IRCAD hosts the European Institute of Telesurgery of Strasbourg. To optimize surgical practice, to introduce new techniques or new technologies, is as important today as initial or ongoing training for the operating room personnel. In fact, surgeons, anesthesiologists, and operating room nurses have been subjected for several years to a technological "stress" that was heretofore unknown and that corresponds to the introduction of laparoscopic surgery. This French technique has no doubt revolutionized the therapeutic approach to the patient. High technology has made its way into the operating room, bringing about the necessary move from manual, tactile surgery to high-tech surgery.

Continuing education today is therefore inseparable from the practice of medicine. The results of medical research and technical innovation require doctors to update their knowledge regularly in terms of new practices (training, instruments, accessories like cameras, monitors, image recorders, cold lighting, ultrasounds, etc.).

Training today cannot be conceived of without the participation of the universities. To be effective, the training must be rigorous, up-to-date, controlled, and validated. Only theoretical and practical exams can confer the legitimacy a surgeon needs. Accreditation for specific procedures, after maintaining a certain basic level, is the next step.

The non-surgical personnel in the operating room are also evolving. In fact, the evolution of the operating room to a high-tech environment is causing a change in the different jobs within the operating room. The operating room assistants need to integrate the technical notions of engineering which did not exist when they were trained initially: robotics, micro-instrumentation, data entry, teletransmission, and sterilization of sensitive equipment are now part of their daily work.

The EITS benefits from an exceptional structure that gives participants access to a totally interactive amphitheater with 140 seats and an operating area with seventeen tables, allowing all forms of video interaction needed for educational purposes. This infrastructure equipment will soon be doubled. More than five hundred surgeons serve on the school's faculty. These experts come from around the world, free of charge, to Strasbourg, to share their experience in laparoscopic surgery. Between June 1994 and June 1999, the EITS trained more than 4,500 surgeons of fifty different nationalities. The cost of this training is high (about 875,000 francs [133,000 euros] per EITS seminar for thirty surgeons); industry contributes significantly to financing this training. This participation is justified because the EITS has a dual role as both experimental laboratory and technological showroom.

Experimental laboratory: at each EITS seminar, one of the industrial partners field tests a new piece of equipment or prototype (instrument, camera, lens, electronic device, etc.). The feedback obtained by the industrial partner is a valuable asset for the company's research and development departments. Some thirty surgeons, "novices" for the most part, and some twenty experts judge the usability and the possible applications of the proposed object. This group provides an ideal sample of the market as well.

Technological showroom: These same industrial players provide the EITS the latest equipment at no cost. This equipment is used both for instruction and for applied research.

The laparoscopic technique was born in Europe. Today, 95 percent of the equipment is manufactured in America. It is difficult for Europe to make inroads in this area. The introduction of European know-how and companies that are ready to rise to this challenge can only happen with the support of a well-known university. This is the case with the EITS today, which can bring university backing to the industrial partners that they will need to penetrate this market.

S.U.: In your case, we see the successful marriage of the public and private cultures, with public interests that are not separate from profitability.

J.M.: Yes, it is precisely for that reason that the experiment has been successful. It is clear that in the field of new information technologies and big Internet projects, the university alone cannot maintain a comprehensive web site (for training, patient information, surgeon education, direct intervention), due to the cost. Millions of dollars are at stake, which no university in the world, even in the United States, can provide, so it is really an invest-ment that companies make, because they know that if they are not in the "Internet" race, they won't survive.

S.U.: I find it amazing that you had this intuition, or this reasoning, already in the early 1990s. . . .

J.M.: . . . and I'm not even from the computer generation (I only started working with the Internet regularly a couple of months ago because I needed to correct some chapters on our web project)! On the other hand, I am con-vinced that in the medical field, it is the biggest change that medicine has ever seen. Because of the precise information that is accessible, because of the transfer of know-how, the full transfer of well-explained medical knowledge to the general public, the public is going to be phenomenally demanding. It is the public that will help us save money in health care, who will consti-tute their own network of the best specialists to go to, and who will make sure that for each illness, the immediate interplay of questions and responses will increase the doctor's level of excellence. This was unthinkable several years ago.

S.U.: This is a form of democratization of social life that is enabled by the new information technologies?

J.M.: In a sense. I clearly think that surgery is a good example to help us understand what is happening in the information age, which is in fact an age of sharing.

2. The Information Age: An Era of Sharing

J.M.: Information technologies enable both the sharing of real and virtual know-how and the sharing of a particular surgical technique at a distance, something that is extraordinary. We will first be able to share data—all that exists now, and that which doesn't exist but is *more than reality* (virtual reality)—and finally we'll share action. That's the ultimate goal in terms of information relating to surgery.

Sharing Real Knowledge with the Development of Videoconferencing

J.M.: To share real skills, there are two revolutions in the area of medi-cine and surgery: the development of videoconferencing and the develop-ment of the Internet.

With the development since 1995 of videoconference capabilities, doctors are no longer isolated from one another, and the mythical isolation of the operating room is gone. This means that simply through telephone lines we are able to link to any other site in the world. With three lines, we arrive at a quality of transmission that is similar to television (not quite yet, but almost) and a sound that is fantastic, which means that you can have a connection between Strasbourg and Tokyo, Strasbourg and New York, with no problem. The repercussions are phenomenal; they occurred because there has been a great deal of progress in the area of "semi-invasive" surgery, in which the surgeon doesn't look at the patient but at a screen; everything is recorded because the camera is present either in the patient's stomach or thorax. So we already have the concept of the image, the image which we will share or send. This has brought about some important revolutions.

First, *before* the surgical act itself and the decision about what is the best type of intervention, we can have therapeutic teleconsultation. This is a European project, Tésus, which we have been operating since 1995. We link six centers in Europe. Of these six centers, at least four are linked before an important surgical decision is made: this occurs over a period of two hours, with about thirty practitioners at each site, which means that every patient's file is reviewed by one-hundred-twenty individuals, which is no doubt amazing for the patient, especially when the problem is complicated. It is obvious that there is more information and there are more skills in many heads than in one, especially in medicine. Each consultation involves the talents of radiologists, histologists, and oncologists, and each team has some additional competencies in one of those areas. We are able to see that arriving at the *best* decision for the patient is possible, particularly since the teams who are not in contact with pressure from the patient's family or with pressure from the doctor treating the patient, make decisions that are very rigorous, very scientific, and often showing good common sense. (For example, a decision that there was no reason to operate on an eighty-five-year-old man with metastasis and in poor health generally, because there would be no benefit to his quality of life.) We created this program in 1995 and it has evolved since then, that is, we have passed from a pre-operation consultation to consultation during the operation itself.

Second, *during* a surgical procedure, images are broadcast over a screen that anyone can see. So we are now able to do operatory teleconsulting. A surgeon who faces a difficult strategic problem during a procedure can be connected with any other expert in the world, who can see what the operating surgeon is doing, what the x-rays show, and can provide immediate surgical advice. We have gone one step further in applying this technique: we can not only ask for advice but we can arrange for a surgeon who is particularly expert in this type of intervention to be connected to the operating room. This way, the surgeon performing the procedure can see how the surgeon providing the advice performs a specific technique. The expert surgeon from another site can guide the procedure; this is called telementoring. The "mentor" can be located in New York and supervise and direct a surgeon operating in Strasbourg or Paris.

Third, we have faced another problem, an enormous one: the evaluation of the surgeon, in this age when we talk so much about accreditation. Currently, it is the hospitals that are accredited, which is already something, but this means that the laundry room, the kitchens, etc. are accredited; this is a global accreditation. But it is becoming more and more difficult to understand that an airplane pilot is accredited, a truck driver is monitored by a black box, but a surgeon is neither controlled nor accredited. Technically, it is possible: a surgeon could be certified for this or that procedure, because everything is recorded. But what is interesting with the new technologies is that we can imagine an accreditation process that is very objective. Right now, in a Latin country like ours, and many other European countries, formal accreditation is difficult to imagine because we all know one another. It is difficult for me to imagine that my colleagues from Paris or Montpelier might accredit me or the other surgeons in my department, or vice versa. Thanks to telesurgery, accreditation—which especially needs to be done for young surgeons who are promoted to the level of senior surgeon after seven years of surgical training—can be done anonymously. In this area, we were able to do a test in 1997 with the United Nations Educational, Scientific, and Cultural Organization (UNESCO) that was fantastic. We linked eight sites in the world, including Sydney, Los Angeles, and Tokyo (with significant time differences to manage), with eight surgeons (most at the end of their surgical studies, and who could begin practicing the next day) and a jury of twenty international experts. We watched all of the procedures of those eight surgeons all over the world through videoconferencing; there was unanimity for accrediting (a "virtual" accreditation) of five of them, but not the other three. There was no disagreement; it was clear that there were three who could not be accredited for the procedure they were asked to do, a surgical procedure between the esophagus and the stomach. Thanks to technological progress we are able to arrange for "anonymous tele-accreditation"; and I think it is a system that will soon enter into general practice.

So this is what is going on with videoconferencing in relation to the practice of surgery. In terms of training, it is the same: video education is revolutionizing the culture of medical training.

Since we know that surgery, especially, is a form of apprenticeship, it can become "tele-apprenticeship." So instead of physically traveling, spending three or four days with a famous surgeon, we connect with one another electronically. Currently, in Strasbourg, we are able to connect regularly with forty-two sites in the world that have compatible technology. We are most frequently connected to sites in Tokyo and New York because we have very strong collegial relationships there. We connect with New York several times a week. This means that when my colleague in New York performs surgery, either a new procedure or one that is somewhat complex, we simply connect and we are in the same operating room, so to speak; we see what he is doing and we can easily share our knowledge. This sharing of knowledge and know-how saves us years, because before the introduction of tele-surgery, the surgeon, usually the chief surgeon, would go to the United States, spend four days, be tired by the trip, come back, not share what he learned right away, and so forth.

Today, with the new information technologies, if there is a new surgical technique that is being developed, twenty of us will go to the auditorium to watch and ask interactive questions, as if we were standing behind the surgeon without disturbing him. So, for me, having seen the "before" and "after," this is something fabulous, because there are no limits to teaching in this system of tele-apprenticeship.

Sharing Real Knowledge with the Internet

J.M.: The second information revolution that is beginning to surpass the one we have just discussed is that of the Internet. We are involved in this as well, after having requested a European program, which was given to us in 1997 as part of an initiative called "Info 2000." This is beginning to take on phenomenal proportions, with the real multimedia Internet now enabling film capabilities (which weren't possible a year ago). Today we can see new video systems with high quality film. There is no better training for a surgeon than that which is available on the Internet, because it corresponds to the best courses. The surgeons who attend a training session at the EITS take theoretical courses at the Institute every morning for a week; we believe they are assured that we aim to be the very best experts, but of course the six hundred experts who travel here each year are not always of the same level. On the Internet, on the other hand, the people who go there for training, those who are taught, only have relations with the very top echelon in the world, which will be a big area of competition for the universities! Whatever the policies of the university, there is henceforth a demand for excellence. There will be no need in education for those individuals who are mediocre.

Why would we connect to someone who is average when we can connect through means of the Internet with the most brilliant surgeons in New York, who invented the last fifteen procedures and who will show you the films, the techniques, and will allow you to talk with them in a forum setting, responding in depth within forty-eight hours? . . . Whoever is not at this level is not in the game. So there is a network of excellence that is being developed. We have greatly developed this teaching on the Internet by conceiving of a real multimedia system that addresses the needs of the surgeon. We do this in several languages, because people prefer to read in their own language, and not only in French or English. So we developed the training materials in nine languages, including Japanese, Russian, and Hindi, so that there is no problem for the surgeon who gets home exhausted at night (which is necessarily the fate of the surgeon); he'll see something that is easy to understand, sound, text, graphics. This is really the best methodology conceivable as compared to traditional books, which are relatively dry, where a surgeon takes three text pages to get across his explanation how he operates. And surgery, beyond strategic choices, is technique. With the image, we understand in two minutes how it should be done. And if, as a bonus, you have the best expert who shares his results, this is indeed fabulous. The end product is extraordinary. We have practically finished all the chapters on digestive surgery, and one tells oneself that it is not normal that people do not take advantage of this information, and that the physician's power is about to be totally lost. Why?

The "physician's power" is very ephemeral, founded solely on a difference in knowledge. The general public respects the physician and surgeon because there is a difference in the knowledge between them. The doctor tells the patient that he knows the answer, that he has performed the diagnosis, which he is in the process of refining, and that he will be able to treat him. Now things are becoming extremely complicated with new treatments, particularly for the general practitioner. Several American studies have shown that in two days on the Internet, the general public, the patient or future patient, could know as much as, if not more than, his general practitioner, particularly if it concerned a rare illness. This is logical. Since it is a rare condition, the doctor may have seen two or three cases in his life, but the individual who has this condition will spend forty-eight hours researching all the people who work on this rare condition, the specialists, all the types of treatment, the research, the results, and will no doubt know more than his doctor, who does not have forty-eight hours to devote to research-ing a rare condition. So there will be two solutions; the doctor will either respond defensively, explaining to the patient that it isn't the patient's role to research the illness and to leave medical care to the medical community, etc., that sort of doctor is obsolete; or the doctor will take the information that the patient gives him and will work with the patient, explaining that he couldn't have already read countless articles on the topic with thirty-five consults that day, but that he will read them and will of course "digest" the information better than someone who hasn't had medical training. He will connect to specialized forums and will get to the point where he can under-stand this phenomenon and know more than the patient does.

We are really convinced that by involving the general public we will raise the level of care throughout the world. It is clear that if the patient is more demanding, he will be demanding about everything the doctor asks of him; we will no longer be able to routinely prescribe tests that are aggressive or present a risk, because the patient will be informed. Take the example of a patient who is being followed for potential colon cancer. In eighty percent of the cases in France, we prescribe *one* colonoscopy per year, although the offi-cial guidelines recommend one procedure every three years. Why? It is not useful to do the procedure every year, the test can be dangerous (one acci-dent per thousand), and can even be fatal (one in ten thousand). When you explain that to a patient, he understands immediately, he understands that it is a necessary test, because in the end he wants to catch any polyp or recur-rence, but also that it's not a test without risks, that there is the possibility of catching a virus, etc., and the patient will understand this himself. So the "medical power" is shifting. I was in the United States last July (1999) and in *USA Today* there were three pages on this topic; on the first page in color there was a scale, just like the scale of justice, with the caduceus in the middle, and the patient in his hospital bed beginning to assume power over the doctor. They also presented the results of a survey that showed a certain traditional temperament of the doctor (one that has already been brought out in Molière's plays): the doctor used complicated words for simple things; it is an unintentional barrier that results in him not being completely under-stood, which is convenient from time to time when the illness is serious or when the patient is afraid to be confronted with problems (and then prefers not to ask questions). Today, the culture has completely changed; in Europe, too, we are getting closer to the American culture. In the United States there are two to three million people who connect each month to medical or sur-gical sites on the Internet; these are, in fact, the sites that are the most frequently visited. Fifty-three percent of Internet users connect to medical reference sites in the United States, visited more than sites about the arts, sports, etc. These "surfers" are thirsty to get more information in this area, and that's phenomenal!

But what is also important, is that the patient doesn't like to be manipulated, or directed to this or that doctor in a network by an insurer who is removed from the patient's situation. This will never work. People want a network, but a network selected by the patient who wants to understand. Why would one go to a doctor only because he is approved? This is not a criterion based on quality. On the contrary, the patient will do research and accept a network that is of good quality. This is extraordinary.

S.U.: The opposite of the post-war system in Britain. . . .

J.M.: Yes, exactly. So this is the first aspect of globalized medicine: we communicate *real* information.

3. The Development of "Virtual Reality"

J.M.: The second aspect of the revolution brought about by the new information and communication technologies, particularly the development of computer technology and the power of computers, is progress in the area of "virtual reality." Thanks to a new language of algorithms and to mathematics, virtual reality is able in fact to prolong the abilities of our five senses and those of the doctor and surgeon; virtual reality will enable us to reconstruct a damaged organ or the organ that needs surgical intervention, in three dimensions. With a three-dimensional (3D) scanner, we are able to see an organ in three dimensions, but that is all. Thanks to this new computer system, it's completely different; we will be able to use three concepts inherent in virtual reality: interaction, immersion and navigation.

Interaction means that we can touch the organ (with a *data glove* or with a virtual instrument), it will change shape, we will feel the counterpressure, we will move around in it, that is, we will enter an organ that is usually opaque, we will see it as if it were transparent, we see the vessels, we direct ourselves, can wander around in the vessels, the artery, the vein, we see if it's far from a tumor, or close to it. And this is fantastic because it enables us to simulate and plan an operation. If you analyze a tumor in the liver, for example, then you can really see the tumor, you see the liver in transparency, you can turn it, see it from the opposite direction, from the top, the bottom, in all the positions to get a good understanding of the situation. Then you have everything in mind, and you can plan the operation. You know exactly what margin of safety you'll need. You put all the data in your computer, and you see the operation; if it doesn't work like you hoped, you can redo the simulation, two, three, four times. Once you have perfected the procedure, you can send it out on the Internet and get another expert who goes through it with you, to plan, to correct, to say "no, given the position of the tumor and this vessel that you need to consider, I'd go for another treatment." This is the virtual sharing of information, but the term "virtual" here must be understood correctly. The "virtual" is more than the here and now, it is the past, present, and future at the same time. With these three temporal dimensions, we enhance the senses; we can see something in transparency that is not. The "virtual" allows you to shift limits: it is more than what really exists; it is an "improved" or "amplified" reality (that would really be the correct term). We then exchange virtual information among experts.

4. Telesurgery and the Global Exchange of Surgical Procedure

J.M.: The third aspect of telesurgery brings us to the exchange of surgical procedure, that is, the application of virtual reality to do a real operation from a distance. With true telesurgery, or automated or computer-assisted surgery, the surgeon is not there with his instruments to operate and look at the screen; he is sitting down and doesn't even touch the patient. Between the surgeon, comfortably seated, and his patient, there is an interface of computers. There is something between the doctor and patient, an additional intelligence that the surgeon will have in order to make the procedure more precise. So the surgeon has two virtual instruments, left and right, providing the virtual information that he will give to the computer. The computer will analyze them in real time, improve them, check them, remove any shaking and anything else that shouldn't be done, will send these orders immediately to two robot arms that will have an arm position, forearm, hand, and then an endo-effector (an instrument) will perform the procedure within less than a millimeter's precision, a precision that a human hand cannot achieve. Here is the ultimate application of telesurgery, the sharing of procedure, since the procedure is performed from a distance. Currently, we do it at a distance of five meters, but as technology progresses we know that very soon we will be able to do it from a greater distance, we will do it from thousands of miles away. This is what is key in the concept, because it is the first time that we have even imagined operating from a distance.

S.U.: *Do you mean that an operation could be done jointly by a surgeon in Strasbourg and a surgeon in New York?*

J.M.: Yes, by two different teams, in different locations. For the "grand opening" I would like to go to New York and operate from there on a patient in Strasbourg (who will have agreed to the experiment), with, of course, my team in place in Strasbourg in case of a computer problem. This first test case will be a common procedure to start with (but will progressively become more complex); it will show symbolically that there are no limits to the sharing of surgical techniques. This, too, is something fascinating in the development of technologies. I don't think any surgeon could have imagined, several years ago, that one day we would be able to operate from Tokyo in Paris, or from New York in Strasbourg. That was unthinkable. But everything is moving quickly, first because of semi-invasive surgery, because of the distance, the screen (that allows us to share images and advice), and then we arrive at the sharing of gestures. In fact there are no limits. This makes me think of a quote by Alan Kay, the head of Research and Development at Apple: "The easiest way to predict the future is to invent it." We are lucky to live in an era where there are no more technological barriers. "To invent the future in surgery" was impossible twenty years ago. Today, we know that it is possible; it's extraordinary! It is also the fruit of a collaboration between the public and private sectors; we have learned to work with large companies, with information technology, robotics, telecommunications, publishing, etc. Engineers have no limits: if we know how to send something to Mars, how difficult can it be to transmit a couple of surgical manipulations across the ocean?

S.U.: *And when you mentioned the future, your going to New York, etc., is this future in several months or several years?*

J.M.: In several months.

S.U.: *So this is really a fabulous speed of evolution?*

J.M.: Yes, I'd say the only problem is that we also have to sleep! You have the impression of never sleeping. Every day, every time you say something, every time you think of something, an amazing response is given. We've never been dissuaded from any idea we have had concerning the evolution of technology. "Virtual reality" is a project that we began three years ago, thinking at the time that it would be six or eight years before we could create a virtual liver using scanner technology, or do a simulated operation. Today, three years later, the prototype is complete. The power of computers is phenomenal and most of all, I think that the intelligence of the programmers is limitless (our computer programmers in France are brilliant).

S.U.: And can this technology be used in other areas?

J.M.: Yes, of course. When robotics were developed, we were among the pioneers to use them in surgery, using them in what's called visceral surgery since 1994. At the time, the manufacturers' concern was that they didn't know whether it involved only digestive surgery, and they wanted larger markets, worldwide markets, etc. In fact, this same technology is also applied to gynecological and opthamological surgery, among others. A robot has the precision of motion that is at the micron level, nothing like the precision of a human. It concerns all the specialities. We will all be confronted by this phenomenal development in information technology; we must accept this, not as an intelligence that will replace our own, but one that will be added to it. . . .

S.U.: . . . a complementary intelligence, so to speak.

J.M.: Yes, complementary to our own. This is clear. Take the case of a liver tumor. With a scanner you look at views in two dimensions; by looking at them all (there are at least sixty to look at at the same time), very carefully, you are almost able to reconstruct the tumor, some vascular connections, but it is very difficult. All of a sudden, in five minutes, a computer does it all for you, you see everything in transparency. If you can't see the back very well, you turn the liver with the computer, and everything is turned around. If you want to see from above, you see from above. If you want to know if the tumor has invaded the artery that is adjacent, you go into the artery and look around. You see the tumor; it is really phenomenal, also for the professor.

S.U.: Yes, it helps hand and mind at the same time. In the future, there must be applications that we have yet to imagine, the evolution is so quick and powerful.

J.M.: Yes, we cannot imagine.

S.U.: Let's return to the patient. For now, in France we have a system of socialized medicine that seems to be very advanced in respect to the rest of the world.

J.M.: Yes, I think it is the system in which the patient has the best chance of being treated properly.

5. The Evolution of the Healthcare System in a Global World

S.U.: So everything that you are developing is obviously marvelous and makes one dream about the possibilities. However, with globalization underway, we are in fact witnessing a competitive race, a reduction in expenditures, budgetary restrictions, and a questioning of the welfare state, and therefore a risk of limiting public assistance for medical care. Is this the tendency you see and which can limit progress toward the democratization of healthcare, or do you think that the technologies that you are developing can help all patients?

J.M.: I think there are two ways to answer this question. The first problem relates to the resources that one wants to allocate to healthcare: it is a political question, a societal choice; it's also a choice for the politicians and therefore for the electorate. If, for example, we spend billions of dollars to construct a highway to go faster to the beach in the summer, if we reduce the number of toll booths so as not to lose time, if we consider that all this is normal, and if we admit that for this reason we need to decrease spending on new technologies that might be promising for a hospital, we arrive at something that is nonsensical! I think that if we are able to clearly explain the choice to the voters, we won't get to that point: the choice will surely be made to benefit the advancement of healthcare. But, we're not able to get that point across very well at present.

There is a second way to respond: it is that the new technologies—which are ultimately not that expensive because virtual reality will be available on any PC, with software that is inexpensive—will allow us to achieve phenomenal savings in healthcare. It is obvious that if you simulate a procedure, if you plan correctly, and if you share your plans with another individual, you are going to do better work, the outcome will be better, the patient will spend less time at the hospital, will have fewer complications, and everything will cost less. The same is true with robotics. Robotics shouldn't be used for a simple procedure (like a vesicle removal, which we used initially to test the technique), but for a more complex surgery like liver surgery. These robots will also have many applications in heart surgery and for sutures in heart bypass surgery. It is obvious that if for the ten minutes it takes to do the suture, this suture is done from a distance by someone who has the best results in coronary suturing (we know that this is what matters, one must be fast and good), the better the suture, the better the follow-up care of the patient. In a few years there will be doctors who will not necessarily have completed the most surgical training or be the most intelligent, the best, etc., but who will be best able to do in fifteen minutes a coronary suture that has been recommended. In this case, again, the patient will have a shorter hospital stay, won't need a coronography dilation, and the postoperative follow-up will be less painful. Overall, the length of hospitalization and recovery will be reduced, and so will the global cost to society because the patient will return to active life more quickly.

S.U.: So it is undeniable that the quality of care is being dramatically improved. However, you've cited Strasbourg, New York, Tokyo, only cities in the developed world, and we understand that you need a considerable infrastructure. But what about less developed countries: will this kind of networking that you have described also play a role in limiting the spread of disease in poor countries, or help prevent the diseases?

J.M.: Yes, of course. With networking programs (particularly European), developing countries will be able to connect and make up for the time they have lost. It is clear that these countries have enormous problems to solve, of all kinds: practical, day-to-day management, poorly equipped hospitals, no money, etc., but also intellectual: they don't have the money to acquire scientific journals, etc. So for now, while waiting for these countries to emerge, it is important that the gap doesn't become wider. Once the video-conference and the Internet have become as common as the telephone, anyone, in any country, will have access to knowledge. Developing countries will then be able to benefit from the technology as well.

S.U.: Returning to the developed countries, can we imagine, thanks to new information and communication technologies, that patients, connected to the Internet, will be able to avoid hospitalization, or to delay the need to go into a nursing home . . . that is, maintain their lifestyle in their homes, their quality of life that is so cherished, indeed, to care for themselves at home?

J.M.: Self-medication, self-treatment, can be a phenomenal source of savings in healthcare by avoiding long-term care, testing, and costly examinations, though there is a risk of missing something that is serious and completely unexpected. Thus this is something that should not be prevented, provided we furnish the patient with the best information from the start. The patient is capable of understanding (at least some illnesses); the patient is not necessarily ignorant and the physician not necessarily intelligent. With the diffusion of information and the new information and communication technologies, self-medication will be justified.

The patient will also be able to make an informed choice about the place where he will be operated on or cared for. In France, the government has been agonizing over the closing of small hospitals, some of which are not equipped to provide care in the year 2000 and beyond. Except for certain useful first aid, these little hospitals do not enable one to give birth with a great deal of safety or to undergo any procedure that is not completely without risk, not because the surgeon isn't competent but because the hospital environment is not satisfactory (no anesthesia available at night, no resuscitation units, lack of specialized equipment, etc.). With better information, the patient will understand the situation; he will decide himself not to be operated on in hospitals that are not able to ensure quality or the best chances for recovery.

S.U.: We will then be able to close the health care centers that are the least productive, reducing the waste of public funds.

J.M.: Yes, because people will no longer be willing to accept waste, nor will healthcare professionals. It will then be more attractive for the surgeon, who likes to operate, but who is located in a small hospital and cannot do a major operation, to be associated with a large medical center, one that is well equipped and has highly qualified surgical teams. The patient will spend several days there and then return to a local hospital or transitional care unit, between a medical center and a rehab center, with fewer nurses, and that will be less expensive.

S.U.: So you are suggesting a new hospital organization: large well-equipped centers for major procedures and local services for less serious problems and for recovery.

J.M.: Yes, because we cannot imagine keeping a large number of hospitals, all equally well equipped in terms of material and people. That's not possible.

S.U.: You have helped us envision a superb "revolution," stimulating for the mind and full of promise both for the patient and for society: a better future. . . . Thank you!

CHAPTER 20

Food:
Language, Thought, Ideology

DAVIDE PAOLINI

Food is language, thought, and even ideology all at the same time. It is definitely a tool, in the media sense of the word, with much as yet unexplored potential. It is capable of touching a transverse target and promoting the integration of peoples. It is sufficient to think of media coverage of events dealing with the phenomenon of food: there is a veritable boom of interest in everything related to taste. But a cultural phenomenon is also appearing that directly affects the history, traditions, and movements of people.

The opening of markets, the speed of information, the rapidity and ease of exchanges of merchandise and ideas, the influence of advertising, the concentration of food power in the hands of a few multinational companies—all this has triggered a completely new phenomenon: the standardization of taste, a child of economic globalization.

Countries which up to a few years ago had been the masters and the cultural reference points in gastronomy, that is, France and Italy, are not exempt from this reality. These countries too have been experiencing a rapid standardization of eating habits, with models arriving, to no one's surprise, from nations that have long been considered the "third world of tastes," such as the United States. The items that come to mind immediately are the Big Mac

Davide Paolini is the head of Idea Plus, a Milan-based advertising company, and a researcher and writer in the field of food and wine. He also writes a column on cultural topics for *Sole 24 Ore*.

and Coke, but we could also mention certain types of "industrial" cheese or the snacks that are already part of the teenage culture, be it French or Italian. And yet, in these two countries there are strong, even spectacular, resistance movements. They range from the violent reactions on the part of French farmers and chefs who protest against the cult of globalization (e.g., McDonald's) to the Italian counter-initiatives (Slow Food, Sapori & Saperi) that have launched campaigns against fast food and that preach in favor of genuine products made according to time-honored methods.

The face of the world map of cuisine is truly changing: on the one hand we see a new trend in cuisine known as "fusion," and on the other hand we see a revival of local dishes and products or, better still, of the "minor gastronomy." These are two extremes that never meet. In fact, they are growing farther and farther apart, creating new modes in eating.

In gastronomy we are witnessing a phenomenon that is entirely comparable to what has happened with respect to languages: the English language (or Esperanto) can be compared to this culinary fusion, while the local idioms or dialects are the equivalent of local cuisine. It is obvious that this fusion is the legitimate child of economic globalization because it is a direct descendant of the free circulation of people and goods and, therefore, of material cultures. If "fusion" is defined as the creation of chefs who use raw materials and ingredients from all over the world, which are now available in their local markets, we can immediately see the potential effects of globalization—and even more than that. If we add in the fact that chefs contribute the various techniques of different countries, we see that we are dealing with a "united cuisine of the world." One outstanding example comes from Australia: in Sydney, Melbourne, or Adelaide, Japanese or Chinese chefs create dishes using local ingredients but follow their "oriental" traditions in preparation. In the United States, in California, for example, you can taste foods made with oriental species, Italian balsamic vinegar, Canadian fish, and Mexican vegetables.

Culinary fusion is a recent development, which began in the 1990s. In previous decades, when chefs went abroad to work they rarely, if ever, used the traditional ingredients of the "new countries" in their recipes. A typical example of this is Italian cuisine. Although it has spread throughout all five continents, the chefs originally tried to use products made in Italy—at any cost. But in the end they created dishes with false Italian ingredients that they obtained in other countries (parmesan cheese, cured ham, tomato sauce, olive oil, etc.). This is a clear case of imitation or, better yet, of "counterfeiting" ingredients. It still occurs, and lawsuits to defend trademarks or production methods are constantly coming up before the courts. The French model is different; over the years French cuisine was distinguished by the fact that it exported recipes created by renowned chefs that absolutely required the use of unique ingredients made in France, such as foie gras and cheeses, wines, and champagne. In contrast, we perhaps see "fusion" in the case of the American chef who uses Hawaiian bread, Mexican chili peppers, Italian balsamic vinegar, and what have you to create his very personal dishes, the fruit of his creativity.

To continue the economic parallels: we are facing a situation resembling that of multinational companies who set up production facilities where labor is cheap. In gastronomy, however, it is a matter of purchasing the product that is most suited to the chefs' tastes with respect to flavor and aroma.

Fusion is also an attitude toward food, which moreover differs from that of *nouvelle cuisine,* even though the latter trend can, in a sense, be considered supranational because of the Japanese contribution to the mode of presentation or the use of certain oriental ingredients. *Nouvelle cuisine* was a French-based approach; once again, French chefs, using mainly ingredients made in France, became the leaders of this new vogue. We must also add that *nouvelle cuisine* did indeed influence many taste-developing nations. It is no coincidence that today many American, Australian, and German chefs are at the forefront of this French-born philosophy. We can say that, in a certain sense, culinary fusion is the illegitimate child of *nouvelle cuisine,* and we must also acknowledge that *nouvelle cuisine* marked the first attempt at uniting several countries "in one dish," as it were.

Globalization has certainly contributed to the growth of culinary fusion, making it possible to develop creativity and genius in all parts of the world. Yet for many, it has also limited the possibilities of lingering with the wonderful, yet "difficult" riches of their homes. In fact, in many cases global dissemination of the same products has initiated young people to facile, identical, and undifferentiated tastes. The fact that you can buy the same food products at home or abroad, whether you go on holiday or to study, strongly orients the choices of the consumer, who in this way runs no risks of "unpleasant surprises" for the palate. On the contrary, sameness offers security. This behavior is leading to the development of the "tourist" who finds, rather than the traveler who discovers. That is, the consumer is increasingly encouraged to eat widely available products (such as those offered in the large vacation clubs and villages, the big hotels, etc.) and to forget about tasting the "local" flavors.

The success of many "global" food products and the growth of the "party" of chefs who are united under the banner of culinary fusion can lead us to assume that the "minorities" in the kitchen and the local or regional products are in danger of extinction. This is not at all true. A full picture of the situation shows that those who support local flavor and regional aromas can indeed rest easy. In fact, it is precisely the overwhelming power of globalization, of taste standardization, that is leading to the rebirth of the "special," of the local. History is merely repeating itself: minorities find the strength to resist and survive when they are threatened with extermination. The future will not belong to the "glocal" (global + local), as some have dismally forecast, but rather to the coexistence, albeit difficult, of the global and the local.

It is almost redundant to set on the table the reasons for the success of the "global" and to state that the future of agricultural products and foodstuffs consists of big numbers, exploitation, big names, and big profits; this is borne out in the economic picture. Perhaps less obvious, therefore, are predictions of a *revival* of the material culture of the land and hence of local agricultural products and foodstuffs.

The positive sign that is cause for hope comes from the country where culinary fusion and the "global" were born: the United States, especially in California. It is precisely on that golden stretch of coast extending from San Francisco to San Diego that many American chefs are using and promoting the products of small farmers from this area where everything grows. The Californian movement is big, and it is being carried under the banner of organic foods, for example, by Alice Waters (of the Chez Panisse restaurant in Berkeley). Optimism for a major recovery and for a victory of the "local" over the colonization of the table by industrial products is coming from this effervescent Californian lady.

It is, in fact, unthinkable that the extraordinary material culture of the Mediterranean area (Italy, Spain, France, etc.) could die out in the face of attempts to level the tastes of Europe and the rest of the world. There are tangible signs of a great reaction underway, beginning in Italy, and it is being instigated precisely by the excessive power of global products. No one can dispute the enormous gastronomic wealth that is scattered throughout Italy. A study paid for by Confartigianato (the confederation that represents the artisans in food production) revealed that there are approximately six hundred different types of processed meats and four hundred different cheeses that are made by at least one producer each. In many cases the quantity of production is extremely limited, and the goods are marketed only where that artisan works; they are unknown in the rest of the country. This "cultural heritage," comprising tradition, wisdom, and skill, was only recently rediscovered by the Italians themselves, as the so-called "global" products began to make inroads. It practically amounts to a reaction against undifferentiated tastes.

But perhaps the factors that more than any others have launched the "quest for the lost taste" are the European Union directives 93/43 and 96/3 concerning the hygiene of food products (and other related provisions). These directives, which, if fully implemented, would have led to the closing of many artisan firms that are the source of the products mentioned above, led to a violent reaction on the part of many consumers and gourmets. They saw in these documents a desire on the part of the European Commission to kill traditional foods in favor of those homogeneous frozen goods manufactured by northern Europe's huge multinationals. Suddenly, a race began to save the "niche products," and it was based on consumption, local research, and the allure of discovery.

We must note, however, that simultaneously with the "hygienic-health" directives, the European Union also issued regulations (2081 and 2082, dated July 14, 1992) that define "protected designation of origin" (PDO) and "protected geographical indication" (PGI). These regulations aim at protecting and highlighting those agricultural products and foodstuffs that are made according to authentic and unvarying local methods, and are the fruit of historic traditions. PDO and PGI are different. For the former to apply, all the phases of production and processing must take place in the specified geographic area. For the latter to apply, it is sufficient that the respective quality and reputation can be attributed to the geographic origin, although the production process itself may take place elsewhere.

But Italy is not the only country to be pervaded by interest in artisan niche-food products. The trend is very strong in Spain, as we can see in Catalonia—a land which, like the Basque country, offers an exciting and delightful regional cuisine.

Not only is there a great dichotomy between the *global* and the *local* throughout the world; we must also note the consequences of economic interdependency in nutrition. Throughout history the movements of peoples—great exoduses, pilgrimages, cultural migrations, workers leaving poor countries and then returning to their countries of origin, mass tourism—have made and are still making an enormous contribution to the development and integration of multicultural cuisines. From the remote past to recent times, Europe has been the theater of continuous migratory movement. In the last two centuries, in addition to the major movements from southern Europe toward the United States and Australia, there have been major population shifts within the continent. In the decades following

World War II (the 1950s and 1960s) there was a great homeward flow of many former European emigrants, and this trend has been accentuated in more recent decades. Moreover, whereas migrations within Europe have decreased, the flow of immigrants from non-European countries has become more pronounced. To these phenomena we must add mass tourism throughout the Mediterranean countries and the hordes of Europeans traveling to so-called "exotic" places.

Migrations have contributed to the diffusion of foods through a bidirectional process. Over the years foods and culinary practices have traveled from south to north and vice versa, and are continuing to do so. Continuous cultural exchanges deriving from various forms of population shifts have led to a dissemination and consolidation of eating habits and customs that have become universal. It is sufficient to mention the growing popularity of what is known as the "Mediterranean diet," which has become a lifestyle in countries such as the United States and Australia: in the latter, the national food is "spaghetti alla bolognese," and the national beverage is cappuccino. Looking in the other direction, we can see the rising popularity of beer in southern lands.

It is obvious that, on the one hand, the movement of peoples brings about the development and affirmation of what have become universal foods and cuisines; on the other hand, we are witnessing the fact that ethnic cuisines are literally bursting onto the European scene. Ten years ago the only "exotic" restaurants in Italy were Chinese, but today there is a literal explosion of Japanese, Arab, Indian, and Eritrean restaurants, which are divided into two categories: one for the ethnic population and one for the Italians. Paradoxically, the emerging cuisines throughout today's world are the Italian and Japanese.

As these two phenomena continue to intertwine, they have given us a series of dishes from different countries that have been widely adopted around the globe. We call them "world food": pasta, pizza, hamburgers, hotdogs, popcorn, sushi, cousous, kebab, moussaka, churrasco, chili and tacos, French croissants, tiramisù.

CHAPTER 21

Mayoral Voices

---

1. European Cities between Supranationality and Subsidiarity

The phenomenon of globalization as it is currently formulated around the world has consequences for cities and social life in the urban milieu, where everyday life reflects the constant pull between what is universal and global, and what is local. The city is also a meeting place for diverse populations (locals, immigrants, tourists, business professionals, artists, etc.) and is thus a home for cultural diversity and a place for change and innovation.

In Europe, with the signing of the Treaty of Amsterdam, the vitality of local groups is developing within a new context of institutional partnership in which mayors have more responsibility and more power.

As a player in this environment, how do you perceive your new role between supranationality and subsidiarity?

Herbert Wagner (Dresden): With the implementation of the principle of supranationality at the level of the European Union, the relations among states, nations, regions, and communities have become more complex, and in many respects must be redefined. Structural decisions are now made in Brussels; the farther one is from this important decision-making center, the deeper subsidiarity must be anchored locally. That which can be regulated on the local level must also be decided on the local level, with the concomitant growth of local diversity. At the same time, information must be able to circulate from the bottom up as well as from the top down, and must be institutionalized. Adequate institutional forms have yet to be identified. I see

At the time of these interviews, the following held mayoral or equivalent positions in their respective towns: Albert Bore (Birmingham), Leoluca Orlando (Palermo), Roland Ries (Strasbourg), Wolfgang Tiefensee (Leipzig), Herbert Wagner (Dresden).

my role in this context as one of a "manager of the transformation" who, on the one hand, must promote in my own city the advantages of a unified but diverse Europe and, on the other hand, must be the advocate for local interests in Brussels, thus contributing to create more effective institutions.

Albert Bore (Birmingham): With regard to the European Union, to date new operational rules for EU institutions have had relatively little affect on the city. However, in an increasingly globalized world there is growing potential for major cities to develop an increased autonomy and exert some increased influence. This will be particularly the case where cities and their immediate regions can coalesce and find some common political voice. It has been on that basis that Birmingham was one of the six founder members of the Eurocities organization. It has the capacity and potential to project the urban voice within Europe that at present is sadly lacking and to help cities and urban areas as a whole to have a much greater say within European affairs and the decisions of the various institutions within the European Union. It is also a network where cities can learn from each other and share best practice.

Leoluca Orlando (Palermo): The implementation of a single European currency, the necessary and desirable prelude to the formation of a larger, borderless Europe, must necessarily be accompanied by the glorification of the identities of local collectivities, including cities. Europe is a huge reality that goes beyond national borders, barriers, and adherence, to create a single market, a single communal politics which cannot, however, be fully glorified without the "protection" of the cultures, traditions, and identities of those who comprise it. For this reason, I believe that the role of the cities, entities that do not mint currency, do not have armies, but that concretely reflect the basic needs of the citizens who live there, is fundamental. In this scenario the role of mayors, who are in turn becoming the primary representatives of citizens and the voices of their requests at both the state and, most importantly, the European level, is even more essential: a clear projection toward the world beyond—this, today more than ever before, characterizes the role of city mayors who have become true ambassadors of the culture and identity of their local constituencies. I, myself, have felt as if I were a "postcard" that the citizens of Palermo send to the entire world to share their history, traditions, cultural wealth, distinctive characteristics, and most of all, the potential they can promise in an increasingly "supranational" environment.

Roland Ries (Strasbourg): An important part of the urban population is at ease in a world where the globalization of communication and exchange has profoundly impacted the content of work, cultural practices, and leisure activities. This population functions in networks of which large cities constitute the major nodes. The city is experienced as a part of the "global village," where communication and exchange are facilitated.

All the same, a large majority of the urban population *endures* this globalization: insufficient education, a rural family background, professional instability—these are all factors that contribute to narrow the horizon for a population that considers globalization as a threat. For this group of individuals, the city is experienced as a place to be near others, a place for a support network and for aid. They wish above all for peace of mind and security.

This duality of the phenomenon of globalization is central to the responsibilities of a mayor of a large European city such as Strasbourg.

The growth of production and service activity, the employment dynamic, and demographic attractiveness are all concentrated in large metropolitan areas. A mayor has little control over the global systems of information and exchange which he witnesses and which impact the development of his city. Yet the regulation of these systems is a major priority of international institutions. By contrast, mayors are increasingly confronted with the regulation of social systems: for example, cities are becoming the right level of subsidiarity for implementing lasting development projects.

This is not, strictly speaking, a new role. In the shadow of the leader of a city council there has always been a referee, a mediator, on whom fell the responsibility for harmony in social life.

In Strasbourg, this will to master the development of the city and its surrounding area, as well as the entire urban region, is being translated into a regional project and a long-term plan to develop the urban environment.

Wolfgang Tiefensee (Leipzig): Regardless of size, a city's resources are limited and it is not in any position to make major structural changes alone. In Leipzig, we are reacting to this new constellation with a double strategy: on the one hand, we are seeking to develop our own identity, our own path in the areas of political participation, of economic development, and of cultural awareness; on the other hand, we rely on regional solidarity.

In the "Europe of Regions" and in a global economy, regions will be competing with one another. A large city by itself, even if it has a strong tradition, can no longer make itself heard in this concert of regions, can no longer assert itself individually as an attractive economic space. By contrast, a region that is reinforced by intensive cooperation among its parts certainly can. The inhabitants of Leipzig are eager to be part of this interactive game, to be in "the major league." This is possible only with the support of the larger economic area comprising Leipzig-Halle-Dessau-Merseburg. Today, a city's politics cannot stop at its own city hall. Rather than competing within a single region, cities must join forces and work toward a division of labor. Only through true cooperation can we reinforce an entire region. From this perspective, our geographic location is a huge advantage. Leipzig is located near many important transportation outlets. The expansion of the European Union toward Eastern Europe and beyond gives us the opportunity to serve as a platform for east-west trade.

2. Challenges of Employment and of the Quality of Social Relations

The phenomenon of globalization has strongly accelerated the rhythm and breadth of change; in many cases, we observe a profound economic and social mutation that must be managed. Employment is one of the most important variables. Most cities throughout the world are familiar with problems linked to unemployment, job insecurity, the quality of urban infrastructures, pollution, etc. Do these issues particularly affect your city? What are the means that have been deployed in an attempt to solve these problems? Have these problems evolved significantly?

Albert Bore (Birmingham): *Unemployment and job instability.* Birmingham has had a hard time over the last twenty years. The economic recessions of the late 1970s and early 1980s had a devastating effect. Two hundred thousand jobs were lost in Birmingham during this period. More jobs were lost in my city in this period than the total number of jobs lost in the whole of Scotland and Wales put together. In 1984 there were twenty-eight unemployed adults for every single job vacancy in Birmingham. And with that economic recession came social turmoil.

The city and the surrounding West Midlands region was a traditional industrial region, heavily reliant upon motor manufacture, component industries, and more generally, metal bashing and engineering. The need to diversify the city's economic base was absolutely overwhelming.

That was the picture fifteen years ago. It is not the image and reality of Birmingham today. During that period the City Council has pursued a diversification strategy that built upon its long-standing role as a regional capital and as the United Kingdom's second city. Many problems still remain, but we have now consolidated and expanded our role as a regional capital for banking, legal services, accountancy, and other professional services. We have science, research, and business parks. We have the largest exhibition center in the UK and one of Europe's largest and best convention centers. In short, what we have seen is a significant diversification of the economy. How has this come about, and why is it of interest for other cities?

I think, above all, the most important reason is that from very early days, Birmingham has realized that the public and private sectors need to work in harness. Together, we have sought to change the economic climate of the city; to boost the confidence of the financial institutions in the future of the city and encourage them to invest in it. Central to this approach has been the development of a series of innovative public/private sector partnerships, which mutually benefit the city, its citizens, and the private sector. These have helped to create conditions for economic growth and increased employment. We have encouraged the private sector to invest in new sectors of the economy. The Council's Economic Development Department and its Property Division have helped companies to find new sites. We have made adroit use of European Union Structural Funds monies to develop the infrastructure and to make new sites accessible and bring old industrial land back into modern use. And the Council has consistently attempted by a variety of ways and means to develop new forms of public/private partnerships.

Partnerships in Practice. Let me give three examples of how these partnerships have helped with the diversification of the city's economy: the National Exhibition Center group, which has promoted Birmingham's exhibition, convention, and business tourism trade; the Aston Science Park, which has seen us develop in the science/technology arena; and the Brindley-place Development, which has boosted our professional services and leisure sector. The National Exhibition Center was established back in 1975 as a partnership between the City Council and the Chamber of Commerce and Industry. Since that date it has gone from strength to strength in both developing the capacity of its exhibition facilities and, from 1991, extending its services into the high-quality convention sector with the enormously successful International Convention Center and National Indoor Arena in the heart of Birmingham.

On a smaller scale, we have applied the same principles to new technology enterprises in the Aston Science Park. This joint venture started in 1982. It was developed as a joint venture between the City Council, Aston University, and Lloyds Bank, encouraging the formation and growth of new businesses in the technologies of tomorrow.

My third example is Brindleyplace. Here the Council assembled unused and derelict land around unused canals and drew up plans for commercial development. We insisted on high quality buildings, new public squares, mixed usage with a range of restaurants and bars, new housing, and an arts facility in a restored historic building, as well as new offices. The outcome is an attractive, welcoming area used in the day, during the evening, and on weekends. It provides 8,000 jobs in the professional and financial services and also provides a new entertainment and leisure quarter for the city and wider region.

We have also undertaken a range of measures to improve the educational attainment, training, and skills levels of our students and young people. We are very anxious to ensure that with the emergence of new job opportunities, Birmingham's work force has the knowledge and skills to do them.

Today, we see a more balanced economy with overall unemployment down from almost 20 percent to around 9 percent. This is still well above the UK average, and there remain pockets of very high male unemployment particularly in some of our inner-city areas, among our black and Asian communities, and in some of our housing districts on the edge of the city.

All the activities I have mentioned here require partnership. I think that is the message for all the cities. Our experiences will be different, but we all know we are moving from the world of bulk mass production, where the majority of people earn their living in large factories, to a more diversified fragmented economy with lots of smaller enterprises and greater reliance on information technology, computing, and technological skills. This move from a Fordist to a post-Fordist economy critically requires flexible partnerships and is best achieved with an active role by local and regional governments.

Cities in Central and Eastern Europe and the former Soviet Union have come out of an era of complete state control. Its failings are so clear that no one calls for a return to that economic system. But the way forward is not its polar opposite. A complete absence of government, whether local, regional, national, or European, from the business of the economy is a neoliberal, utopian delusion. Rather, what we need to deal with the complexities of the modern globalizing world are a range of flexible partnerships.

These will differ from city to city and region to region, but nevertheless, we must always recognize that to make progress and ensure sustainable economic development we need meaningful partnerships between the public and private sector which bring benefits to citizens and the wider economy.

Wolfgang Tiefensee (Leipzig): The evolution of employment is expressed in numbers: in 1989, about 120,000 people were employed in the manufacturing sector in Leipzig; today [2000] there are only 12,000. The reduction in the size of the industrial sector has left vacant jobs that are far from being replaced. It is difficult to assimilate this sudden void overnight, even more so today since the growth rate of the new *Länder* scarcely exceeds that of West Germany.

Despite undeniable successes and the potential revealed through transfers arranged by the German state, which continue to be necessary for our development, it should be emphasized that we face numerous problems in terms of historical wounds. Last year [1999], the unemployment rate rose, on average, to about 17 percent. For the year 1998, the city of Leipzig—contrary to the tendency in West Germany—had to increase its budget for social programs from 93 to 116 million deutschmarks (DM).

To resolve this difficult situation, we trust in our own strength. For example, in 1998 the City Council of Leipzig, despite a healthy financial situation, decided to sell 40 percent of the capital of the city electric company to an energy company called MEAG. A large part of the funds raised from this sale, a total of 420 million DM, was used to attract new companies and to stimulate the expansion of existing companies.

To this end, we have created a technological foundation endowed with some 100 million DM. An additional 50 million DM have been put into a technological fund to adapt the infrastructures to the needs of new "future growth" companies. For the creation of new companies, we have put into place, in collaboration with the savings and loan bank, a fund for high risk capital. At the same time, our new, recently opened Business Innovation Center offers favorable conditions for young companies that are ready to launch into risky ventures.

Past experience has shown that the possibility of attracting an important investor to Leipzig, creating thousands of jobs at once, is not likely. To count on one large investor is a bad policy. We need to diversify the odds. The assistance accorded to companies must above all reinforce the "endogenous factors," that is, build on the city's existing potential.

In the framework of the successful public relations campaign "Leipzig's on its way!" (*Leipzig kommt*), intended to improve the image of our city, we recently put a program in place called "Leipzig—a city for entrepreneurs." The goal is to augment the means of transferring know-how and capital, to make land and buildings available, and to stimulate useful professional contacts. We want each resident of Leipzig who has a promising business idea and a serious entrepreneurial concept to obtain the highest level of support from our city.

But we also support existing companies by providing access to high-risk capital through banks and private investors. Mid-size companies, the trades and businesses, have created numerous jobs. These companies are at the core of the German economy in general, but this is particularly true for Leipzig. More than 95 percent of our companies employ fewer than ten individuals. These young companies depend on the large financial and personal commitment of their founders. We support them, as this is also in our own best interest.

The development of Leipzig as a city for media illustrates the success of our program in support of companies. Here we have an example of a successful structural transformation. Leipzig, "the city of books," has become "the city of media." More than 33,000 inhabitants of Leipzig are employed in this sector; the annual sales figures of this industry is some 4 billion DM. Nearly two thirds of the media companies have been created since 1990. These are usually small companies that use ultramodern technical equipment and a highly developed telecommunications platform. But we also vigorously support new information and communications technologies: multimedia; the development of software or of new forms of services aided by computers, such as telemedicine. A growing number of computer companies are now located in and around the city, and Leipzig is gradually becoming the service provider for the entire region.

But we do not exclusively depend on the areas of activity and the jobs provided by the new economy, though they are full of potential. So long as the more traditional job market is not satisfactory, we need to develop an intelligent political strategy on every front. The city of Leipzig, therefore, in the early 1990s created a useful operational tool for employment called the "Office for the Promotion of Employment." This service offers a second chance to people who have lost their jobs in the traditional labor market to retrain to obtain new qualifications. Currently, some 5,000 people are taking advantage of this new service, which has become a model for all of Germany in the revitalizing of employment.

Leoluca Orlando (Palermo): The city of Palermo suffers from the endemic plague of unemployment resulting from decades of clientelism and poor management. We are now trying to bring a concrete response to this penury of jobs among the residents of Palermo, thanks to a range of initiatives designed to define new development factors.

Every day we receive entrepreneurs who wish to begin production activities in Palermo, and we offer concrete responses to their needs in a "European" timeframe. The experience of Sportello Unico per le Imprese (a dedicated office for business representatives) is in this sense emblematic. Today, an individual who wants to undertake an activity in Palermo is not thrust against the wall of bureaucracy but finds a special government office that helps him deal with the administrative process, by accelerating to whatever extent possible the time needed to get the venture underway. These are small steps whose effects are nonetheless visible and that contribute decisively in bringing about a solution to the employment needs of Palermo's citizens.

Herbert Wagner (Dresden): Our city is now undergoing a dramatic process of transformation due to the passage from a socialist economy with authoritative central direction to a social market economy. The globalization process makes this transition even more complex and difficult.

Our city sees its path toward successful development as being a symbiotic relationship between economics and culture. And it is especially in the area of high technology that Dresden has been able to attract important business.

Do you think that the need for new forms of collective well-being (in terms of solidarity and security, for example) has arisen, at the level of local government?

Leoluca Orlando (Palermo): As I mentioned earlier, regarding the new and very important role cities play in the new Europe, now more than ever we must focus on quality of life issues for those who live in urban areas. This is what we have tried to do these last few years in Palermo. We have succeeded, thanks to a circumspect and profitable use of funds made available through European community programs like Urbs, Medea, Urban, and Zeus, in offering our residents a higher quality of life, one that is remarkable, unmatched, and respected throughout all Europe and the world. Cities have to be particularly watchful of solidarity issues and look after the least protected, those who in our society are not heard; this is one issue that Palermo has been addressing for some time already, with extremely positive results. We need to be particularly attentive to safety in our cities. Security is an essential element not only for arriving at an optimal quality of life but also for fully guaranteeing social and economic development. In this regard, Palermo's experience can be considered representative: the city, once freed from the cultural hegemony of the Mafia, has finally become a safer city with a much lower crime rate than in the past. As a consequence of this "rediscovered" security, thanks to the commitment of honest politicians and the work of investigators and law enforcement officials who, in too many cases, gave up their lives in the quest, we are beginning to see the arrival in Palermo of an increasing number of foreign and Italian entrepreneurs, all seeking to invest in the city. This tendency was certainly influenced by the safer conditions in the city, and also by the realization on the part of investors who have selected Palermo, that Sicily is an integral part of Europe, with all the legal and commercial guarantees on investments that Europe implies.

Albert Bore (Birmingham): This is just one of a wide variety of ways in which we have responded to the needs of those people and communities who have migrated to Birmingham from other parts of the world over the last three or four decades. In Birmingham today more than 20 percent of the population is of black or ethnic minority origin. In particular, we had large successive waves of settlement of people from the West Indies, the Indian subcontinent, and East Africa during the late 1950s, 1960s, and 1970s. This population is heavily concentrated in the inner-city districts. It is a relatively young population, and nearly 50 percent of our school children come from black and ethnic minority backgrounds. Our response as a city has been to welcome our new citizens and to seek to integrate them within every aspect of the life of Birmingham, but also to recognize their need for their own autonomy and space within which to develop and sustain their own religion and culture.

We have experienced outbursts of racism. However, these outbursts have been significantly marginalized, and important progress has been made over these decades in the development of harmonious, multiracial city.

All black citizens from the former Commonwealth have the right to vote, and we have significant involvement from black and Asian councilors and voluntary groups in the political and civic life of the city. Within the Local Authority we have set targets for the employment of staff from black and Asian communities; developed services addressed to the distinctive needs of these communities, for example, English as a special language course and women-only swimming sessions at set times within our swimming-pools; and given support to a wide range of black and Asian voluntary groups. We have established a range of forums and other consultation processes through which we can work with minority ethnic groups to develop services that are sensitive to their particular needs. The limited resources that are directly available to the City Council have been allocated on the basis of defined needs, and therefore we have concentrated a greater amount of our resources on the poorer areas where these communities are concentrated. At the same time, within the economic arena, we have made specific efforts to develop Asian and black businesses and provided training and employment opportunities for people from these communities. In these ways the past decades have seen significant positive advances within the city, and its black and Asian communities have increasingly contributed to the dynamism, vibrancy, and cosmopolitan character of Birmingham.

The socioeconomic system of the German Democratic Republic (GDR) highlighted the principle of social solidarity. The current system places more emphasis on satisfaction drawn from individual advantages and the merits of competition. In an economy in transition, what form can the new types of collective well-being take?

Wolfgang Tiefensee (Leipzig): I have always considered the so-called "social warmth" of the GDR to be the result of a view about life that turned poverty into a virtue. Because many things were absent in everyday life, one simply depended more on other people. We should also recall the collective rallies organized by the central government in which "mandatory" participation was considered proof of political loyalty. But you are no doubt correct: the current way of thinking in terms of competition risks leading to a loss in social substance that is indispensable to a community. The citizens of the former GDR are undeniably very sensitive to this issue.

This exposes our city politics to new specific demands. The transformation of Leipzig into a city that is modern and open to the world must benefit all of its citizens. Our common desire is that now, as in the past, Leipzig remain a city with a good quality of life for all its citizens. I emphasize the ideal of social solidarity because it is in contradiction with certain schools of thought and action that are popular today which do not expressly condemn exclusion, or which accept exclusion all too easily.

Henceforth, since the "Peaceful Revolution" (of 1989), in Leipzig we have sought to reach a consensus on all political and economic decisions. This has been possible because all the political players in our city were aware from the beginning that there was no alternative to the process of modernization. In all of the discussions or debates, all of the players have been persuaded of the need to work together to make the city move forward. This has been the cement of the "Leipzig model:" to bring to the forefront the development of "our" city, superseding individual, group, or party interests defending divergent points of view.

The expression "transition from a planned economy to the market economy" is simple! But the concept is not! It conceals a thousand small revolutions with endless learning processes, with fundamental changes in behavior, with gigantic ruptures in mentality. The population of the GDR has been forced overnight to learn new forms of work, political administration, and judicial culture. The old world was profoundly transformed, up to the smallest details of daily life, both for the so-called "regular citizen" and for the corporate director and the elected official. No stone was left unturned.

This process undeniably has not been painless. How could it be otherwise! Such a transformation, rapid and deep, is a unique example in modern European history. As a political leader in one of the new *Länder,* I recognize that one element has been fundamental in this regard: if this process has been a success in spite of all opposing forces, it is because the notion of "social equilibrium" was never lost from sight. All of those involved have always been aware that this enormous effort was only possible by combining all forces. This was true whether it concerned an employee or a boss, a citizen or a politician, a "Wessi" or an "Ossi."

Roland Ries (Strasbourg): In the realm of public expectation, to talk about aspirations toward new forms of collective good would probably be an exaggeration. On the other hand, it is clear that the priorities today are no longer the same. Just a few years ago, the priorities of the population were related to municipal facilities: swimming pools, playgrounds, sporting and cultural spaces. Even though all of these needs have not yet been met, today the priorities of the population have shifted to more intangible areas.

Public peace and the quality of the everyday environment are top priority in all the surveys or sociological polls. Next is the goal to be active in the city in a range of forms: access to information, participation in local life, neighborhood advocacy, the need to understand the significance of political choices, etc. Responding to these new aspirations presents a certain number of challenges to the mayors of large cities. The local administrations are organized to manage communal facilities, public services (water, sanitation, public transport, etc.) or the large public works projects. Public peace and citizen participation require a different structure, still embryonic in local governments.

Strasbourg is affected, like other large cities, by the flipside of the phenomenon of urbanization: atmospheric pollution and exclusion. One must, however, be mindful of seasonal phenomena and the media focus on certain events such as the summer pollution levels or nights of urban violence.

Strasbourg experiences what all other cities experience. The difference is that it has been among the first to precisely measure the levels of atmospheric pollution, and its public housing is located in large part in the city center rather than in the outskirts, as in many cities.

In these areas, the principal significant evolution is that these phenomena have reached a plateau and are stabilizing. It is our hope that this stabilization will mark a starting point for a significant decline in the problems at issue.

Regarding atmospheric pollution, a vigorous policy of limiting the use of personal automobiles, particularly in the historic city center, has begun to bear fruit thanks to alternatives like the tramway and a strong network of bicycle paths. Here, we have developed a long-term strategy. It is the very conception of the city of tomorrow that is being redefined, a city reined in, organized around public transportation networks.

In the realm of social exclusion, the most notable progress has been in the birth of initiatives on the part of associations of citizens with humanitarian or social concerns. These have woven a new social instinct and a new social life in the various neighborhoods. The mayors of large cities are observing the emergence of this new urban environment without really having the means to precisely evaluate its impact on the life of the city. We know how to measure delinquency and urban violence, but not yet this new urban solidarity.

If I were to evoke new significant evolutions, they are here: a new attitude among citizens relating to the transportation and how one lives in the city, a new culture of citizenship and of urban life that is emerging across a myriad of solidarity initiatives.

Cities, like other entities, must take competition into account. In your opinion, what are the most important factors in making a city attractive?

Leoluca Orlando (Palermo): Cities above all can offer—for those who want to invest in high-quality service—cultural activities of a high level, overall cultural dynamism, efficient infrastructures, and especially a large zone of interest to workers and consumers: essential elements to a "complete" developmental approach that isn't limited only to the economic aspect but encompasses social and cultural aspects as well.

Wolfgang Tiefensee (Leipzig): Every city is characterized by a certain spirit and possesses a certain charisma, a force of influence. This perception of the city results both from historical tradition and the current situation. It is always the people who create their city's image and atmosphere. Despite all the agitation associated with the globalization process, we cannot forget that our cities are places where our citizens *live*. Possibilities for work, housing, and leisure must be conceived in response to their needs.

Moreover, the infrastructures should respond to the needs of potential investors. Billions of deutschmarks have already been and continue to be invested in this area. Our transportation—land, air, underground—and communication networks (Leipzig has the densest and most modern fiber optic connections in Europe) are excellent. Henceforth, the private and public highway and train connections are facilitated. The Leipzig airport is an important factor for the establishment of new activities.

Investments, in billions of deutschmarks, have been and continue to be made for the modernization of the economic environment, the construction of a new convention center and electrical plants, the renovation of public transportation and office and commercial space, the restoration of schools and universities, the expansion of hospitals, the improvement of social structures, etc.

But our largest asset is the quality of the Leipzig residents: they are involved in the life of their city. The city's residents are its most important assets. Employees are well trained. The men and women of Leipzig are proud of their city. Individuals who are involved have ideas and stamina. Many of them work toward the collective good in an exemplary manner and hope that our city will continue to progress. We can count on them.

Albert Bore (Birmingham): Your wider question on globalization presumes that there is only one model. I would dispute this. Certainly the components of a neoliberal model of globalization would call into question all of the achievements of the welfare state and steer us down an American-type road. I do not think this need be the case, and I know this view is shared by my colleagues within the European Socialist Group of both the Committee of the Regions and the European Parliament. Certainly, in a fast-changing world, one could and would expect the models of welfare and collective provision that have been developed over the past half-century to be altered and amended. It may be that new forms of collective welfare will appear at the local level, although there is little immediate sign of this within the United Kingdom. Such provision would require a shift in the tax-raising powers of local and regional authorities which, at the present time, the UK government certainly does not appear eager to propose. I would also be wary of such developments if they could lead to serious significant variations in levels of provision across the country for such basic services as schools and hospitals, where I think there needs to be a basic uniform standard.

Your question focuses on the impact of globalization on cities, particularly with regard to competition. It is clearly a factor that we are all facing in one way or another, although I think it important to recognize that there is increasing acknowledgement of the importance of collaboration and cooperation as well.

You ask for the most important factors with regard to the attractiveness of cities. I think a number of issues are crucial here. Firstly, clear political leadership and a clear strategic sense of where the city is going. These two factors can help instill a dynamism within the city and a logic and direction to its development. These need to be worked out and developed in partnership between the elected municipal authority and the key local stakeholders, notably, the business and financial community, the universities and higher education institutions, and the other public agencies. Added to this there needs to be some concentration on softer factors: an environmentally attractive city, easy to travel around in, with good parks, attractive housing, good quality cultural facilities, and attractive night-life. More generally, a city of social cohesion which feels and acts as if it is at ease with itself. These are clearly tough aspirations but they are important quality of life factors which are crucial in considering the attractiveness of cities.

Roland Ries (Strasbourg): What characterizes competition in the new context of global communication systems and exchanges is mobility. We have the impression that we live in a world where everything is in motion, where nothing is ever a given. Thus, competition for a large city is not based solely on its attractiveness. It requires a constant vigilance to ensure its performance in the network of communication and exchange. International accessibility, the quality of urban life, density of services and cultural life, availability of professional services, etc. certainly remain factors of attractiveness.

At the same time, it is still the strong involvement of women and men in the life of a city that makes the greatest difference in terms of a city's development. To attract a new scientific team, showcase development potential, or retain the headquarters of a large organization or company, the will of the individuals in the city is more important than the other features of attractiveness. The attractiveness of a city is above all in the quality of the social life of that city.

Herbert Wagner (Dresden): Based on my concrete experience, each individual, each event can change the course of things. Democracy can be lived and fashioned right in front of our eyes (*hautnah*). Cities are able to satisfy most of the needs expressed by its citizens in terms of work, culture, leisure, and social relations, so long as they have the optimal size of about a half million inhabitants. In the larger cities, the danger is increased that individuals will be lost in anonymity.

3. Culture: The Role of Cities

Culture is often cited as an essential element in the development of individuals and of cities. Does this seem like a well-founded position to you? Is it truer today than in the past?

Herbert Wagner (Dresden): Yes, culture enables us to escape from uniformity and to compensate for the monotony of the work world, just as it is furthermore a source of inspiration and promotion of technological development.

Leoluca Orlando (Palermo): We have recently been involved in a real cultural battle in Palermo. It has been deemed necessary, in fact, to liberate the city and its residents from the cultural hegemony of the Mafia that too long blocked its development and compromised all positive projection to the outside world.

In the recent past, the citizens of Palermo were ashamed of their history, culture, and traditions. Today, we have finally won this battle and the Mafia no longer controls the spirit of Palermo's residents. At the start of my mandate as mayor of Palermo, I constantly repeated that culture has to be an economic resource and not the opposite. The recent history of Palermo, a city whose "Renaissance" is now the subject of in-depth studies and is discussed in the media around the world, and has been recognized by prestigious international political, cultural, and economic representatives, is the best proof of what I just said. It is thanks to culture and the promotion of it that Palermo has been freed from the cultural hegemony of the Mafia. In this regard, there is an anecdote that I find emblematic. At the reopening of the Teatro Massimo, the third largest lyric theater in Europe, which was closed for twenty years, the conductor of the Berlin Philharmonic, Claudio Abbado, proudly revealed to the press that he felt as if he were Palermitan himself because his mother came from the Sicilian capital. I don't think that it was a coincidence that Claudio Abbado wanted to make this detail known at the very moment when, after such a long time, Palermo was reappropriating one of its symbols, at the very moment when Palermo was affirming itself, once again, as one of the cultural capitals of Europe and the world. "I am Palermitan," is the phrase that U.S. first lady Hillary Clinton used in Palermo, at the Teatro Massimo in fact, in her opening address at the conference for the international promotion and diffusion of a culture of legality and democracy, of which Palermo is now a capital. Palermo is no longer a problem, but a model, a resource for the international community.

Wolfgang Tiefensee (Leipzig): On this question, we can clearly respond in the affirmative. When we consider the history of our city, we can make the following assertion: through all time periods and regardless of the form of government, the identity of Leipzig has always been expressed by a diversified culture that has always given the city strength and self-confidence. Even, indeed particularly during this period of globalization, it is important to know one's background and identity. In this sense, culture is a good indicator, a kind of compass.

Moreover, the transregional perception of Leipzig is one of a cultural metropolis. The 250th anniversary of the death of Johann Sebastian Bach in 2000 confirms this and reinforces Leipzig's reputation all over the world. Our major cultural institutions—such as the Gewandhaus [symphony hall], the Opera, and the Thomanerchor [St. Thomas Choir]—have an international reputation. We are doing everything we can to retain and enlarge that reputation.

Culture constitutes, henceforth, an important point of attraction for our city. In addition, artistic creation mirrors reality and delivers a critical image that politics needs to address. Art generates imagination and visions that allow us to see beyond our everyday activities and emphasizes the real problems of an era. Let us beware of a mode of thought that is too conformist! The atmosphere of a city, its flair, does not come from statistical grandeur that can be measured in economic terms. Culture is not a product and not just a game for our enjoyment.

Albert Bore (Birmingham): Culture is increasingly and rightly seen as an essential element for the well-being of individuals and cities, and this is more important today than in the past. There are both economic and social reasons for this. On the one hand, within the population as a whole there is more disposable income and in these changed conditions people are both able and keen to spend their income on cultural and leisure pursuits. The growing involvement and participation of women in society, as compared to forty years ago, means there is a larger potential audience for culture. Broader social changes with more importance given to choice means that there is more interest in and a wider-range of diverse activities.

The political leadership in Birmingham believes that the promotion and encouragement of culture in its broadest sense is a key component within the city's overall rejuvenation and regeneration. We feel this requires both the encouragement and development of high-quality, prestigious facilities and groups such as the magnificent concert hall at the International Convention Center, the home of the City of Birmingham Symphony Orchestra, and the development of the Hippodrome as the home for the prestigious Birmingham Royal Ballet. But we have sought to combine support for these and other high-quality developments with support for multipurpose, community-based facilities such as those at the Midlands Art Center and the Drum—a center built purposely for the Afro-Caribbean community—and other community initiatives designed to ensure that young people and new talent have plenty of opportunities for cultural development.

Within tight budgets it will always be hard to have the right balance between support given to high-profile, city-wide initiatives and those seeking to develop new talent and give voice to a new generation of cultural work within the districts and communities. However, our ongoing commitment is to do both. We think this is crucial to the vibrancy and vitality of the city as a whole and we think it particularly important that through this route we are able to demonstrate the multiracial character of Birmingham.

Roland Ries (Strasbourg): Culture expresses individual identity, as well as that of a community or city. In this sense, the city is a multicultural and mixed society. The mission of mayors of large cities is to support diverse cultural expressions. This happens sometimes through new cultural practices. This requires the recognition in Strasbourg of the Alsatian culture and dialect, Islamic religious practices, Yiddish culture, or gypsy tradition. This leads us also to value the presence of the European nationalities that make Strasbourg a European city, through festivals, events, celebrations. This commitment is visible in the significant budget allocated to the creative cultural institutions that make Strasbourg a city of cultural excellence.

Culture is also the sharing and a respect for the identity and the expression of others. A fee structure facilitating access to contemporary cultural events, the creation of events that cultivate cultural expression, the opening of cybercenters that allow for access to information, all contribute to this sharing and respect.

More generally, when a mayor of a city like Strasbourg aims to place his city within the global systems of communication and exchange, the city's culture remains the most solid anchor. If the city is the place where relations between the universal and the local are arranged, everyone does it in his own way, forging both his culture and his identity.

From this point of view it is interesting to note the extent to which the culture of a city is capable of making its mark on the social, economic, and political life of a city. A free city for three centuries, a city of humanism and tolerance, a city for commercial trade open to the world, Strasbourg remains profoundly marked by this culture: it projects its future into a global world as a crossroads for Europe, a city of international exchange, a university town, a tolerant and multicultural city.

CHAPTER 22

Considerations on
Method and Events

MARINA RICCIARDELLI

The many questions on the trends of globalization have provided the stimulus for preparing and collecting the essays featured in this book. Given the multidisciplinary nature of reality, the scope of the topics treated here extends far beyond the purely economic aspects of globalization. The introduction explains this clearly, and I need not revisit it. I prefer instead to consider the consensus in some of the "basic assumptions" found in the various essays, from which I shall draw some points for consideration while raising a few questions.

I consider this consensus a significant and useful aspect of the book. It is significant because we did not deliberately aim for it or propose it to the contributors. And precisely for this reason, this book may be more convincing (and valuable). Its utility derives, in my opinion, from giving the book the form of a "user's manual": the ideas in these essays can easily be "linked" to other interlocutors and subjects that are not specifically covered here but are central to scientific, institutional, and "everyday" debates on globalization.

I. The Concept of Time

The first basic assumption I would like to discuss is the concept of time. Among the various conceptual categories on which the analyses in these

Marina Ricciardelli teaches political economics and monetary economics at the University of Rome "La Sapienza" and at the University of L'Aquila.

essays depend, "time" is the most general, the one found in all. My attention is focused on the common approach that emerges, albeit through the authors' purely autonomous choices and decisions. In each of the essays, time is considered not as a sequence in which to place events, but as the phenomenon that causes events and is essential to their occurrence, their existence, and their identity.

As Prigogine has explained over the years, and as he reminds us in the opening chapter, this view of time is not a "given" and hence univocal methodological hypothesis. It summarizes the history of a basic problem in debates on scientific method—starting from ancient Greece, we might say! More recently it has fueled an epistemological debate going beyond "determinism," to use the expression coined by Western culture at the end of the eighteenth century (Pomian 1991). And what does this term mean? I will briefly discuss it in order to show how it fits within the logic of my argument.

Speculative creativity and attention to experience allowed Newton to develop a synthesis in the field of physics between Bacon's empirical method and the deductive method of Descartes. This brought about the birth of classic mechanics. In the study of the solar system, the basic idea and the related mathematical construction permitted exact predictions of the planets' future orbits. In this methodological approach, the current state of the universe is considered both the effect of the previous state and the cause of the next. Thus, predictability is an inherent property of the universe itself: there are no breaks between the past and the future.

But Heisenberg's principle of indetermination and quantum mechanics in the physical sciences, the study of dissipative structures and of entropy in chemical sciences, and the reconsideration of causality in evolutionary process have raised doubts, through probabilism, about the deterministic hypothesis (Forti 1998). Science has introduced the concepts of instability and nonlinearity of behavior for a system with internal fluctuations that move away from the point of equilibrium. This can mean either a change in the preexisting structure or its chaotic breakup. The evolutionary process presents a point of bifurcation, where it is impossible to predict the direction of change. Entropy is understood as generating not only disorder, but order as well. Among the principal characteristics of science in the past decades is the discovery of complexity, with a role of its own that includes the revision of the laws of nature (Prigogine 1993).

Chance is not an intruder, as in classical mechanics, but an element that is as uncertain and unpredictable as it is important, and that must be situated in time in order to occur. The concept of chaos, in the broadest sense of the term, is related to that of chance. Chaos is not the antithesis of symmetry—a condition or place of disorder and featureless confusion—but, rather, as it was regarded in the primitive cosmogonies, the initial figuration (Koyré 1966), a reality that is opening.

As I write this [July 2000], the newspapers are saying that a new comet is crossing the sky at slightly more than one hundred times the distance between the Earth and the Moon: "That is as if to say, it is just around the corner."[1] The message this brings us is that of gravitational instability, which permitted the comet's nucleus to leave the stable orbit it had been in for millions of years and move toward the sun. The comet may revolve around the sun or land on it or on one of its satellites—including Earth—and disappear forever. Who knows? The event has not yet occurred and the result is uncertain. Complexity and uncertainty are indissolubly linked to the life and history of the universe. "The universe is too complex to be able to do without time."[2]

2. The Concept of Science

The second basic assumption concerns our view of science. If by scientific research we mean the "traditional" study of the laws of the universe, drawing an acceptable picture of the world, making discoveries which by their nature are not predictable, and providing interpretative schemes for solving problems born outside the domain of research, then today we must include in the scope of science—and this becomes explicitly clear in our book—not only the conceptual phase of technology which can be derived from it, but also the subsequent application phase, namely, the byproduct of the exploitation of this knowledge (Rubbia 1993).

Let us start with the last point. Progress, not merely technological progress, can be attributed to man's creative ability to produce added value that becomes stratified over time. In this sense, progress is considered a process in history, inserted into the path of time, that moves toward "the best," even though progress is not linear and does not always accumulate positive elements (Bodei 1987). The idea of scientific and technological progress therefore rejects the myth (or legend) of a happier age in the past. I tend to agree, but it is also important to avoid making science a lay religion, fueling the belief in a miraculous future golden age produced by it and by its applications. We can take a closer look at this issue by selecting certain situations as a "framework for understanding"—understanding, for example, the possibilities of controlling science and its applications by nonscientists, and the times and methods by which nonscientists can increase knowledge and make use of science.

The Control of Scientific Results

Perhaps it is not the duty of scientists to question themselves and raise doubts about the social consequences of their ideas and discoveries. But the most scrupulous among them are the first to state that it is their direct duty and responsibility to inform society about the content and technical aspects of potential scientific solutions, if for no other reason than the fact that society provides the resources to finance research without obtaining any immediate advantage in exchange (Dulbecco 1995).

Scientific discoveries and their applications have impacted human existence and the world. The new millennium has inherited many significant and positive, as well as negative, phenomena. Many of the latter (pollution, excessive exploitation of scarce natural resources, and so on) were generated by technological progress.

Whether and how to solve or at least address these problems requires the will and the sense of responsibility of society and its political institutions. This is not a statement of principle. There is more to it. Consider one current example from a field of many such examples. The result of a very important biological research project was announced in the summer of 2000: the decoding of the human genome. We can roughly define the genome as the organized arrangement of genes that directs the construction of biological structures and, at the same time, defines their characteristics. This discovery is at the heart of the current debate on the role of biological contributions in determining certain human character traits. This debate illustrates the great interest that a scientific event can arouse in the lay world, since it can be translated into a model for interpreting social behavior. The knowledge of genetics permits greater effectiveness in the prevention, diagnosis, and cure of many diseases. But at the same time, in dealing with genetic differences among individuals as well as the respective alterations, this knowledge could be used as a basis for discrimination against one individual with respect to other members of the group.

I believe we can say that an increase in knowledge and social awareness leads to a better understanding of the potential and the risks of this union of science and technology, and furthermore, that society expects to participate in decision making without trusting in the mere "internal logic" of the scientific method. And there is more. An issue that is so important to everyone directly affects the political world. A conflict could be created between the regulation of society's broad interests (for example, the defense of the fundamental rights of mankind) and the attempts to convert the results of this scientific discovery into economic profit as quickly as possible, on the basis of the vast range of potential uses.

The Speed of Information

The second "framework of understanding" concerns the methods through which we learn about scientific results. We are entering the field of information, which is a strange kind of reality. It is a resource that seems exempt from all limits posed by the scarcity or rigidity of supply; a resource that seems to disorient or rather displace the classic resources of land, capital, and labor, and that matches or replaces the exchange of goods with the increasing distribution and exchange of symbols and messages. In the era of the integrated global market, the interaction and spread of scientific research and related technologies comprise a very complex real and interpretive structure. How can we live in harmony with it? I relate this question to "time," a very important conceptual category for us. Today, information travels at the speed of light and has already become globalized. Are the tools and languages of information systems so innovative (some rapid changes can be seen and measured from day to day) as to create new conceptual and learning frameworks? Can we assume that they can change the relationship between physical and philosophical time and even affect some methodological assumptions? The future often seems farther from the past, and experience based on previous events no longer seems to have the time to become consolidated. The idea of putting experience to use seems superfluous, because experience has already become outdated. In the words of Serres,

> In which time are we living? The universal response today is in the very short term. In order to protect the earth . . . we propose . . . short-term solutions because we are living with immediate deadlines, and it is from those that we draw the essentials of our power . . . there is [a] cultural contamination, which we have extended to long term thoughts, the guardians of the earth. How can we succeed in a long-term undertaking with short-term means? We will have to pay for this through a drastic, and perhaps painful, revision of today's culture.[3]

The Thoughts of Economic Science

Let me add a few words on economic studies, which first of all, following liberal doctrine, are engaged in guiding the integration of the world's markets as well as methodically highlighting the obstacles in all areas to universal free trade.

A strange dilemma (a point of bifurcation!) affects this field of science. For a long time, even its nature as a "science" was contested on the grounds that the continued presence, in its field of interest, of a critical analysis of the bases of social function made it impossible to develop new theories according to rigorous analytical methods (Popper 1989). On the other hand, the formulation and doctrinaire assumptions of the dominant intellectual paradigm have made it possible to embark on the road of methodological reliability precisely by adopting the same determinist model as that constructed by the natural sciences. The conceptual framework of the initial, dominant paradigm affirms the separation of the world of values (hence values are not subject to analysis) from the intrinsically value-neutral and logically "mechanical" behavior of the rational economic actor. In this way, the rules of economics take on the characteristics of truth and universality for market systems. A fundamental disregard for the complexity, the dynamics, and hence the obvious interdisciplinary bonds that exist among all phenomena related to living beings is inherent in these assumptions.

And what is the state of things today? Those in research areas that are involved in the globalization process frequently raise questions about the role and mode of expression of the "uncertainty" factor in the decision-making methods adopted by the various economic actors. In this book, Modigliani explains the meaning of the hypothesis of rational expectations in the theoretical models and how it can be correlated with the interpretation of real phenomena, since the role of economic science is precisely that of dealing with real problems in order to solve them. An example is the development of free trade, which, according to its method of implementation, may or may not be transformed into a mechanism for exacerbating inequalities and thus increasing unemployment and exclusion.

Modigliani's important stand fits into a lively debate among economists; the debate reintroduces the relationships between complexity, uncertainty, and the future—involving methodological assumptions and components— into various interpretive schemes. The wealth of analyses and debates is not matched by univocal conclusions. We cannot but agree with the statement, "We would say that the discussion was fruitful when the conflict of opinion led the participants to produce new and interesting arguments."[4]

There does seem to be some reticence about abandoning the deterministic method, and it is defended in various ways. Some of those who consider the personal beliefs of economic actors, including their behavior in the face of risk, as one of the causes of uncertainty in decision making emphasize that a large number of the related problems derive from the actors' ignorance of what science has clarified and hence of the possible consequences of their own actions. In other words, they suppose that the spread of scientific information and education could attenuate or correct (Debreu 1994) this feature that is so typical of human decision making. The hypothesis that uncertainty is fueled or driven by complex economic systems, which are influenced by external policies, follows a similar line of reasoning.

Other interpretive schemes emphasize that subjective uncertainty would correspond to the subjective values of the deterministic model without adding anything new to the framework of analysis. They add that the uncertainty linked to the nature of certain economic transactions—such as the fact that the clauses of an insurance policy only become applicable following the occurrence of an event, or that a financial contract with clearly defined indications of place, quantity, and price has a future deadline—does not contradict the market axioms which were developed by the theoretical model of rational choice and were designed for a world of certainties. For instance, these interpretive schemes emphasize that the different distribution of probabilities for these situations can vary significantly from one economic actor to the next, but would not impede the development of a single balanced price for every good on the market (Arrow 1963).

Other interpretive schemes, which refuse to employ a priori assumptions for interpreting social phenomena, propose a recourse to "methodological individualism." They affirm that we must take into account the "good reasons" that an individual has for believing in certain ideas or for taking certain actions, as well as the results of cognitive psychology and neurophysiology (Boudon and Viale 2000). Such a view goes beyond both the "holistic" interpretation of social phenomena, as well as the dichotomy between the behavior of the economic subject based on a priori principles of rationality (i.e., based on the theory of rational choice) and the indeterminate behavior of the social subject. In other words, in these interpretive schemes a basic hypothesis of rationality is adopted that is "limited" not only by the constraints of the external world, but also by the respective knowledge and evaluations of those who link the consequences of their economic decisions to it (Simon 2000).

3. The Space for Participation

"We have embarked on an adventure of economics, science and technology."[5] I would add: we also have embarked on an adventure of culture, politics, and a great deal more. The future is going to touch a much more integrated world. It is a common future. Can its realization depend on the contributions of everyone, or will it be increasingly in the hands of the protagonists of market globalization, that is, the "global players"? How can we work together to achieve global equilibrium, defined as the coordinated interconnection that Prigogine mentions among the many states of equilibrium described by the natural sciences and achieved by human sciences and cultures?

There are too many issues for this essay to address. I will limit myself to a short list of questions concerning individual commitment, collective commitment, and the work of institutions.

I begin with the statement that the rational mind can indeed be of help to the creative mind, in the sense that the study of the creative spirit's basic principles and imagination can give rise to new ideas and "leave the beaten path to enter the forest."[6] Arno Penzias would ask that the researchers be allowed to keep their "messy corners" in carrying out their projects, harvesting the fruits of chance as well as following clearly defined guidelines.

Can we fit Prigogine's statement, "It is not an impossible utopia to hypothesize that each person can be creative in his own way,"[7] together with facts and ideas in the category of uncertainty, and thus create maneuvering space based on an optimism of will?

The growth of knowledge for all, in my view, is the crux of the matter. On this point, it is essential that the enormous potential of the communications media—even if they focus primarily on images—is used to intensify and improve the way in which the ideas of different speakers can confront one another, without diminishing the substance of dialogue or blocking one of the channels of democracy (Paz 1995). I understand Chomsky's fears that in a mass society where everyone participates and everyone believes himself to be equally competent, a democratic dialogue could only be conducted about sports, an inoffensive topic.

The problem of collective participation, however, is subject to many other tensions. Faced with a multitude of actors, the many representational models and schemes we have inherited from the past are no longer functional. Furthermore, there is also the question of content. If globalization is a structural evolution, a large process of change that we try to control and master with a view toward "building the future," a frame of reference that comprises value judgments, behavioral standards, and procedures for regulating the activities of institutions will indeed be necessary. But first, we have to ascertain whether or not there is homogeneity and agreement among our values and aims, as well as determining the manner of establishing relations among individuals, society, and institutions. For example, is it possible and indispensable to arrive at "global governance"? In other words could we construct a global politics in which the various communities are willing or encouraged to incur costs to support each other? What means of control and orientation, and what type of coordination should there be among them? What kind of new democratic procedures will be needed to carry out a program of reforms? We could believe that "if good will on the part of all and much effort are combined, far-reaching understanding will indeed be possible."[8]

International interdependencies are such that the destinies of today's society are not strictly and solely linked to national decisions. For some time now, technological and scientific applications have reinforced and emphasized this fact (it is sufficient to mention nuclear experiments). The democratic order is increasingly separated from the state, whose political sovereignty is becoming weaker on both the domestic and international front. What new problems does a postnational arrangement raise for the future of democracy (Habermas and Taylor 1998; Habermas 1999)?

I believe that there is much that political science can do in this regard, combining reason and imagination. The very special place that we have dedicated in this book to the European economic and monetary union derives from the importance and ambition of this project, which must traverse a rough and rocky road on a daily basis.

The EMU wants to participate in globalization under its own rules. It is using sophisticated economic and institutional models that closely link positive and predictive analyses and gradually implementing the institutional bodies and procedures deemed necessary for the new economic and political reality it wishes to achieve. Currently, the EMU is an extremely broad and important observatory for the contradictory and complex affirmation of a supranational power, as well as a power capable of levying sanctions on its member states. The assimilation of national territory and of social and political identity has been and will continue to be greatly modified. The "axiom of territorial action" (Beck 2000) is being shifted toward subnational decentralization. However, it is still impossible to understand fully the roles of local institutions and the plurality of contracts and players in the process of drafting regulations and public actions that concern them, or whether local institutions and players are, regarding global EMU policies and measures, partners merely obliged to implement in their respective territories decisions made elsewhere.

Democratic participation plays a role in another fundamental problem that goes well beyond Europe's boundaries. The concept of "crimes against humanity" has its roots in ancient Greece, where the principle of human equality was affirmed in a context that was independent of recourse to a state order (through the doctrine of natural law). The shift from philosophy to criminal law within a country (which involves hierarchization, that is, the state becomes the guardian of order) opens the way for the subsequent separation between domestic and international criminal law. Since the latter refers to an equal relationship (the "international community"), a failure of democracy may appear—for example, at the level of guarantees (if the elected representatives of the people do not administer justice, and so forth).

I have raised several questions, and I could add many others to which I have no definite or even indefinite answers. In general terms, I believe that we must not mythicize or defend a single, unique frame of reference. I am also convinced that we must not turn to rhetoric or catchwords for or against a given thing. I agree with Boyer: "The method recommends the maximum freedom of invention, exchange and criticism by proposing mainly that we do not cease controlling our statements by their consequences and comparing them according to their merits."[9]

I favor adopting the conclusions of our "user's manual" and expanding the horizons of our expectations, by taking advantage of uncertainty, the unforeseeable, and every potential area of freedom that will allow our ideas to mold the shape of the future.

"Uncertainty. A balm for headaches."[10] In the light of the beauty offered by an uncertain and asymmetrical future, I have but one regret—growing old.

NOTES

1. Zichichi (2000): "Come dire dietro l'angolo di casa nostra."
2. Prigogine (1993): "L'universo è troppo complesso per poter fare a meno del tempo."
3. Serres (1990), p. 57.
4. Popper (1989), p. 17.
5. Serres (1990), p. 19.
6. Esaki (1995): "lasciare la strada vecchia per addentrarsi nella foresta."
7. Prigogine, in *Tempo ed entropia*: ". . . si tratta di un'utopia non impossibile ipotizzare che ognuno a suo modo possa essere creativo."
8. Popper (1989), p. 13.
9. Boyer (1989), p. 99.
10. Enzensberger (1993): "Ungewissheit. Balsam für die Migräne."

REFERENCES

Arrow, K. "Uncertainty and the Welfare Economics of Medical Care." *American Economic Review* 52, no. 6 (1963).
Bartoli, H. *L'économie multidimensionelle*. Paris: Economica, 1991.

Beck, U. "Libertà e democrazia in pericolo se vincono quelli 'senza principi.'" *Reset* no. 60 (June 2000).

Bell, D., and I. Bristol. *Crise et renouveau de la théorie économique*. Paris: Bonnel & Publisud, 1986.

Bodei, R. *Scomposizioni: Forme dell'individuo moderno*. Turin: Einaudi, 1987.

Boudon, R., and R. Viale. "Reason, Cognition and Society." *Mind and Society* no. 1 (2000).

Boyer, A. "La méthode en perspective." In *Karl Popper et la science d'aujourd'hui: actes du colloque au Centre culturel de Ceresy-la-Salle 1981,* edited by R. Bouveresse. Paris: Aubier, 1989.

Cleveland, H. "Trecento anni dopo Newton." In *La morte di Newton,* edited by A. Forti. N.p., 1998.

Chomsky, N. *Intervista su linguaggio e ideologia a cura di Mitsou Ronat*. Bari: Laterza, 1977.

Debreu, G. "Innovation and Research: An Economist's Viewpoint on Uncertainty." In *Dieci Nobel per il futuro: Scienza, economia, etica per il prossimo secolo*. Milan, n.p., 1994.

Dulbecco, R. "Libertà della ricerca e timori della società." In *Dieci Nobel per il futuro: Scienza, economia, etica per il prossimo secolo*. Milan, n.p., 1995.

Elster, J. *Ulysses Unbound: Studies in Rationality, Precommitment and Constraints*. Cambridge: Cambridge University Press, 2000.

Enzensberger, H. M. *Zukunftsmusik*. Frankfurt: Suhrkamp Taschenbuch, 1993.

Esaki, L. "Preparare menti e cuori al XXI secolo." In *Dieci Nobel per il futuro: Scienza, economia, etica per il prossimo secolo*. Milan, n.p., 1995.

Field, M., and M. Golubitsky. *Symmetry in Chaos*. Oxford: Oxford University Press, 1992.

Fitoussi, J. *Rapport sur l'état de l'Union européenne*. Paris: Fayard, 1999.

Forti, A. Introduction to *La morte di Newton*. Edited by A. Forti. N.p., 1998.

Gell-Mann, M. "Information versus Knowledge and Understanding." In *Dieci Nobel per il futuro: Scienza, economia, etica per il prossimo secolo*. Milan, n.p., 1995.

Girard, R. *Le bouc émissaire*. Paris: Grasset, 1982.

Habermas, J., and C. Taylor. *Multiculturalismo: Lotte per il riconoscimento*. Milan: Feltrinelli, 1998.

Habermas, J. *La costellazione postnazionale: Mercato globale, nazioni e democrazia*. Milan: Feltrinelli, 1999.

Hayek, F. A. *L'abuso della ragione*. Milan: Edizioni Seam, 1997.

International Monetary Fund. *World Economic Outlook,* May 1997.

Koyré, A. *Études galiléennes*. Paris: Hermann, 1966.

Jonas, H. *Il principio di responsabilità*. Turin: Einaudi, 1990.

Jurdant, B. "Popper entre la science et les scientifiques." In *Karl Popper et la science d'aujourd'hui: actes du colloque au Centre culturel de Ceresy-la-Salle 1981,* edited by R. Bouveresse. Paris: Aubier, 1989.

Mandelbrot, B. *Fractales, hasard et finance*. Paris: Flammarion, 1997.

Merton, R. K. *On the Shoulders of Giants*. New York: Free Press, 1965.

Paz, O. "Il patto verbale." In *Dieci Nobel per il futuro: Scienza, economia, etica per il prossimo secolo*. Milan, n.p., 1995.

Pomian, K. *Sul determinismo: La filosofia della scienza oggi*. Milan: Il Saggiatore & Mondadori, 1991.

Popper, K. "Le mythe du cadre de référence." In *Karl Popper et la science d'aujourd'hui: actes du colloque au Centre culturel de Ceresy-la-Salle 1981*, edited by R. Bouveresse. Paris: Aubier, 1989.

Porter, G. "Comunicare attraversando i confini culturali." In *Dieci Nobel per il futuro: Scienza, economia, etica per il prossimo secolo*. Milan, n.p., 1995.

Prigogine, I. "The Open Universe." In *L'infinito in una scienza finita*, edited by G. Toraldo di Francia. Florence: Istituto dell'enciclopedia Treccani, 1987.

———. *Tra il tempo e l'eternità*. Milan: Bollati Boringhieri, 1989.

———. "Le frontiere della complessità." In *Dieci Nobel per il futuro: Scienza, economia, etica per il prossimo secolo*. Milan, n.p., 1995.

———. *Le leggi del caos*. Bari: Edizioni Laterza, 1993.

———. *Tempo ed entropia*. Rai-Italia, Enciclopedia multimediale delle scienze filosofiche, Video.

Richter, B. "From Science to New Technologies." In *Dieci Nobel per il futuro: Scienza, economia, etica per il prossimo secolo*. Milan, n.p., 1993.

Rubbia, C. "The Main Role of Science in the 1990s." In *Dieci Nobel per il futuro: Scienza, economia, etica per il prossimo secolo*. Milan, n.p., 1993.

Serres, M. *Le contrat naturel*. Paris: Editions François Bourin, 1990.

Simon, H. "Bounded Rationality in Social Science: Today and Tomorrow." *Mind and Society* no. 1 (2000).

Simon, H. A. *Scienza economica e comportamento umano*. Turin: Edizioni di Comunità, 2000.

Steinberger, J. "The Responsibility of the Scientist on a Finite Globe." In *Dieci Nobel per il futuro: Scienza, economia, etica per il prossimo secolo*. Milan, n.p., 1993.

Thom, R. *Prédire n'est pas expliquer*. Paris: Flammarion, 1991.

Zichichi, A. "Arriva una nuova cometa: Tornerà tra 21 milioni di anni." *Il Messaggero*, 14 July 2000.